KT-226-736

Dion Fortune's
THE
MYSTICAL
QABALAH

THE AQUARIAN PRESS

First published 1935
First paperback edition 1987

© THE SOCIETY OF THE INNER LIGHT 1957, 1987

All rights reserved. No part of this book may be reproduced or utilized in any form or by any means, electronic or mechanical, including photocopying, recording or by any information storage and retrieval system, without permission in writing from the Publisher.

British Library Cataloguing in Publication Data

Fortune, Dion
The mystical qabalah.
1. Cabala
Rn: Violet Mary Firth   I. Title
135'.4   BF1611

ISBN 0-85030-355-4

*The Aquarian Press is part of the Thorsons Publishing Group,
Wellingborough, Northamptonshire, NN8 2RQ, England*

Printed in Great Britain by Woolnough Bookbinding Limited,
Irthlingborough, Northamptonshire

3 5 7 9 10 8 6 4 2

f 12

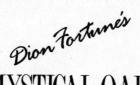

THE MYSTICAL QABALAH

FOREWORD

THE Tree of Life forms the ground-plan of the Western Esoteric Tradition and is the system upon which pupils are trained in the Society of the Inner Light.

This volume, and others which are to follow, are used as the basis of the tutorial system of the Society. Particulars of the Society will be sent to anyone who cares to write to the author, in the care of the Society of the Inner Light, 38 Steele's Road, London, N.W.3.

The transliteration of Hebrew words into English is the subject of much diversity of opinion, every scholar appearing to have his own system. In these pages I have availed myself of the alphabetical table given by MacGregor Mathers in *The Kabbalah Unveiled* because this book is the one generally used by esoteric students. He himself does not adhere to his own table systematically, however, and even uses different spellings for the same words. This is very confusing for anyone who wishes to use the Gematric method of elucidation, in which letters are turned into numbers. When, therefore, Mathers gives alternative transliterations, I have followed the one which coincides with that given in his own table.

The capitalisation employed in these pages may also appear unusual, but it is the one traditionally used among students of the Western Esoteric Tradition. In this system, common words, such as earth or path, are used in a technical sense to denote spiritual principles. When this is done, a capital is used to indicate the fact. When a capital is not used, it may be taken that the word is to be understood in its ordinary sense.

As I have frequently referred to the authority of MacGregor Mathers and Aleister Crowley in matters of Qabalistic mysticism, it may be as well to explain my position in relation to these two writers.

I was at one time a member of the organisation founded by the former, but have never been associated with the latter. I have never known either of these gentlemen personally, MacGregor Mathers having died before I joined his organisation, and Aleister Crowley having then ceased to be associated with it.

CONTENTS

PART I

PART IV

DIAGRAMS

THE MYSTICAL QABALAH

PART I

CHAPTER I

THE YOGA OF THE WEST

1. Very few students of occultism know anything at all about the fountain-head whence their tradition springs. Many of them do not even know there is a Western Tradition. Scholarship is baffled by the intentional blinds and defences with which initiates both ancient and modern have wrapped themselves about, and concludes that the few fragments of a literature which have come down to us are mediæval forgeries. They would be greatly surprised if they knew that these fragments, supplemented by manuscripts that have never been allowed to pass out of the hands of initiates, and completed by an oral tradition, are handed down in schools of initiation to this day, and are used as the bases of the practical work of the Yoga of the West.

2. The adepts of those races whose evolutionary destiny is to conquer the physical plane have evolved a Yoga technique of their own which is adapted to their special problems and peculiar needs. This technique is based upon the well-known but little understood Qabalah, the Wisdom of Israel.

3. It may be asked why it is that the Western nations should go to the Hebrew culture for their mystical tradition ? The answer to this question will be readily understood by those who are acquainted with the esoteric theory concerning races and sub-races. Everything must have a source. Cultures do not spring out of nothing. The seed-bearers of each new phase of culture must of necessity arise within the preceding culture. No one can deny that Judaism was the matrix of the

European spiritual culture when they recall the fact that Jesus and Paul were both Jews. No race except the Jewish race could possibly have served as the stock upon which the new dispensation was to be grafted because no other race was monotheistic. Pantheism and polytheism had had their day and a new and more spiritual culture was due. The Christian races owe their religion to the Jewish culture as surely as the Buddhist races of the East owe theirs to the Hindu culture.

4. The mysticism of Israel supplies the foundation of modern Western occultism. It forms the theoretical basis upon which all ceremonial is developed. Its famous glyph, the Tree of Life, is the best meditation-symbol we possess because it is the most comprehensive.

5. It is not my intention to write a historical study of the sources of the Qabalah, but rather to show the uses that are made of it by modern students of the Mysteries. For although the roots of our system are in tradition, there is no reason why we should be hidebound by tradition. A technique that is being actually practised is a growing thing, for the experience of each worker enriches it and becomes part of the common heritage.

6. It is not necessarily incumbent upon us to do certain things or hold certain ideas because the Rabbis who lived before Christ had certain views. The world has moved on since those days and we are under a new dispensation. But what was true in principle then will be true in principle now, and of value to us. The modern Qabalist is the heir of the ancient Qabalist, but he must re-interpret doctrine and re-formulate method in the light of the present dispensation if the heritage he has received is to be of any practical value to him.

7. I do not claim that the modern Qabalistic teachings as I have learnt them are identical with those of the pre-Christian Rabbis, but I claim that they are the legitimate descendants thereof and the natural development therefrom.

8. The nearer the source the purer the stream. In order to discover first principles we must go to the fountain-head. But

a river receives many tributaries in the course of its flow, and these need not necessarily be polluted. If we want to discover whether they are pure or not, we compare them with the pristine stream, and if they pass this test they may well be permitted to mingle with the main body of waters and swell their strength. So it is with a tradition: that which is not antagonistic will be assimilated. We must always test the purity of a tradition by reference to first principles, but we shall equally judge of the vitality of a tradition by its power to assimilate. It is only a dead faith which remains uninfluenced by contemporary thought.

9. The original stream of Hebraic mysticism has received many tributaries. We see its rise among the nomad star-worshippers of Chaldea, where Abraham in his tent among his flocks hears the voice of God. But Abraham has a shadowy background in which vast forms move half-seen. The mysterious figure of a great Priest-king, "born without father, without mother, without descent; having neither beginning of days nor end of life," administers to him the first Eucharistic feast of bread and wine after the battle with the Kings in the valley, the sinister Kings of Edom, "who ruled ere there was a king in Israel, whose kingdoms are unbalanced force."

10. Generation by generation we trace the intercourse of the princes of Israel with the priest-kings of Egypt. Abraham and Jacob went thither; Joseph and Moses were intimately associated with the court of the royal adepts. When we read of Solomon sending to Hiram, King of Tyre, for men and materials to aid in the building of the Temple we know that the famous Tyrian Mysteries must have profoundly influenced the Hebrew esotericism. When we read of Daniel being educated in the palaces of Babylon we know that the wisdom of the Magi must have been accessible to Hebrew illuminati.

11. This ancient mystical tradition of the Hebrews possessed three literatures: the Books of the Law and the Prophets, which are known to us as the Old Testament; the Talmud, or

collection of learned commentaries thereon; and the Qabalah, or mystical interpretation thereof. Of these three the ancient Rabbis say that the first is the body of the tradition, the second its rational soul, and the third its immortal spirit. Ignorant men may with profit read the first; learned men study the second; but the wise meditate upon the third. It is a strange thing that Christian exegesis has never sought the keys to the Old Testament in the Qabalah.

12. In Our Lord's day there were three schools of religious thought in Palestine: the Pharisees and the Sadducees, of whom we read so frequently in the Gospels; and the Essenes, who are never referred to. Esoteric tradition avers that the boy Jesus ben Joseph, when His calibre was recognised by the learned doctors of the Law who heard Him speak in the Temple at the age of twelve, was sent by them to the Essenian community near the Dead Sea to be trained in the mystical tradition of Israel, and that He remained there until He came to John to be baptised in the Jordan before commencing His mission at the age of thirty. Be that as it may, the closing clause of the Lord's Prayer is pure Qabalism. Malkuth, the Kingdom, Hod, the Glory, Netzach, the Power, form the basal triangle of the Tree of Life, with Yesod, the Foundation, or Receptacle of Influences, as the central point. Whoever formulated that prayer knew his Qabalah.

13. Christianity had its esotericism in the Gnosis, which owed much to both Greek and Egyptian thought. In the system of Pythagoras we see an adaptation of the Qabalistic principles to Greek mysticism.

14. The exoteric, state-organised section of the Christian Church persecuted and stamped out the esoteric section, destroying every trace of its literature upon which it could lay hands in striving to eradicate the very memory of a gnosis from human history. It is recorded that the baths and bakehouses of Alexandria were fired for six months with the manuscripts from the great library. Very little remains to us of our spiritual heritage in the ancient wisdom. Everything that was above ground was swept away, and it is only with the excavation of

ancient monuments the sands have swallowed that we are beginning to rediscover its fragments.

15. It was not until the fifteenth century, when the power of the Church was beginning to show signs of weakening, that men dared to commit to paper the traditional Wisdom of Israel. Scholars declare that the Qabalah is a mediæval forgery because they cannot trace a succession of early manuscripts, but those who know the manner of working of esoteric fraternities know that a whole cosmogony and psychology can be conveyed in a glyph which means nothing to the uninitiated. These strange old charts could be handed on from generation to generation, their explanation being communicated verbally, and the true interpretation would never be lost. When in doubt as to the explanation of some abstruse point, reference would be made to the sacred glyph, and meditation thereon would unfold what generations of meditation had ensouled therein. It is well known to mystics that if a man meditates upon a symbol around which certain ideas have been associated by past meditation, he will obtain access to those ideas, even if the glyph has never been elucidated to him by those who have received the oral tradition "by mouth to ear."

16. The organised temporal force of the Church availed to drive all rivals from the field and destroy their traces. We little know what seeds of mystical tradition sprang up only to be cut down during the Dark Ages; but mysticism is inherent in the human race, and although the Church had destroyed all roots of tradition in her group-soul, nevertheless devout spirits within her fold rediscovered the technique of the soul's approach to God and developed a characteristic Yoga of their own, closely akin to the Bhakti Yoga of the East. The literature of Catholicism is rich in treatises on mystical theology which reveal practical acquaintance with the higher states of consciousness though a somewhat naïve conception of the psychology thereof, thus revealing the poverty of a system which does not avail itself of the experience of tradition.

17. The Bhakti Yoga of the Catholic Church is only suitable for those whose temperament is naturally devotional

and who find their readiest expression in loving self-sacrifice. But it is not everybody who is of this type, and Christianity is unfortunate in not having any choice of systems to offer its aspirants. The East, being tolerant, is wise, and has developed various Yoga methods, each of which is pursued by its adherents to the exclusion of the others, and yet none would deny that the other methods are also paths to God for those to whom they are suited.

18. In consequence of this deplorable limitation on the part of our theology many Western aspirants take up Eastern methods. For those who are able to live in Eastern conditions and work under the immediate supervision of a guru, this may prove satisfactory, but it seldom gives good results when the various systems are pursued with no other guide than a book and under unmodified Western conditions.

19. It is for this reason that I would recommend to the white races the traditional Western system, which is admirably adapted to their psychic constitution. It gives immediate results, and if done under proper supervision, not only does it not disturb the mental or physical equipoise, as happens with regrettable frequency when unsuitable systems are used, but it produces a unique vitality. It is this peculiar vitality of the adepts which led to the tradition of the elixir of life. I have known a number of people in my time who might justly be considered adepts, and I have always been struck by that peculiar ageless vitality they all possessed.

20. On the other hand, however, I can only endorse what all the gurus of the Eastern Tradition have always averred—that any system of psycho-spiritual development can only be safely and adequately carried on under the personal supervision of an experienced teacher. For this reason, although I shall give in these pages the principles of the mystical Qabalah, I do not consider it would be in anybody's interest to give the keys to its practice even if by the terms of the obligation of my own initiation I were not forbidden to do so. But, on the other hand, I do not consider it fair to the reader to introduce intentional blinds and misinformation, and to the best of my know-

ledge and belief the information I give is accurate, even if incomplete.

21. The Thirty-two Mystical Paths of the Concealed Glory are ways of life, and those who want to unravel their secrets must tread them. As I myself was trained, so can anyone be trained who is willing to undergo the discipline, and I will gladly indicate the way to any earnest seeker.

CHAPTER II

1. No student will ever make any progress in spiritual development who flits from system to sytsem; first using some New Thought affirmations, then some Yoga breathing-exercises and meditation-postures, and following these by an attempt at the mystical methods of prayer. Each of these systems has its value, but that value can only be realised if the system is carried out in its entirety. They are the calisthenics of consciousness, and aim at gradually developing the powers of the mind. The value does not lie in the prescribed exercises as ends in themselves, but in the powers that will be developed if they are persevered with. If we intend to take our occult studies seriously and make of them anything more than desultory light reading, we must choose our system and carry it out faithfully until we arrive, if not at its ultimate goal, at any rate at definite practical results and a permanent enhancement of consciousness. After this has been achieved we may, not without advantage, experiment with the methods that have been developed upon other Paths, and build up an eclectic technique and philosophy therefrom; but the student who sets out to be an eclectic before he has made himself an expert will never be anything more than a dabbler.

2. Whoever has any practical experience of the different methods of spiritual development knows that the method must fit the temperament, and that it must also be adapted to the grade of development of the student. Westerners, especially such as prefer the occult to the mystic Path, often come seeking initiation at a stage of spiritual development which an Eastern guru would consider exceedingly immature.

Any method that is to be available for the West must have in its lower grades a technique which can be used as a stepping-stone by these undeveloped students; to ask them to rise immediately to metaphysical heights is useless in the case of the great majority, and prevents a start from being made.

3. For a system of spiritual development to be applicable in the West it must fulfil certain well-defined requirements. To begin with, its elementary technique must be such that it is readily grasped by minds that have in them nothing of the mystic. Secondly, the forces it brings to bear to stimulate the development of the higher aspects of consciousness must be sufficiently powerful and concentrated to penetrate the relatively dense vehicles of the average Westerner, who makes nothing whatever of subtle vibrations. Thirdly, as few Europeans, following a racial dharma of material development, have either the opportunity or the inclination to lead the life of a recluse, the forces employed must be handled in such a way that they can be made available during the brief periods that the modern man or woman can, at the commencement of the Path, snatch from their daily avocations to give to the pursuit. They must, that is to say, be handled by a technique which enables them to be readily concentrated and equally readily dispersed, because it is not possible to maintain these high psychic tensions while living the hard-driving life of the citizen of a European city. Experience proves with un-failing regularity that the methods of psychic development which are effectual and satisfactory for the recluse produce neurotic conditions and breakdowns in the person who pur-sues them while compelled to endure the strain of modern life.

4. So much the worse for modern life, some may say, and adduce this undeniable fact as an argument for modifying our Western ways of living. Far be it from me to maintain that our civilisation is perfect, or that wisdom originated and will die with us, but it appears to me that if our karma (or destiny) has caused us to be incarnated in a body of a certain racial type and temperament, it may be concluded that that is

the discipline and experience which the Lords of Karma consider we need in this incarnation, and that we shall not advance
the cause of our evolution by avoiding or evading it.   I have
seen so many attempts at spiritual development that were
simply evasions of life's problems that I am suspicious of any
system which involves a breach with the group-soul of the
race.   Nor am I impressed by a dedication to the higher
life which manifests itself by peculiarities of clothing and
bearing and by the manner of cutting, or omitting to cut, the
hair.   True spirituality never advertises itself.

5. The racial dharma of the West is the conquest of dense
matter.   If this were realised it would explain many problems
in the relationships of West and East.   In order that we may
conquer dense matter and develop the concrete mind we are
endowed by our racial heritage with a particular type of
physical body and nervous system, just as other races, such as
the Mongolian and the Negro, are endowed with other types.

6. It is injudicious to apply to one type of psycho-physical
make-up the developing methods adapted to another; they
will either fail to produce adequate results, or produce unfore-
seen and possibly undesirable results.   To say this is not to
condemn the Eastern methods, nor decry the Western constitution, which is as God made it, but to reaffirm the old adage
that one man's meat is another man's poison.

7. The dharma of the West differs from that of the East;
is it therefore desirable to try and implant Eastern ideals in a
Westerner?   Withdrawal from the earth-plane is not his line
of progress.   The normal, healthy Westerner has no desire
to escape from life, his urge is to conquer it and reduce it to
order and harmony.   It is only the pathological types who
long to "cease upon the midnight with no pain," to be free
from the wheel of birth and death;   the normal Western
temperament demands "life, more life."

8. It is this concentration of life-force that the Western
occultist seeks in his operations.   He does not try to escape
from matter into spirit, leaving an unconquered country
behind him to get on as best it may;   he wants to bring the

Godhead down into manhood and make Divine Law prevail even in the Kingdom of the Shades. This is the root-motive for the acquisition of occult powers upon the Right-hand Path, and explains why initiates do not abandon all for the mystic Divine Union, but cultivate a White Magic.

9. It is this White Magic, which consists in the application of occult powers to spiritual ends, by means of which a large proportion of the training and development of the Western aspirant is carried out. I have seen something of a good many different systems, and in my opinion the person who tries to dispense with ceremonial is working at a great disadvantage. Development by meditation alone is a slow process in the West, because the mind-stuff upon which it has to work, and the mental atmosphere in which the work has to be done, are very resistant. The only purely meditative school of Western Yoga is that of the Quakers, and I think that they would agree that their path is for the few; the Catholic Church combines Mantra Yoga with its Bhakti Yoga.

10. It is by means of formulæ that the occultist selects and concentrates the forces he wishes to work with. These formulæ are based upon the Qabalistic Tree of Life, and whatever system he may be working, whether he be assuming the God-forms of Egypt or evoking the inspiration of Iacchus with chant and dance, he has the diagram of the Tree at the back of his mind. It is in the symbolism of the Tree that Western initiates are drilled, and it supplies the essential ground-plan of classification to which all other systems can be related. The Ray upon which the Western aspirant works has manifested itself through many different cultures and developed a characteristic technique in each. The modern initiate works a synthetic system, sometimes using an Egyptian, a Greek, or even a Druidic method, for different methods are best suited for different purposes and conditions. In all cases, however, the operation he designs is strictly related to the Paths of the Tree of which he is master. If he possesses the grade which corresponds to the Sephirah Netzach, he can work with the manifestation of the force of that aspect of the

Godhead (distinguished by the Qabalists by the name of Tetra-grammaton Elohim) in whatever system he may select.   In the Egyptian system it will be the Isis of Nature; in the Greek, Aphrodite; in the Nordic, Freya; in the Druidic, Keridwen. In other words, he possesses the powers of the Sphere of Venus in whatever traditional system he may be using.   Having attained a grade in one system, he has access to the equivalent grades of all the other systems of his Tradition.

11. But although he may use these other systems as occasion serves, experience proves that the Qabalah supplies the best groundwork and the best system upon which to train a student before he begins to experiment with the pagan systems.   The Qabalah is essentially monotheistic; the potencies it classifies are always regarded as the messengers of God and not His fellow-workers.   This principle enforces the concept of a centralised government of the Cosmos and of the grip of the Divine Law upon the whole of manifestation—a very necessary principle with which to imbue any student of the Arcane forces.   It is the purity, sanity, and clarity of the Qabalistic concepts as resumed in the formula of the Tree of Life which makes that glyph such an admirable one for the meditations that exalt consciousness and justify us in calling the Qabalah the Yoga of the West.

CHAPTER III

THE METHOD OF THE QABALAH

1. Speaking of the method of the Qabalah, one of the ancient Rabbis says that an angel coming down to earth would have to take on human form in order to converse with men. The curious symbol-system known to us as the Tree of Life is an attempt to reduce to diagrammatic form every force and factor in the manifested universe and the soul of man; to correlate them one to another and reveal them spread out as on a map so that the relative positions of each unit can be seen and the relations between them traced. In brief, the Tree of Life is a compendium of science, psychology, philosophy, and theology.

2. The student of the Qabalah goes to work in exactly the opposite way to the student of natural science; the latter builds up synthetic concepts; the former analyses abstract concepts. It goes without saying, however, that before a concept can be analysed it must first be assembled. Someone must have thought out the principles that are resumed in the symbol which is the object of meditation of the Qabalist. Who then were the first Qabalists who built up the whole scheme? The Rabbis are unanimous upon this point, they were angels. In other words, it was beings of another order of creation than humanity who gave the Chosen People their Qabalah.

3. To the modern mind this may seem as absurd a statement as the doctrine that babies are found under gooseberry bushes; but if we study the many mystical systems of comparative religion we find that all the illuminati are in agreement upon this point. All men and women who have had practical experience of the spiritual life tell us that they are taught by

13

Divine beings. We shall be very foolish if we altogether dis-
regard such a cloud of witnesses, especially those of us who
never have had any personal experience of the higher states of
consciousness.

4. There are some psychologists who will tell us that the
Angels of the Qabalists and the Gods and Manus of other
systems are our own repressed complexes; there are others
with less limited outlook who will tell us that these Divine
beings are the latent capacities of our own higher selves. To
the devotional mystic this is not a point of any great moment;
he gets his results, and that is all he cares about; but the
philosophical mystic, in other words the occultist, thinks the
matter out and arrives at certain conclusions. These conclusions, however, can only be understood when we know
what we mean by reality and have a clear line of demarcation
between the subjective and the objective. Any one who is
trained in philosophical method knows that this is asking a
good deal.

5. The Indian schools of metaphysics have most elaborate
and intricate systems of philosophy which attempt to define
these ideas and render them thinkable; and though generations
of seers have given their lives to the task, the concepts still
remain so abstract that it is only after a long course of discipline, called Yoga in the East, that the mind is able to apprehend them at all.

6. The Qabalist goes to work in a different way. He does
not attempt to make the mind rise up on the wings of metaphysics into the rarefied air of abstract reality; he formulates
a concrete symbol that the eye can see, and lets it represent
the abstract reality that no untrained human mind can
grasp.

7. It is exactly the same principle as algebra. Let X represent the unknown quantity, let Y represent the half of X,
and let Z represent something we know. If we begin to
experiment with Y, to find out its relation to Z, and in what
proportions, it soon ceases to be entirely unknown; we have
learnt something at any rate about it; and if we are sufficiently

skilful we may in the end be able to express Y in terms of Z, and then we shall begin to understand X.

8. There are a great many symbols which are used as objects of meditation; the Cross in Christendom; the God-forms in the Egyptian system; phallic symbols in other faiths. These symbols are used by the uninitiated as a means of concentrating the mind and introducing into it certain thoughts, calling up certain associated ideas, and stimulating certain feelings. The initiate, however, uses a symbol-system differently; he uses it as an algebra by means of which he will read the secrets of unknown potencies; in other words, he uses the symbol as a means of guiding thought out into the Unseen and Incomprehensible.

9. And how does he do this? He does it by using a composite symbol; a symbol which is an unattached unit would not serve his purpose. In contemplating such a composite symbol as the Tree of Life he observes that there are definite relations between its parts. There are some parts of which he knows something; there are others of which he can intuit something, or, more crudely, make a guess, reasoning from first principles. The mind leaps from one known to another known and in so doing traverses certain distances, metaphorically speaking; it is like a traveller in the desert who knows the situation of two oases and makes a forced march between them. He would never have dared to push out into the desert from the first oasis if he had not known the location of the second; but at the end of his journey he not only knows much more about the characteristics of the second oasis, but he has also observed the country lying between them. Thus, making forced marches from oasis to oasis, backwards and forwards across the desert, he gradually explores it; nevertheless, the desert is incapable of supporting life.

10. So it is with the Qabalistic system of notation. The things it renders are unthinkable—and yet the mind, tracking from symbol to symbol, manages to think about them; and although we have to be content to see in a glass darkly, yet we have every reason to hope that ultimately we shall see face to

face and know even as we are known; for the human mind
grows by exercise, and that which was at first as unthinkable
as mathematics to the child who cannot manage his sums,
finally comes within the range of our realisation. By thinking
about a thing, we build concepts of it.

11. It is said that thought grew out of language, not
language out of thought. What words are to thought,
symbols are to intuition. Curious as it may seem, the symbol
precedes the elucidation; that is why we declare that the
Qabalah is a growing system, not a historic monument.
There is more to be got out of the Qabalistic symbols to-day
than there was in the time of the old dispensation because our
mental content is richer in ideas. How much more, for
instance, does the Sephirah Yesod, wherein work the forces
of growth and reproduction, mean to the biologist than to the
ancient rabbi? Everything that has to do with growth and
reproduction is resumed in the Sphere of the Moon. But
this Sphere, as represented upon the Tree of Life, is set about
with Paths leading to other Sephiroth; therefore the biological
Qabalist knows that there must be certain definite relationships between the forces subsumed in Yesod and those represented by the symbols assigned to these Paths. Brooding
over these symbols, he gets glimpses of relationships that do
not reveal themselves when the material aspect of things is
considered; and when he comes to work these out in the
material of his studies he finds that therein are hidden important
clues; and so upon the Tree, one thing leads to another,
explanation of hidden causes arising out of the proportions
and relations of the various individual symbols composing
this mighty synthetic glyph.

12. Each symbol, moreover, admits of interpretation upon
the different planes, and through its astrological associations
can be related to the gods of any pantheon, thus opening up
vast new fields of implication in which the mind ranges end-
lessly, symbol leading on to symbol in an unbroken chain of
associations; symbol confirming symbol as the many-branch-
ing threads gather themselves together into a synthetic glyph

once more, and each symbol capable of interpretation in terms of whatever plane the mind may be functioning upon.

13. This mighty, all-embracing glyph of the soul of man and of the universe, by virtue of its logical association of symbols, evokes images in the mind; but these images are not randomly evolved, but follow along well-defined association-tracks in the Universal Mind. The symbol of the Tree is to the Universal Mind what the dream is to the individual ego—it is a glyph synthetised from subconsciousness to represent the hidden forces.

14. The universe is really a thought-form projected from the mind of God. The Qabalistic Tree might be likened to a dream-picture arising from the subconsciousness of God and dramatising the subconscious content of Deity. In other words, if the universe is the conscious end-product of the mental activity of the Logos, the Tree is the symbolic representation of the raw material of the Divine consciousness and of the processes whereby the universe came into being.

15. But the Tree applies not only to the Macrocosm but to the Microcosm which, as all occultists realise, is a replica in miniature. It is for this reason that divination is possible. That little-understood and much-maligned art has for its philosophical basis the System of Correspondences represented by symbols. The correspondences between the soul of man and the universe are not arbitrary, but arise out of developmental identities. Certain aspects of consciousness were developed in response to certain phases of evolution, and therefore embody the same principles; consequently they react to the same influences. A man's soul is like a lagoon connected with the sea by a submerged channel; although to all outward seeming it is land-locked, nevertheless its water-level rises and falls with the tides of the sea because of the hidden connection. So it is with human consciousness, there is a subconscious connection between each individual soul and the World-soul deep hidden in the most primitive depths of subconsciousness, and in consequence we share in the rise and fall of the cosmic tides.

16. Each symbol upon the Tree represents a cosmic force or factor. When the mind concentrates upon it, it comes into touch with that force; in other words, a surface channel, a channel in consciousness, has been made between the conscious mind of the individual and a particular factor in the world-soul, and through this channel the waters of the ocean pour into the lagoon. The aspirant who uses the Tree as his meditation-symbol establishes point by point the union between his soul and the world-soul. This results in a tremendous access of energy to the individual soul; it is this which endows it with magical powers.

17. But just as the universe must be ruled by God, so must the many-sided soul of man be ruled by its god—the spirit of man. The Higher Self must dominate its universe or there will be unbalanced force; each factor will rule its own aspect, and they will war among themselves. Then do we have the rule of the Kings of Edom, whose kingdoms are unbalanced force.

18. Thus do we see in the Tree a glyph of the soul of man and the universe, and in the legends associated with it the history of the evolution of the soul and the Way of Initiation.

CHAPTER IV

1. The point of view from which I approach the Holy Qabalah in these pages differs, so far as I know, from that of all other writers on the subject, for to me it is a living system of spiritual development, not a historical curiosity. Few people, even among those interested in occultism, realise that there is an active Esoteric Tradition in our midst, handed down in private manuscripts and by "mouth to ear." Still fewer know that it is the Holy Qabalah, the mystic system of Israel, which forms its basis. But where may we look more aptly for our occult inspiration than to the Tradition which gave us the Christ?

2. The interpretation of the Qabalah is not to be found, however, among the Rabbis of the Outer Israel, who are Hebrews after the flesh, but among those who are the Chosen People after the spirit—in other words, the initiates. Neither is the Qabalah, as I have learnt it, a purely Hebraic system, for it has been supplemented during mediæval times by much alchemical lore and by the intimate association with it of that most marvellous system of symbolism, the Tarot.

3. In my presentation of the subject, therefore, I do not appeal so much to tradition in support of my views, as to modern practice among those who make use of the Qabalah as their method of occult technique. It may be alleged against me that the ancient Rabbis knew nothing of some of the concepts here set forth; to this I reply that it is hardly to be expected that they should, as these things were not known in their day, but are the work of their successors of the Spiritual Israel. For my part, although I would not willingly mislead

anyone concerning the teachings of those of ancient days, and upon matters of historical accuracy stand subject to correction from any who are better informed than I am in these matters (and their name is legion), I care not one jot for the authority of tradition if it hampers the free development of a system of such practical value as the Holy Qabalah, and I use the work of my predecessors as a quarry whence I fetch the stone to build my city.   Neither am I limited to this quarry by any ordinance that I know of, but fetch also cedar from Lebanon and gold from Ophir if it suits my purpose.

4. Let it be clearly understood, therefore, that I do not say, This is the teaching of the ancient Rabbis; rather do I say, This is the practice of the modern Qabalists, and for us a much more vital matter, for it is a practical system of spiritual unfoldment; it is the Yoga of the West.

5. Having thus guarded myself as far as possible against blame for not having done what I never undertook to do, let me now define my own position in the matter of scholarship and general qualifications for the task in hand.   So far as actual scholarship goes, I am in the same class as William Shakespeare, having little Latin and less Greek, and of Hebrew only that peculiar portion which is cultivated by occultists— the ability to transliterate unpointed Hebrew script for the purposes of Gematric calculations.   Of any knowledge of Hebrew as a language I am guiltless.

6. Whether such frank acknowledgment of my deficiencies will serve to disarm criticism I do not know; no doubt it will be alleged against me, and not without justification, that one so ill-equipped should not have undertaken the task at all.   To this I reply that if one saw a man lying injured, should the admitted absence of a medical qualification debar one from going to his assistance and giving him what help one could, pending the arrival of qualified attention?   My work upon the Qabalah is of the nature of first aid.   I find an invaluable system lying neglected, and ill-qualified for the task as I may be, I am striving to draw attention to its possibilities and restore it to its proper place as the key to Western occultism;

and it is my chief hope in so doing that it may attract the attention of scholars, and that they will continue the task of translation and investigation of the Qabalistic manuscripts, which are as yet a vein of which only the outcroppings have been worked.

7. One qualification for my task I can plead in justification, however. For the last ten years I have lived and moved and had my being in the Practical Qabalah; I have used its methods both subjectively and objectively till they have become a part of myself, and I know from experience what they yield in psychic and spiritual results, and their incalculable value as a method of using the mind.

8. It is not required of those who would use the Qabalah as their Yoga that they should acquire any extensive knowledge of the Hebrew language; all they need is to be able to read and write the Hebrew characters. The modern Qabalah has been pretty thoroughly naturalised in the English language, but it retains, and must ever retain, all its Words of Power in Hebrew, which is the sacred language of the West just as Sanscrit is the sacred language of the East. There are those who have objected to the free employment of Sanscrit terms in occult literature, and no doubt they will object even more strongly to the employment of Hebrew characters, but their use is unavoidable, for every letter in Hebrew is also a number, and the numbers to which words add up are not only an important clue to their significance, but can also be used to express the relationships existing between different ideas and potencies.

9. According to MacGregor Mathers, in the admirable essay which forms the introduction to his book, the Qabalah is usually classed under four heads:

The Practical Qabalah, which deals with talismanic and ceremonial magic.

The Dogmatic Qabalah, which consists of the Qabalistic literature.

The Literal Qabalah, which deals with the use of letters and numbers.

The Unwritten Qabalah, which consists of a correct knowledge of the manner in which the symbol-systems are arranged on the Tree of Life, and concerning which MacGregor Mathers says, "I may say no more on this point, not even whether I myself have or have not received it." But as this portentous hint is elaborated by the late Mrs MacGregor Mathers in her introduction to the new edition of his book in the following plain-spoken words, "Simultaneously with the publication of the *Qabalah* in 1887, he received instructions from his occult teachers to prepare what was eventually to become his esoteric school," it may be justifiable to say that if he did receive the Unwritten Qabalah, it has for some years ceased to be unwritten, for after a quarrel with MacGregor Mathers, Aleister Crowley, the well-known author and scholar, published the lot. His books are now rare and hard to come by, and being much valued by the more scholarly of esotericists, their price has gone up out of sight, and they seldom come into the second-hand book market.

10. The breaking of an initiation oath is a serious matter, and a thing that I, for my part, do not care to do; but I admit of no authority that debars me from collecting and collating all available material that has been published upon any subject, and interpreting it according to the best of my understanding. In these pages it is the system given by Crowley of which I shall avail myself to supplement the points upon which MacGregor Mathers, Wynn Westcott, and A. E. Waite, the principal modern authorities upon the Qabalah, are silent.

11. As to whether I myself have received any knowledge of the Unwritten Qabalah, it would as ill beseem me as Mac-Gregor Mathers to be explicit upon this point, and having followed his classic example of burying my head in the sand and waving my tail, I will return to the consideration of the matter in hand.

12. The essence of the Unwritten Qabalah lies in the know-

ledge of the order in which certain sets of symbols are arranged upon the Tree of Life. This Tree, Ets Chayyim, consists of the Ten Holy Sephiroth arranged in a particular pattern and connected by lines which are called the Thirty-two Paths of the Sepher Yetzirah, or Divine Emanations (see *The Sepher Yetzirah*, by Wynn Westcott). Here there exists one of the "blinds," or traps for the uninitiated, in which the ancient Rabbis delighted. We find, if we count them, that there are twenty-two, not thirty-two Paths upon the Tree; but for their purposes the Rabbis treated the Ten Sephiroth themselves as Paths, thus misleading the uninitiated. Thus the first ten Paths of the Sepher Yetzirah are assigned to the Ten Sephiroth, and the following twenty-two to the actual Paths themselves. It will then be seen how the twenty-two letters of the Hebrew alphabet can be associated with the Paths without discrepancy or overlapping. With them also are associated the twenty-two Tarot trumps, the Atus, or Abodes of Thoth. Concerning the Tarot cards there are three modern authorities of note: Dr Encausse, or "Papus," the French writer; Mr A. E. Waite; and the MSS. of MacGregor Mathers' Order of the Golden Dawn, which Crowley published upon his own authority. All three are different. Concerning the system Mr Waite gives, he himself says, "There is another method known to initiates." There is reason to suppose that this is the method used by Mathers. Papus disagrees with both these writers in his method, but as his system does violence to many of the correspondences when placed upon the Tree, the final test of all systems, and as the Mathers-Crowley system fits admirably, I think we may justly conclude that the latter is the correct traditional order, and I propose to adhere to it in these pages.

13. The Qabalists further placed upon the Paths of the Tree the Signs of the Zodiac, the Planets, and the Elements. Now there are twelve Signs, seven Planets, and four Elements, making twenty-three symbols in all. How are these to be fitted on to the Twenty-two Paths? Herein is another "blind," but the solution is simple. Upon the physical plane

we are ourselves in the Element of Earth, therefore that symbol does not appear upon the Paths which lead into the Unseen. Remove this, and we are left with twenty-two symbols, which fit accurately and, correctly placed, are found to correspond perfectly with the Tarot trumps, each elucidating the other in the most remarkable fashion, and giving the keys to esoteric astrology and Tarot divination.

14. The essence of each Path is to be found in the fact that it connects two of the Sephiroth, and we can only understand its significance by taking into account the nature of the linked Spheres upon the Tree. But a Sephirah cannot be understood upon a single plane; it has a fourfold nature. The Qabalists express this by saying that there are four worlds:

Atziluth, the Archetypal World, or World of Emanations; the Divine World.

Briah, the World of Creation, also called Kursiya, the World of Thrones.

Yetzirah, the World of Formation and of Angels.

Assiah, the World of Action; the World of Matter.
(See MacGregor Mathers, *The Qabalah Unveiled.*)

15. The Ten Holy Sephiroth are held to have each its own point of contact with each of the four Worlds of the Qabalists. In the Atziluthic World they manifest through the Ten Holy Names of God; in other words, the Great Unmanifest, shadowed forth through the Three Negative Veils of Existence which hang behind the Crown, declares itself in manifestation as ten different aspects which are represented by the different names used to denote Deity in the Hebrew Scriptures. These are variously rendered in the Authorised Version, and a knowledge of their true significance and the spheres to which they belong enables us to read many of the riddles of the Old Testament.

16. In the Briatic World the Divine Emanations are held to manifest through the Ten Mighty Archangels, whose names play such an important part in ceremonial magic; it is the worn and effaced remnants of these Words of Power that are the

"barbarous names of evocation" of mediæval magic, "not one letter of which may be changed." Why this is so may readily be seen when we remember that in Hebrew a letter is also a number, and the numbers of a Name have an important significance.

17. In the Yetziratic World the Divine Emanations manifest, not through a single Being, but through different types of beings, which are called the Angelic Hosts or Choirs.

18. The Assiatic World is not, strictly speaking, the World of Matter when viewed from the Sephirotic standpoint, but rather the Lower Astral and Etheric Planes which, together, form the background of matter. Upon the physical plane the Divine Emanations manifest through what may not inaptly be called the Ten Mundane Chakras, likening these centres of manifestation to the centres that exist in the human body, an exact analogy. These Chakras are the Primum Mobile or First Swirlings, the Sphere of the Zodiac, the seven planets, and the Elements taken together—ten in all.

19. It will be seen from the foregoing that each Sephirah will therefore consist, firstly, of its Mundane Chakra; secondly, of an angelic host of beings, Devas or Archons, Principalities or Powers, according to the terminology used; thirdly, an Archangelic Consciousness, or Throne; and fourthly, a special aspect of the Deity. God as He is, in His entirety, being hidden behind the Negative Veils of Existence, incomprehensible to unenlightened human consciousness.

20. The Sephiroth may justly be considered macrocosmic, and the Paths microcosmic; for the Sephiroth, connected as they sometimes are in old diagrams by a flash of lightning, which is often depicted as hilted like a fiery sword, represent the successive Divine Emanations which constitute creative evolution; whereas the Paths represent the successive stages of the unfolding of cosmic realisation in human consciousness; in old pictures a serpent is often depicted as twined about the boughs of the Tree. This is the serpent Nechushtan "who holdeth his tail in his mouth," the symbol of wisdom and initiation. The coils of this serpent, when correctly arranged

upon the Tree, cross each of the Paths in succession and serve to indicate the order in which they should be numbered. With the help of this glyph, then, it is a simple matter to arrange all the tables of symbols in their correct positions upon the Tree, granted that the symbols are given in their correct order in the tables. In certain modern books which rank as authorities upon the subject the correct order is not given, the writers apparently holding that this should not be revealed to the uninitiated. But as this order is given correctly in certain older books, and, for the matter of that, in the Bible itself and the Qabalistic literature, there seems to me no point in deliberately misleading students with spurious information. To refuse to divulge anything may be justifiable, but how is it possible to justify the handing on of misleading statements? No one is going to be persecuted nowadays for their studies in unorthodox sciences, so there can be but one purpose in withholding teaching that relates solely to the theory of the universe and the philosophy arising therefrom, and in no way to the methods of practical magic, and that purpose is to retain a monopoly of the knowledge which confers prestige, if not power.

21. For my part I believe that this selfishness and exclusiveness is the bane of the occult movement rather than its safeguard. It is the old sin of retaining the knowledge of God in the hands of a priesthood and denying it to all outside the sacred clan; justifiable enough when the people were savages, but unjustifiable in the case of the modern student. For when all is said and done, the desired information can be worked out from existing literature by those who care to take the trouble, or purchased plainly set forth by those who can afford high prices for books now rare. Surely the possession of ample time and ample cash should not be the test of the fitness to obtain the Sacred Wisdom?

22. No doubt I shall expose myself to a shower of abuse from the self-constituted guardians of this knowledge who may hold that their precious secrets have been betrayed. To this I reply that I am not betraying anything that is secret, but

collecting that which has already been given to the world and is of a simple and well-known nature. When I first had access to certain manuscripts, I believed them to be secret, and unknown to the world at large, but a wider acquaintance with occult literature has revealed to me that the information is to be found scattered broadcast through it. Much, in fact, to which the initiate is sworn to secrecy has been published by Mathers and Wynn Westcott themselves, and as recently as 1926 a new edition of Mathers' work on the Qabalah was brought out under the editorship of his widow (who may be assumed to have known his wishes), and in that work will be found most of the tables that I give in these pages. As these catalogues of beings were originally given to the world by Isaiah, Ezekiel, and various mediæval Rabbis, it may justly be held that the copyright in them has lapsed owing to the passage of time. In any case such ownership as there may be in these ideas is vested in the original author and not in any subsequent commentator, and that author, according to the Qabalah itself, is the Archangel Metatron.

23. Much that was once common knowledge has been gathered up and confined under the initiate's oath of secrecy. It is Crowley's jibe at his teachers that they bound him to secrecy with terrible oaths and then "confided the Hebrew alphabet to his safe keeping."

24. The philosophy of the Qabalah is the esotericism óf the West. In it we find such a cosmogony as is found in the Stanzas of Dyzan, which were the basis of Mme Blavatsky's work. Herein she found the framework of traditional doctrine which she expounded in her great book, *The Secret Doctrine*. This Qabalistic Cosmogony is the Christian Gnosis. Without it we have an incomplete system in our religion, and it is this incomplete system which has been the weakness of Christianity. The Early Fathers, in the homely metaphor, threw away the baby with the bath-water. A very cursory acquaintance with the Qabalah serves to show that here we have the essential keys to the riddles of Scripture in general and the prophetic books in particular. Is there any good

reason why initiates of the present day should put all this knowledge into a secret box and sit upon the lid? If they consider that I am wrong to give accurate information upon matters which they consider their private preserve, I reply that this is a free country and they are entitled to their opinion.

CHAPTER V

1. The esotericist, when endeavouring to formulate his philosophy for communication to others, is confronted by the fact that his knowledge of the higher forms of existence is obtained by a process other than thought; and this process only commences when thought is left behind. Consequently it is only in that region of consciousness which transcends thought that the highest form of transcendental ideas is known and understood; and it is only to those who are able to use this aspect of consciousness that he can communicate his ideas in their original form. When he wants to communicate these ideas to those who have had no experience of this mode of consciousness, he must either crystallise them into form or fail to convey any adequate impression. Mystics have used every imaginable simile in the endeavour to convey their impressions; philosophers have lost themselves in a maze of words; and all to no purpose so far as the unilluminated soul is concerned. The Qabalists, however, use another method. They do not try to explain to the mind that which the mind is not equipped to deal with; they give it a series of symbols to meditate upon, and these enable it to build the stairway of realisation step by step and to climb where it cannot fly. The mind can no more grasp transcendent philosophy than the eye can see music.

2. The Tree of Life, as cannot too often be emphasised, is not so much a system as a method; those who formulated it realised the important truth that in order to obtain clarity of vision one must circumscribe the field of vision. Most philosophers founded their systems upon the Absolute; but

this is a shifting foundation, for the human mind can neither define nor grasp the Absolute. Some others try to use a negation for their foundation, declaring that the Absolute is, and must ever be, unknowable. The Qabalists do neither of these things. They content themselves with saying that the Absolute is unknown to the state of consciousness which is normal to human beings.

3. For the purposes of their system, therefore, they draw a veil at a certain point in manifestation, not because there is nothing there, but because the mind, as such, must stop there. When the human mind has been brought to its highest stage of development, and consciousness can detach itself therefrom and, as it were, stand upon its own shoulders, we may be able to penetrate the Veils of Negative Existence, as they are called. But for all practical purposes we can understand the nature of the cosmos if we are content to accept the Veils as philosophical conventions, and realise that they correspond to human limitations, not to cosmic conditions. The origin of things is inexplicable in terms of our philosophy. However far we push our inquiries back into origins in the world of manifestation, we find a preceding existence. It is only when we are content to draw the Veil of Negative Existence across the path which leads back to beginnings that we get a background against which a First Cause becomes visible. And this First Cause is not a rootless origin, but a First Appearance on the Plane of Manifestation. Thus far and no farther can the mind go back; but we must always remember that different minds go back different distances, and that for some the Veil is drawn in one place, and for others in another. The ignorant man goes no further than the concept of God as an old man with a long white beard who sat on a golden throne and gave orders for creation. The scientist will go back a little further before he is compelled to draw a veil called the ether; and the philosopher will go back yet further before he draws a veil called the Absolute; but the initiate will go back furthest of all because he has learnt to do his thinking in symbols, and symbols are to the mind

what tools are to the hand—an extended application of its powers.

4. The Qabalist takes for his starting-point Kether, the Crown, the first Sephirah, which he symbolises by the figure One, Unity, and by the Point within the Circle. From this he traces backward the three Veils of Negative Existence. This is quite a different matter from starting at the Absolute and trying to work forwards into evolution. It may not yield immediately accurate and complete knowledge of the origin of all things, but it enables the mind to make a start; and unless we can make a start we have no hope of a finish.

5. The Qabalist, then, starts where he can—at the first point that is within the reach of finite consciousness. Kether is equated with the most transcendent form of God that we can conceive, Whose name is Ehyeh, translated in the Authorised Version of the Bible as "I am," or, more explicitly, the Self-Existing One, Pure Being.

6. But these words are words and nothing more unless they convey an impression to the mind, and in themselves they cannot do that. They must be related to other ideas before they have any significance. We only begin to understand Kether when we study Chokmah, the Second Sephirah, its emanation; it is only when we see the full unfoldment of the Ten Sephiroth that we are ready to approach Kether, and then we approach it with the data that gives us the key to its nature. In working with the Tree it is wisest to keep on going over it, rather than to concentrate upon a single point until it is mastered, for one thing explains another, and it is out of the perception of the relationships between the different symbols that enlightenment arises. Again we say, the Tree is a method of using the mind, not a system of knowledge.

7. But at the moment we are not engaged in the study of the Emanations, but of origins, so far as the human mind may hope to penetrate them; and paradoxical as it may appear, we shall penetrate further when we draw the Veils across them than when we try to pierce the darkness. We will, then, sum up the position of Kether in one sentence, a sentence

that can have but little significance for the student approaching the subject for the first time, but which must be borne in mind, for its significance will begin to dawn presently.   In so doing, we are adhering to the ancient esoteric tradition of giving the student a symbol to incubate till it hatches in his mind, rather than explicit instruction which would convey nothing to him. The seed-sentence then, which we cast into the subconscious mind of the reader, is this: "Kether is the Malkuth of the Unmanifest."   Mathers says (*op. cit.*): "The limitless ocean of negative light does not proceed from a centre, for it is centreless, but it concentrates a centre, which is the number One of the manifested Sephiroth, Kether, the Crown, the First Sephirah."

8. These words in themselves contain contradictions and are unthinkable; negative light is simply a way of saying that the thing described, though having certain qualities in common with light, is nevertheless not light as we know it.   This tells us very little about that which it is intended to describe.   We are told not to make the mistake of thinking of it as light, but we are not told how to think of it as it really is, and for the very good reason that the mind is not equipped with any images under which to represent it, and must therefore let it alone till growth takes place.   Nevertheless, although these words do not tell us all that we would like to know, they convey certain images to the imagination; these sink into the subconscious mind and thence are evoked when ideas enter the conscious mind which are related to them.   Thus knowledge grows from more to more when the Qabalistic method is given its practical application as the Yoga of the West.

9. The Qabalists recognise four planes of manifestation, and three planes of unmanifestation, or Negative Existence. The first of these is called AYIN, Negativity; the second, EN SOPH, the Limitless; the third, OR EN SOPH, the Limitless Light.   It is out of this last that Kether is concentrated. These three terms are called the three Veils of Negative Existence depending back from Kether; in other words, they are the algebraic symbols that enable us to think of that

which transcends thought, and which at the same time hide
that which they represent; they are the masks of transcendent
realities. If we think of the states of negative existence in
terms of anything that we know, we shall err, for whatever
else they may be, they cannot be that, being unmanifest.
The expression "Veils," therefore, teaches us to use these
ideas as counters, of no value in themselves, but useful to us
in our calculations. This is the true use of all symbols;
they veil that which they represent until we can reduce them
to terms we can comprehend; nevertheless they enable us to
use in our calculations ideas which would otherwise be unthinkable. And as the essence of the Tree lies in the fact that
it causes its symbols to elucidate one another by means of
their relative positions, these Veils serve as the scaffolding
of thought, enabling us to take our bearings in regions as
yet uncharted. Such Veils, or non-concrete symbols, are,
however, of no value to us unless one side of the Veil abuts
upon known country. The Veils, in fact, while they conceal
that which they represent, enable us to see clearly that to which
they form a background. This is their function, and the only
reason they are referred to. It is only by reason of our infirmi-
ties that we need to have these unresolvable symbols presented
to us, and the mind disciplined in esoteric philosophy soon
learns to work within these limitations and accept as a painted
veil the symbol of that which lies beyond its ken. This way
lies the unfoldment of wisdom, for the mind grows with what
it feeds upon, and one of these days, when we have climbed
to Kether, we may hope to stretch out our hands and rend the
Veil and look through into the Limitless Light. The esotericist does not limit himself by declaring the Unknown to be the
Unknowable, for he is above all things an evolutionist, and
knows that that which we cannot compass to-day we may
achieve in the to-morrow of cosmic time. He knows, too,
that evolutionary time is an individual matter upon the inner
planes, and is measured, not regulated, by the revolution of
the earth upon its axis.

10. These three Veils—AYIN, Negativity; EN SOPH, the

Limitless ; and OR EN SOPH, the Limitless Light—though we cannot hope to understand them, nevertheless suggest to our minds certain ideas. Negativity implies Being or existence of a nature which we cannot comprehend. We cannot conceive of a thing which is, and yet is not; therefore we must conceive of a form of being of which we have never had any conscious experience; a form of being which, according to our concepts of existence, does not exist, and yet, if one may express it so, exists according to its own idea of existence. In the words of a very wise man: There are more things in heaven and earth than are dreamt of in your philosophy.

11. But although we say that Negative Existence is outside the range of our realisation, it does not mean that we are outside the range of its influence. If this were so, we could dismiss it as non-existent so far as we are concerned, and our interest in it would be at an end. On the contrary, although we have not direct access to its being, all that we know as existing has its roots in this Negative Existence, so that, although we cannot know it directly, we have experience of it at one remove. That is to say, although we cannot know its nature, we know its effects, in the same way as we are ignorant of the nature of electricity yet are able to turn it to good account in our lives, and from our experience of its effects we are able to come to certain conclusions concerning some at least of the qualities it must possess. Those who have penetrated furthest into the Unseen have given us symbolic descriptions by means of which we may turn our minds in the *direction* of the Absolute, even if we cannot reach it. They have spoken of Negative Existence as Light: "Or En Soph, the Limitless Light." They have spoken of the First Manifest as Sound: "In the beginning was the Word." I remember once hearing a man, who was an adept if ever there was one, say, "If you want to know what God is, I can tell you in one word: God is pressure." And immediately an image leapt to my mind and a realisation followed. I could conceive the outflowing of life through every channel of existence. I felt that a genuine realisation of

the nature of God had been conveyed to me.   And yet, if one
came to analyse the words, there was nothing in them; nevertheless they had the power to convey an image, a symbol, to the
mind, and the mind, working upon it in the realm of intuition
beyond the sphere of reason, achieved a realisation, even if that
realisation could only be reduced to the sphere of concrete
thought as an image.

12. We must clearly realise that in these highly abstract
regions the mind can use nothing but symbols; but these
symbols have the power to convey realisations to minds that
know how to use them; these symbols are the seeds of thought
whence understanding arises, even if we are not able to expand
the symbol itself into a concrete realisation.

13. Little by little, like a rising tide, realisation is concreting
the Abstract, assimilating and expressing in terms of its own
nature things which belong to another sphere; and we shall
make a great mistake if we try to prove with Herbert Spencer
that because a thing is unknown by any capacity of the mind
we at present possess, that it must for ever be Unknowable.
Time is not only increasing our knowledge, but evolution is
increasing our capacity; and initiation, which is the forcing-
house of evolution, bringing faculties to birth out of due season,
brings the consciousness of the adept within reach of vast
apprehensions which are as yet below the horizon of the
human mind.   These ideas, though clearly apprehended by
himself after another mode of consciousness, cannot be conveyed by him to anyone who does not share this mode of consciousness.   He can only put them forth in symbolic form;
but any mind that has in any way had experience of this wider
mode of functioning will be able to lay hold on these ideas on
their own plane, although it may be unable to translate them
into the sphere of conscious thought.   In this way, therefore,
in the literature of esoteric science there are scattered seed-
ideas such as "God is pressure" and "Kether is the Malkuth
of Negative Existence."   These images, whose content does
not belong to our sphere at all, are as the male germs of thought
which fecundate the ova of concrete realisation.   In them-

selves they are incapable of maintaining more than the most fugitive existence in consciousness as a flash of realisation, but without them the ova of philosophical thought will be infertile. Impregnated by them, however, though their substance is absorbed and lost in the very act of impregnation, growth takes place within the formless germ of thought, and ultimately, after due gestation beyond the threshold of consciousness, the mind gives birth to an idea.

14. If we want to get the best out of our minds, we must learn to allow for this period of latency, this impregnation of our minds by something outside our plane of existence, and its gestation beyond the threshold of consciousness. The invocations of an initiation ceremony are designed to call down this impregnating influence upon the consciousness of the candidate. Hence it is that the Paths of the Tree, which are the stages of illumination of the soul, are intimately associated with the symbolism of initiation ceremonies.

CHAPTER VI

ETS CHAYYIM, THE TREE OF LIFE

1. Before we can understand the significance of any in-individual Sephirah, we must grasp the broad outlines of the ETS CHAYYIM, the Tree of Life, as a whole.

2. It is a glyph, that is to say a composite symbol, which is intended to represent the cosmos in its entirety and the soul of man as related thereto; and the more we study it, the more we see that it is an amazingly adequate representation; we use it as the engineer or the mathematician uses his sliding-rule, to scan and calculate the intricacies of existence, visible and invisible, in external nature or the hidden depth of the soul.

3. It is represented, as will be seen from diagram III, as a set of ten circles arranged in a certain pattern, and connected among themselves by lines. The circles are the Ten Holy Sephiroth, and the connecting lines are the Paths, twenty-two in number.

4. Each Sephirah (which is the singular form of the word of which Sephiroth is the plural) is a phase of evolution, and in the language of the Rabbis they are called the Ten Holy Emanations. The Paths between them are phases of subjective consciousness, the Paths or grades (Latin, *gradus*, step) by which the soul unfolds its realisation of the cosmos. The Sephiroth are objective; the Paths are subjective.

5. Let it be recalled again that I am not expounding the traditional Qabalah of the Rabbis as a historical curio, but the structure that has been raised upon it by generations of students, initiates all of them, adepts some of them, who have made the Tree of Life their instrument of spiritual development and magical work. This is the modern Qabalah, the

37

Alchemical Qabalah as it has sometimes been called, and it contains all manner of things beside traditional Rabbinical lore, as will be seen in due course.

6. Let us now consider the general lay-out and significance of the Tree. It will be seen that the circles which represent the Sephiroth are arranged in three vertical columns (see diagram I), and that at the head of the centre, higher than any other, forming the apex of the topmost triangle of Sephiroth, is the Sephirah Kether, to which we referred in the previous chapter. To quote again the words of MacGregor Mathers, "The limitless ocean of negative light does not proceed from a centre, for it is centreless, but it concentrates a centre, which is the number one of the manifested Sephiroth, Kether, the Crown, the First Sephirah."

7. Mme Blavatsky draws from Eastern sources the term "The point within the circle" to express the First Becoming of manifestation, and the idea is contained in the Rabbinical term, Nequdah Rashunah, the Primal Point, a name applied to Kether.

8. But Kether does not represent a position in space. The Ain Soph Aur has been called a circle whose centre is everywhere and whose circumference is nowhere, a statement which, like so many in occultism, is inconceivable, yet nevertheless presents an image to the mind and therefore serves its purpose. Kether, then (and for the matter of that, all the other Sephiroth), is a state or condition of existence. We must always bear in mind that the planes do not tower up one above another into the empyrean like the storeys of a building, but are conditions of being, states of existence of different types, and though they developed successively in time, they occur simultaneously in space; existence of all types being present in a single being, as we realise when we remember that the being of man is made up of a physical body, emotions, mind, and spirit, all occupying the same space at the same time.

9. If anyone has ever watched a heated liquid, at saturation point, crystallise out as it cools, they will have a useful symbol of Kether. Fill a tumbler with boiling water and dissolve in

it as much sugar as it will take up, and then, as the mixture cools, watch the sugar crystals appearing. When you have done this in actuality, and not merely read about it, you will have a concept under which you can think of the First Manifest coming into existence out of the Primordial Unmanifest. The liquid is transparent and formless, but a change occurs within it, and crystals, solid, visible, and of a definite form, begin to appear. Equally may we conceive that a change occurs within the Limitless Light, and Kether crystallises out.

10. I do not propose at the present moment to go deeply into the nature of any of the Sephiroth, but merely to indicate the general scheme of the Tree. We shall go over the ground again and again in the course of these pages until a comprehensive concept is built up. This can only be done gradually, and if we spend a great deal of time upon an individual point before the student has a general concept, much of that time will be wasted because the bearing of that concept on the scheme as a whole will not be understood. The Rabbis themselves apply to Kether the titles, Concealed of the Concealed, and the Inscrutable Height, hinting that there is not a great deal that the human mind can hope to know about Kether.

11. It is worthy of note that Exoteric Judaism, to whose liabilities Christianity is the not altogether fortunate heir, does not contain any concept of the Emanations, or overflowing of the Sephiroth one from another. It declares that God made the sea and the hills and the beasts of the field, and we visualise this process, if we visualise it at all, as the work of a celestial craftsman fashioning each new phase of manifestation and putting the finished product in its place in the world. This concept kept science back for hundreds of years in Western Europe, and in the end men of science had to break with religion and endure persecution as heretics in order to arrive at that conception of evolution which was explicitly taught in the Mystic Tradition of Israel, a tradition with which the writers of the Old Testament were unquestionably familiar, for their works are full of Qabalistic references and implications.

12. The Qabalah does not conceive of God as fabricating creation stage by stage, but thinks of the different phases of manifestation as evolving one from another, as if each Sephirah were a pool which, being filled, overflowed into a lower pool. To borrow again from MacGregor Mathers, hidden in an acorn is an oak with its acorns, and hidden in each of these is an oak with *its* acorns. So each Sephirah contains the potentiality of all that come after it in the scale of downflowing manifestation. Kether contains the rest of the Sephiroth, nine in number; and Chokmah, the second, contains the potentialities of all its successors, eight in number. But in each Sephirah only one aspect of manifestation is unfolded; the subsequent ones remain latent, and the preceding ones are received by reflection. Each Sephirah, then, is a pure form of existence in its essence; the influence of preceding phases of evolution is external to it, being reflected. These aspects, as it were, having been crystallised out in the previous stages, are no longer in solution in the outflowing stream of manifestation which ever proceedeth from the Unmanifest through the channel of Kether. When therefore we want to find the essential nature, the basis of manifestation, of a particular type of existence, we get it in the Sephirah to which it corresponds when we meditate upon that Sephirah in its primal form; for there are four forms, or worlds, under which the Qabalists conceive of the Tree, and these we will consider in due course. They are only referred to now in order that the student may have enough background to see his picture in perspective.

13. The student will find it very helpful to refer to the chapters in *The Ancient Wisdom*, by Annie Besant, which deal with the phases of evolution. These throw much light upon the subject with which we are dealing, though the system of classification is not the same.

14. Let us conceive of Kether, then, as a fountain which fills its basin, and the overflow therefrom feeds another fountain, which in its turn fills its basin and overflows. The Unmanifest for ever flows under pressure into Kether, and there comes a time when evolution has gone as far as it can

in the extreme simplicity of the form of existence of the First
Manifest.   All possible combinations have been formed, and
they have undergone all possible permutations.   Action and
reaction are stereotyped, there can be no new development
save the combining of the combinations among themselves.
Force has formed all possible units; the next phase of development is for these units to combine into more complex structures.
When this occurs, a new and more highly organised phase of
existence begins; all that has already been evolved remains,
but that which evolves now is more than the sum of the
previously existing parts, for new capacities come into being.

15. This new phase represents a change of mode of existence.
Just as Kether crystallised out of the Limitless Light, so the
second Sephirah, Chokmah, crystallises out of Kether in this
new mode of being, this new system of actions and reactions
which have ceased to be simple and direct and become complex
and tangential.   We now have two modes of existence, the
simplicity of Kether and the relative complexity of Chokmah;
both these are so simple that no kind of life known to us could
be maintained in them ; nevertheless, they are the forerunners
of organic life.   We might say that Kether is the first activity of
manifestation, movement; it is a condition of pure becoming,
Reshith ha-Gilgulim, the First Swirlings, the commencement
of Whirling Motions as it is called by the Qabalists—Primum
Mobile as it is called by the Alchemists.   Chokmah, the
Second Sephirah, is called by the Rabbis Mazzaloth, the Sphere
of the Zodiac.   Here we have introduced the concept of the
circle with its segments.   Creation has moved onwards.   Out
of the primordial Egg has developed the Serpent that holdeth
his tail in his mouth, as Mme Blavatsky chronicles in her
invaluable storehouses of archaic symbolism, the *Secret
Doctrine* and *Isis Unveiled*.

16. In a similar manner to that in which Kether overflowed
into Chokmah does Chokmah overflow into Binah, the Third
Sephirah.   The Paths pursued by the Emanations in these
successive overflowings is represented upon the Tree of Life
by a Lightning Flash, or in some diagrams by a Flaming

Sword. It will be observed by reference to diagram I that the Lightning Flash must proceed from Kether outwards and downwards to the right to reach Chokmah, and then turns on a level course to the left and proceeds an equal distance beyond Kether upon that side, and there establishes Binah. The result is a triangular figure upon the glyph, and it is called the Triangle of the Three Supernals, or the First Trinity, and is separated from the rest of the Sephiroth by the Abyss, which normal human consciousness cannot cross. Here are the roots of existence, hidden from our eyes.

CHAPTER VII

THE THREE SUPERNALS

1. Having considered in outline the development of the three first Divine Emanations, we are now in a position to obtain a deeper insight into their nature and significance, for we can study them in relation to each other.   This is the only way to study the Sephiroth, for a single Sephirah, taken by itself, is barren of significance.   The Tree of Life is essentially a scheme of relationships, stresses, and reflections (see diagram II).

2. The Rabbinical books apply many curious appellations to the Sephiroth, and we learn much from considering these; for every word in these books has a weighty significance, and none are used lightly or for the sake of idle poetic imagery; all are as precise as scientific terms, which, in fact, is what they are.

3. The meaning of the word Kether, we have already noted, is Crown. Chokmah means Wisdom, and Binah means Understanding.   But pendent to these two latter Sephiroth is a curious and mysterious third, which is never represented in the glyph of the Tree; this is the invisible Sephirah, Daath, Knowledge, and it is said to be formed out of the conjunction of Chokmah and Binah and is situated astride the Abyss. Crowley tells us that Daath is in another dimension to the other Sephiroth, and forms the apex of a pyramid of which Kether, Chokmah, and Binah form the three basal angles. To me, Daath presents the idea of realisation and consciousness.

4. Let us now proceed to elucidate the Three Supernals according to the method of the mystical Qabalah, which consists in filling the mind with all the correspondences and

symbols assigned thereto and letting contemplation work among them.

5. It will be observed that these three and their mysterious fourth all contain symbolism relating to the head, which in the archetypal man represents the highest level of consciousness. When we seek in the Rabbinical literature to see what further names may have been applied to them, we find yet more head symbolism applied to Kether; this, although not specifically referred to them, may be taken to embrace the other two Supernals also, for they are aspects of Kether on a lower plane.

6. The Rabbis called Kether, among other titles, which we need not consider now, Arik Anpin, The Vast Countenance, The White Head, The Head Which Is Not. The magical symbol of Kether, according to Crowley, is an ancient bearded king seen in profile. MacGregor Mathers says: "The symbolism of the Vast Countenance is that of a profile in which one side only of the countenance is seen; or as it is said in the Qabalah, 'In him is all right side.'" The left side, being turned towards the Unmanifest, is for us like the dark side of the moon.

7. But Kether is primarily the Crown. Now the Crown is not the head, but rests upon it and above it. Therefore Kether cannot be consciousness, but the raw material of consciousness when considered microcosmically, and the raw material of existence when considered macrocosmically. For there is this twofold way of considering the Tree, as we have already noted; it can be regarded as the universe and as the soul of man, and these two aspects throw light upon each other. In the words of the Emerald Tablet of Hermes: "As above, so below."

8. Kether differentiates into Chokmah and Binah before it achieves phenomenal existence, and these two are called by the Qabalists, Abba, the Supernal Father, and Ama, the Supernal Mother. Binah is also called the Great Sea, and Shabathai, the Sphere of Saturn. As we continue, we shall find that the Sephiroth are called successively the Spheres of the planets, but Binah is the first of the Emanations to be so assigned; Kether

is called the First Whirlings, and Chokmah the Sphere of the Zodiac.

9. Now Saturn is the Father of the Gods; he is the greatest of the old gods that were the predecessors of the Olympians over which Jupiter rules. In the secret titles attributed to the Tarot trumps, the Path of Saturn is called, according to Crowley, The Great One of the Night of Time.

10. We have, then, Kether differentiating into an active male potency, Chokmah, and a passive female potency, Binah, and these are placed at the head of the two side columns formed by the vertical alignment of the Sephiroth in their spacing on the Tree of Life. Of these two columns, the left-hand one under Binah is called Severity; the right-hand one under Chokmah is called Mercy; the middle one under Kether is called Mildness, and it is said to be the Column of Equilibrium. These two side columns are the two pillars that stand at the entrance to King Solomon's Temple and are represented in all Lodges of the Mysteries, the candidate himself, when he stands between them, is the Middle Pillar of Equilibrium.

11. Here we meet with the idea put forth by Mme Blavatsky, that there can be no manifestation without differentiation into the Pairs of Opposites. Kether differentiates its two aspects as Chokmah and Binah, and manifestation is in being. Now in this supernal triangle, The Head Which Is Not, the Father and the Mother, we have the root concept of our cosmogony, and we shall return to it again and again under innumerable aspects, and each time that we return to it we shall receive illumination. These earlier chapters do not attempt to deal with any of the points exhaustively for reasons already noted, for the student unfamiliar with the subject (and there are very few students who are familiar with it) has not yet got the necessary mental furniture of facts to enable him to appreciate the significance of a more detailed study; we are at the present moment engaged in assembling this furniture; in due course we shall begin to arrange it into a house of life, and study it in detail.

12. Binah, the Superior Mother (as distinguished from Mal kuth, the Inferior Mother, the Bride of Microprosopos, the Isis of Nature, the Tenth Sephirah), is two-aspected, and these aspects are distinguished as Ama, the Dark Sterile Mother, and Aima, the Bright Fertile Mother. We have already noted that she is called the Great Sea, Marah, which not only means Bitter, but also is the root of Mary; and here we meet again the idea of the Mother, at first virgin, and then with child by the Holy Spirit.

13. By the association of Binah with the sea we are reminded that life had its primordial beginnings in the waters; from the sea arose Venus, the archetypal woman. The association of Saturn suggests the idea of primordial age: "Before the gods that made the gods had drunk at eve their fill——" It suggests the most ancient rocks: "Within the shady still-ness of the vale . . . sat grey-haired Saturn, quiet as a stone." Max Heindel speaks of the Lords of Form as among the earliest phases of evoluation, and an inspirational work, *The Cosmic Doctrine* speaks of the Lords of Form as the Laws of Geology.

14. Considering again the symbolism of the two lateral columns of the Tree, we see Chokmah and Binah as Force and Form, the two units of manifestation.

15. It would not profit us to go more deeply into the endless ramifications of this symbolism at the present moment, for it is carrying us beyond the three Sephiroth we have already studied. Let us proceed to a further consideration of the mysterious Daath, which never appears on the Tree, and to which no Deity-name or angelic host is assigned and which has no mundane symbol in planet or element, as have all the other stations on the Tree.

16. Daath is produced by the conjunction of Chokmah and Binah, as has been already noted. The Supernal Father, Abba, marries the Supernal Mother, Ama, and Daath is the issue. Now Daath is called some curious things by the Qabalists; we will note a few of them.

17. In verse 38 of the *Book of Concealed Mystery* (Mathers'

English translation from the Latin translation of Knorr von
Rosenroth) it says: "For Father and Mother are perpetually
conjoined in Yesod, the Foundation (the ninth Sephirah), but
concealed under the mystery of Daath or Knowledge"; and in
verse 40 we read concerning Daath: "The man that shall say,
I am the Lord's, he descendeth. . . . Yod (the tenth letter of
the Hebrew alphabet) is the foundation of Knowledge of the
Father; but all things are called BYODO, that is, all things are
applied to Yod concerning which this discourse is. All
things cohere in the tongue which is concealed in the mother.
That is, through Daath or Knowledge, whereby Wisdom is
combined with Understanding, and the Beautiful Path (Tiphareth, the Sixth Sephirah) with his bride the Queen (Malkuth,
the Tenth Sephirah); and this is the concealed idea, or soul,
pervading the whole emanation. Since it is opened for that
which proceedeth from itself; that is, Daath is itself the
beautiful path, but also the inner, whereto Moses referred;
and that Path lieth hid within the mother, and is the medium
of its conjunction." When it is noted that Yod is identical
with the Lingam in the Hindu system; and that Kether, Daath,
and the Beautiful Path, Tiphareth, the Sixth Sephirah, are in a
line on the Middle Pillar of the Tree, which equates with the
spine in man, the microcosm; and that Kundalini is coiled in
Yesod, also on the Middle Pillar, we shall see that we have here
an important key for those who are equipped to use it.

18. In the *Greater Holy Assembly*, verse 566 (Mathers'
translation), we read concerning the Head of Microprosopos,
whose whole body is being taken as a glyph of the cosmos:
"From the Third Cavity there goes forth a thousand times a
thousand conclaves and assemblies, wherein Daath, Knowledge, is contained and dwelleth. And the hollow place of
this cavity is between the other two cavities; and all these
conclaves are filled from either side. This is that which is
written in Proverbs, 'And in knowledge (Daath) shall the
conclaves be filled.' And those three are expanded over the
whole body, on this side and on that, and with them does
the whole body cohere, and the body is contained by them on

every side, and through the whole body are they expanded and diffused."

19. When it is recalled that Daath is situated at the point where the Abyss bisects the Middle Pillar, and that up the Middle Pillar lies the Path of the Arrow, the way by which consciousness goes when the psychic rises on the planes, and that here also is Kundalini, we see that in Daath is the secret of both generation and regeneration, the key to the manifestation of all things through the differentiation into pairs of Opposites and their union in a Third.

20. Thus doth the Tree unfold its secrets to the Qabalists.

21. The Second Triangle upon the Tree of Life is formed of the Sephiroth Chesed, Geburah, and Tiphareth. Chesed is formed by the overflowing of Binah, and is situated in the Right-hand Pillar of Mercy, immediately below Chokmah; the angle of the Lightning Flash, which is used to indicate the course of the emanations upon the Tree, slopes downwards to the right across the glyph, from Binah at the head of the Pillar of Severity to Chesed, which occupies the middle section of the Pillar of Mercy. Then the Flash turns and goes horizontally across the glyph back again to the Pillar of Severity, in the middle section of which is found the Sephirah Geburah. Down and to the right slopes once more the symbol of emanating force, and indicates the Sephirah Tiphareth, which occupies the very centre of the Tree in the Pillar of Mildness or Equilibrium. These three Sephiroth constitute the next functional triangle we have to consider, and although we do not intend to go exhaustively into their symbolism until we have completed our schematic survey of the whole system, it is necessary to say enough to give some clue to their significance and enable them to be assigned to a place in the concept we are building up. This concept is so vast and so infinite in its elaboration of detail that to attempt to teach it exhaustively from A to Z must end in confusion. Only gradually can it reveal its significance to the student as one aspect interprets another. My method of teaching the Tree may not be ideal from the point of view of systematic thought,

but I believe it is the only one which will enable the beginner to "get the hang" of the subject. It was upon the Tree that I got my own mystical training, and I have lived and moved and had my being in its company for a good many years now, so I feel that I am competent to speak upon it from the point of view of practical mysticism; for I know from my own experience the difficulties of getting hold of the Qabalistic system, so intricate, abstract, and voluminous, and yet so comprehensive and satisfactory when once it is mastered.

22. Before we can consider the Second Triangle of the Tree as a unit, we must know the meaning of its component Sephiroth. Chesed means Mercy or Love; it is also called Gedullah, Greatness of Magnificence, and to it is assigned the Sphere of the planet Jupiter. Geburah means Strength; it is also called Pachad, Fear; to it is assigned the Sphere of the planet Mars. Tiphareth means Beauty, and to it is assigned the Sphere of the Sun. When the gods of the various pagan pantheons are being correlated with the Spheres on the Tree, it will be found that the sacrificed gods invariably come on to Tiphareth, and for this reason it has been called the Christ-centre in the Christian Qabalah.

23. We now have sufficient material to make a survey of the Second Triangle. Jupiter, the beneficent ruler and law-giver, is balanced by Mars the Warrior, the fiery and destructive force, and the two are equilibrated in Tiphareth, the Redeemer. In the Supernal Triangle we see the primary Sephirah emanating a pair of opposites which express the two sides of its nature, Chokmah, Force, and Binah, Form, masculine and feminine Sephiroth respectively. In the Second Triangle we have the pairs of opposites which find their equilibrium in a third, placed upon the Middle Pillar of the Tree. From this we deduce that the First Triangle derives its significance from that which lies behind it, and the Second Triangle derives its significance from that into which it issues forth. In the First Triangle we find a representation of the creative forces of the substance of the universe; in the Second we have a representation of the governing forces of evolving

life.   In Chesed is the wise and kindly king, the father of his people, organising his realm, building up industry, fostering learning, and bringing the gifts of civilisation.   In Geburah we have a warrior king, leading his people in battle, defending his kingdom from the assaults of the enemy, extending his boundaries by conquest, punishing crime, and destroying evil-doers.   In Tiphareth we have the Saviour, sacrificed upon the Cross for the salvation of his people, and thereby bringing Geburah into equilibrium with Gedulah, or Chesed. Here we find the sphere of all the beneficent sun-gods and healing gods.   Thus we see that the mercies of Gedulah and the severities of Geburah unite for the healing of the nations.

24. Behind Tiphareth, traversing the Tree, is drawn Parokheth, the Veil of the Temple, the analogue, on a lower plane, of the Abyss which separates the Three Supernals from the rest of the Tree.   Like the Abyss, the Veil marks a chasm in consciousness.   The mode of mentation on one side of the chasm differs in kind from the mode of mentation prevailing upon the other.   Tiphareth is the highest sphere to which normal human consciousness can rise.   When Philip said to Our Lord, "Show us the Father," Jesus replied, "He that hath seen Me hath seen the Father."   All the human mind can know of Kether is its reflection in Tiphareth, the Christ-centre, the Sphere of the Son.   Paroketh is the Veil of the Temple which was rent asunder at the Crucifixion.

25. We now come in our brief preliminary survey to the Third Triangle composed of the Sephiroth Netzach, Hod, and Yesod.   Netzach is the basal Sephirah of the Pillar of Mercy, Hod is the basal Sephirah of the Pillar of Severity, and Yesod is upon the Middle Pillar of Mildness or Equilibrium, in direct alignment with Kether and Tiphareth.   Thus the Third Triangle is an exact replica of the Second Triangle upon a lower arc.

26. The meaning of Netzach is Victory, and to it is assigned the Sphere of the planet Venus; the meaning of Hod is Glory, and to it is assigned the Sphere of the planet Mercury; the meaning of Yesod is Foundation, and to it is assigned the Sphere of the Moon.

27. While the Second Triangle might not inaptly be termed the Ethical Triangle, the Third may well be called the Magical Triangle; and if we assign to Kether the Sphere of the Three in One, the undivided Unity, and to Tiphareth the Sphere of the Redeemer or Son, we may be justified in referring to Yesod the Sphere of the Holy Spirit, the Enlightener; this is an attribution of the Christian Trinity that fits better upon the Tree than its assignation to the Three Supernals, which brings the Son in the place of Abba, the Father, and the Holy Spirit in the place of Ama, the Mother, and is obviously irrelevant and productive of innumerable discrepancies in the correspondences and symbolisms. In this we see an example of the value of the Tree as a method of counterchecking vision or meditation; correct attributions fit upon the Tree through endless ramifications of symbolism, as we saw when considering Binah as the Mother; incorrect symbolism breaks down and reveals its bizarre associations at the first attempt to follow out a chain of correspondences. It is amazing what ramifications of association-chains can be followed when the attribution is correct. It seems as if it were only the extent of our knowledge which limits the length of the chain that can be linked logically together; it will extend through science, art, mathematics, and the epochs of history; through ethics, psychology, and physiology. It was this peculiar method of using the mind which in all probability gave the ancients their premature knowledge of natural science, knowledge which has had to await the invention of instruments of precision for its confirmation. We get clues to this method in the dream-analysis of analytical psychology. We might describe it as the symbol-using power of the subconscious mind. It is an instructive experiment to toss a mass of irrelevant symbolism into the mind and watch it sort itself out in meditation upon the Tree, rising into consciousness in long association-chains like dream analysis.

28. Netzach is the Sphere of the Goddess of Nature, Venus. Hod is the Sphere of Mercury, the Greek analogue of the Egyptian Thoth, Lord of Books and Learning. Observing

their opposition, we shall expect to find two different aspects represented in them, these finding their equilibrium in a third, Yesod, the Sphere of Luna.   We see then a Triangle composed of the Lady of Nature, the Lord of Books, and the Mistress of Witchcraft; in other words, subconsciousness and super-consciousness correlate in psychism.

29. Anyone who is familiar with practical mysticism knows that there are three paths of superconsciousness—devotional mysticism, which correlates with Tiphareth; nature mysticism, of the inebriating Dionysian type, which equates with the Venus Sphere of Netzach; and intellectual mysticism of the occult type, which equates with Hod, the Sphere of Thoth, Lord of Magic.   Tiphareth, as will be seen by reference to the diagram of the Tree, belongs to a higher plane than any member of the Third Triangle; Yesod, on the other hand, is drawing very near to the Sphere of Earth.

30. To Yesod are assigned all the deities that have the moon in their symbolism: Luna herself; Hecate, with her dominion over evil magic ; and Diana, with her presidency over child-birth.   The physical moon, Yesod in Assiah, as the Qabalists would say, with its twenty-eight day cycle, correlates with the reproductive cycle of the human female.   If the symbolism of the luna crescent be traced through the various pantheons it will be found that the deities associated with it are predominantly female; it is interesting to note in confirmation of our assignation of the Holy Spirit to Yesod that according to MacGregor Mathers the Holy Spirit is a feminine force.   He says (*Kabbalah Unveiled,* p. 22): "We are usually told that the Holy Spirit is masculine.   But the word Ruach, Spirit, is feminine, as appears from the following passage of the Sepher Yetzirah, 'Achath (feminine, not Achad, masculine), ruach elohim chiim: One is *she*, the Spirit of the Elohim of Life.'" When we consider the Middle Pillar as referring to levels of consciousness we shall find further confirmation of this view.

31. There remains for our final consideration the Sephirah Malkuth, the Kingdom of Earth.   This Sephirah differs from

the others in several respects. Firstly, it is not part of any equilibrated triangle, but is said to be the receptacle of the influences of all the others. Secondly, it is a fallen Sephirah, for it was cut off from the rest of the Tree by the Fall, and the coils of the Stooping Dragon arising from the World of Shells, the Kingdoms of Unbalanced Force, separate it from its brethren. Behind the shoulder of the Queen, the Bride of Microprosopos (Malkuth), the Serpent rears his head, and here is said to be the place of severest judgments. The Sphere of Malkuth abuts upon the Hells of the Averse Sephiroth, the Qliphoth, or evil demons. It is the firmament whereby Elohim separated the supernal waters of Binah from the infernal waters of Leviathan.

32. The signification of the Qliphoth must be considered fully in due course; but having referred to them here in order to explain the position of Malkuth, we must say something further in order to render the explanation intelligible.

33. The Qliphoth (singular Qliphah, an immodest woman or harlot) are the Evil or Averse Sephiroth, each an emanation of unbalanced force from its corresponding Sphere upon the Holy Tree; these emanations took place during the critical periods of evolution when the Sephiroth were not in equilibrium. For this reason they are referred to as the Kings of Unbalanced Force, the Kings of Edom, "who ruled before there was a king in Israel," as the Bible puts it; and in the words of the *Siphra Ditsni'utha*, the *Book of Concealed Mystery* (Mathers' translation), "For before there was equilibrium, countenance beheld not countenance. And the kings of ancient time were dead, and their crowns were found no more; and the earth was desolate."

34. We have now completed our preliminary survey of the Tree of Life, and the arrangement of the Ten Holy Sephiroth thereon; we also have some clue to their significance and have been given a hint or two of the manner in which the mind works when it uses these cosmic symbols for its meditations. Consequently we are now in a position to assign each fresh bit of information to its correct position in our scheme; we

are building up the jigsaw puzzle with a knowledge of the outlines of the picture. Crowley has aptly likened the Tree to a card-index file, in which each symbol is an envelope. This is a simile which it would be difficult to improve upon. In the course of our studies we shall begin to fill these filing-cases, and to find the cross-indexing among them indicated by the appearance of the same symbol in other associations.

CHAPTER VIII

1. There are various methods by which the Ten Holy Sephiroth can be grouped upon the Tree of Life. Of these it cannot be said that one is correct and another incorrect; they serve different purposes and throw much light upon the meaning of the individual Sephiroth by revealing their associations and equilibrium.

2. They are also of value because they enable the decimal system of the Tree to be equated with the three, four, and sevenfold systems.

3. The primary conformation of the Tree is into three Pillars. It will be observed by reference to the diagrams that the Sephiroth readily lend themselves to this threefold vertical division, for they are arranged in three columns. These are called the Right-hand Pillar of Mercy, the Left-hand Pillar of Severity, and the Middle Pillar of Mildness or Equilibrium (see diagram I).

4. Before proceeding any further we must make clear the significance of the right and left sides of the Tree. As we look at the Tree in the diagram we see Binah, Geburah, and Hod upon the left side, and Chokmah, Chesed, and Netzach upon the right side; this is the way we view the Tree when we are using it to represent the Macrocosm. But when we are using it to represent the Microcosm, that is our own being, we, as it were, back into it, so that the Middle Pillar equates with the spine, and the Pillar that contains Binah, Geburah, and Hod with the right side, and the Pillar that contains Chokmah, Chesed, and Netzach with the left side. These three Pillars can also be equated with the Shushumna, Ida, and Pingala of the Yoga system. It is very important to remember

the reversal of the Tree when it is used as a subjective symbol, otherwise confusion results. In his valuable book upon the literature of the Qabalah, *The Holy Qabalah*, Mr Waite, in the frontispiece, for some reason best known to himself, reverses the usual presentation of the Tree; but it may be taken for granted that most representations of the symbol give the objective Tree, not the subjective. When the Tree is being used to indicate the lines of force in the aura, it is the subjective Tree that must be used, so that Geburah equates with the right arm. In all cases, of course, the Middle Pillar remains steadfast.

5. The Pillar of Severity is considered to be negative or feminine, and the Pillar of Mercy to be positive or masculine. Superficially it may be thought that these attributions lead to incompatible symbolism, but a study of the Pillars in the light of what we now know concerning the individual Sephiroth will reveal that the incompatibilities are purely superficial and that the deeper significance of the symbolism is entirely consonant.

6. It will be observed that the line which indicates the successive development of the Sephiroth zigzags from side to side of the glyph and has been aptly named the Lightning Flash in consequence. This indicates graphically that the Sephiroth are successively positive, negative, and equilibrated. This is a far better representation of the process of creation than if the Spheres were represented one above another in a straight line, for it indicates the difference in the nature of the Divine Emanations and their relations to each other; for when we look at the glyph of the Tree we readily perceive the relations existing between the different Sephiroth, and see how they group, reflect, and react upon each other.

7. At the head of the Pillar of Severity, the negative, feminine Pillar, is Binah, the Great Mother. Now to Binah is assigned the Sphere of Saturn, and Saturn is the Giver of Form. At the head of the Pillar of Mercy is Chokmah, the Supernal Father, a male potency. Thus we see that we have here the apposition of Form and Force.

8. In the Second Trinity we have the apposition of Chesed (Jupiter) and Geburah (Mars). Again we have the pairs of opposites of construction in Jupiter, the lawgiver and beneficent ruler, and destruction in Mars, the warrior and destroyer of evil. It may be asked why such a male potency as Geburah should be placed in the feminine Pillar. It must be remembered that Mars is a destructive potency, one of the infortunes in astrology. The positive builds up, the negative breaks down; the positive is a kinetic force, the negative is a static force.

9. These aspects appear again in Netzach at the base of the Pillar of Mercy, and Hod at the base of the Pillar of Severity. Netzach is Venus, the Green Nature Ray, elemental force, the initiation of the emotions. Hod is Mercury, Hermes, the initiation of knowledge. Netzach is instinct and emotion, a kinetic force; Hod is intellect, concrete thought, the reduction of intuitive knowledge to form.

10. We must remember, however, that each Sephirah is negative, that is to say feminine, in relation to its predecessor, whence it emanates and whence it receives the Divine Influence; and positive, masculine, or stimulating in respect of its successor, to whom it transmits the Divine Influence. Therefore each Sephirah is bi-sexual, like a magnet of which one pole must of necessity be negative and the other positive. We may perhaps explain matters further by an analogy with astrology, and say that a Sephirah in the feminine Pillar is well-dignified when it is functioning in its negative aspect, and ill-dignified when functioning positively ; and that in the masculine Pillar the position is reversed. Thus Binah, Saturn, is well-dignified when providing stability and endurance, but ill-dignified when the overplus of resistance causes it to become actively aggressive and we get obstruction and the accretion of effete matter. On the other hand, Chesed, Mercy, is well-dignified when ordering and preserving all things harmoniously; but ill-dignified when mercy becomes sentimentality and it usurps the Sphere of Saturn, preserving that which the fiery energy of Mars, its opposite number, the Sephirah Geburah, should sweep out of existence.

5

11. The two Pillars, then, represent the positive and negative forces in Nature, the active and passive, the destructive and constructive, concreting form and free-moving force.

12. The Sephiroth on the Middle Pillar may be taken as representing levels of consciousness and the planes on which they operate. Malkuth is sensory consciousness; Yesod is astral psychism; Tiphareth is illuminated consciousness, the highest aspect of the personality with which the individuality has coalesced; this is the condition which really constitutes initiation; it is the consciousness of the higher self brought through into the personality. It is a gleam of higher consciousness coming from behind the veil Parokheth. It is for this reason that the Messiahs and Saviours of the world are assigned to Tiphareth in the symbolism of the Tree, for they were the Light-Bringers to humanity; and as all who bring fire from heaven must do, they died the sacrificial death for the sake of mankind. It is here, too, that we die to the lower self in order that we may rise in the higher self. "In Jesu morimur."

13. The Middle Pillar rises through Daath, the Invisible Sephirah, which we have already seen is Knowledge according to the Rabbis, and conscious awareness or apprehension according to the terminology of the psychologist. At the head of this Pillar is Kether, the Crown, the Root of all Being. Consciousness, then, reaches from the spiritual essence of Kether, through the realisation of Daath, which carries it across the Abyss, into the translated consciousness of Tiphareth, whither it is brought by the sacrifice of the Christ which rends the veil Paroketh; then on into the psychic consciousness of Yesod, the Sphere of the Moon, and thence to the sensory brain consciousness of Malkuth.

14. Thus does consciousness descend in the course of involution, which is the term applied to that phase of evolution which leads down from the First Manifest through the subtle planes of existence to dense matter; the esotericist should, strictly speaking, only use the term evolution when describing

the ascent from matter back to spirit, for then is evolved that which was involved in the descent through the subtle phases of development. It is obvious that nothing can be evolved, unfolded, which was not previously involved, infolded. The actual course of evolution follows the track of the Lightning Flash or Flaming Sword, from Kether to Malkuth in the order of development of the Sephiroth previously described; but consciousness descends plane by plane, and only begins to manifest when the polarising Sephiroth are in equilibrium; therefore the modes of consciousness are assigned to the Equilibrating Sephiroth upon the Middle Pillar, but the magical powers are assigned to the opposing Sephiroth, each at the end of the beam of the balance of the pairs of opposites.

15. The Way of Initiation follows the coilings of the Serpent of Wisdom upon the Tree; but the Way of Illumination follows the Path of the Arrow which is shot from the Bow of Promise, Qesheth, the rainbow of astral colours that spreads like a halo behind Yesod. This is the way of the mystic as distinguished from that of the occultist; it is swift and direct, and free from the danger of the temptation of unbalanced force that is met with in either pillar, but it confers no magical powers save those of sacrifice in Tiphareth and psychism in Yesod.

16. We have noted the Three Trinities of the Tree in our preliminary discussion of the Ten Sephiroth. Let us recapitulate these again for clearness' sake. Mathers calls the First Trinity of Kether, Chokmah, and Binah the Intellectual World; the Second Trinity of Chesed, Geburah, and Tiphareth the Moral World; and the Third Trinity of Netzach, Hod, and Yesod the Material World. To my way of thinking, this terminology is misleading, for these words do not connote in our minds what is meant by these Worlds. The intellect is essentially a concreting of intuition and apprehension, and as such is an unsuitable term for the World of the Three Supernals. With the use of the term Moral World for Chesed, Geburah, and Tiphareth I agree; it is identical with my term, Ethical Triangle; but with the term Material World for the Trinity

of Netzach, Hod, and Yesod I emphatically disagree, for this term belongs exclusively to Malkuth. These three Sephiroth are not material but astral, and for this Trinity I propose the term Astral, or Magical World; it is not well to wrest words from their dictionary meaning, even if you define your use of them, and this Mathers has not troubled to do.

17. The Intellectual Sphere is not so much a level as a Pillar, for the intellect, being the content of consciousness, is essentially synthetic. These terms, however, are apparently taken from a somewhat crude translation of the Hebrew names given to the four levels into which the Qabalists divide manifestation.

18. These four levels permit of yet another grouping of the Sephiroth. The highest of these is Atziluth, the Archetypal World, consisting of Kether. The second, Briah, called the Creative World, consists of Chokmah and Binah, the Supernal Abba and Ama, Father and Mother. The third level is that of Yetzirah, the Formative World, consisting of the six central Sephiroth, viz. Chesed, Geburah, Tiphareth, Netzach, Hod, and Yesod. The fourth World is Assiah, the Material World, represented by Malkuth.

19. The Ten Sephiroth are also conformed into Seven Palaces. In the First Palace are the Three Supernals; in the Seventh Palace are Yesod and Malkuth ; and the rest of the Sephiroth each has a Palace to itself. The grouping is of interest as revealing the intimate relationship of Yesod and Malkuth, and enabling the tenfold scale of the Qabalah to be equated with the sevenfold scale of Theosophy.

20. There is also a threefold division of the Sephiroth which is very important in Qabalistic symbolism. In this system Kether is given the title of Arik Anpin, the Vast Countenance. This is manifested as Abba, the Supernal Father, Chokmah, and Ama, the Supernal Mother, Binah, these being the positive and negative aspects of the Three in One. These two differentiated aspects, when united, are, according to Mathers, Elohim, that curious Divine Name which is a feminine noun with a masculine plural attached to it. This union takes place in Daath, the invisible Sephirah.

21. The next six Sephiroth are conformed into Zeir Anpin, the Lesser Countenance, or Microprosopos, whose special Sephirah is Tiphareth. The remaining Sephirah, Malkuth, is called the Bride of Microprosopos.

22. Microprosopos is also sometimes called the King; Malkuth is then called the Queen. She is also called the Lesser Mother or Terrestrial Eve as distinguished from Binah, the Supernal Mother.

23. These different methods of classifying the Sephiroth are not competing systems, but are designed to enable the decimal system of the Qabalists to be equated with other systems, using a threefold notation, such as the Christian, or as we have already noted, a sevenfold system like Theosophy; they are also valuable as indicating functional affiliations among the Sephiroth themselves.

24. The final system of classification which we must note is under the presidency of the Three Mother Letters of the Hebrew alphabet: Aleph, A; Mem, M; and Shin, Sh. These three, according to the Yetziratic attribution of the Hebrew alphabet, are assigned to the three elements of Air, Water, and Fire. Under the presidency of Aleph is the Airy triad of Kether, in which is the Root of Air, reflecting downward through Tiphareth, the Solar Fire, into Yesod, the Lunar radiance. In Binah is the Root of Water (Marah, the Great Sea), reflected through Chesed into Hod, under the presidency of Mem, the Mother of Water. In Chokmah is the Root of Fire, reflected downwards through Geburah into Netzach, under the presidency of Shin, the Mother of Fire.

25. These groupings must be borne in mind, for they aid greatly in understanding the significance of individual Sephiroth, for, as we have already pointed out in various connections, a Sephirah is best interpreted by its affiliations.

CHAPTER IX

THE TEN SEPHIROTH IN THE FOUR WORLDS

1. We have already noted the division of the Sephiroth into the Four Worlds of the Qabalists, for this is one of the methods of classification much employed in Qabalistic thought and of great value when studying evolution. We must remember, however, that the Tree is not an arbitrary method of classification, and because a thing is classified under one head in one system it does not mean that it cannot equally properly be classified under another head in another system. The reappearance of the same symbol in a different Sphere often affords valuable clues.

2. Under another method of classification the Ten Holy Sephiroth are considered as appearing in each Qabalistic World upon another arc or level of manifestation; so that just as Or En Soph, the Limitless Light of the Unmanifest, concentrated a point, which was Kether, and the emanations worked down through increasing grades of density to Malkuth, so the Malkuth of Atziluth is conceived of as giving rise to the Kether of Briah, and so on consecutively down the planes, the Malkuth of Briah giving rise to the Kether of Yetzirah, the Malkuth of Yetzirah giving rise to the Kether of Assiah, and the Malkuth of Assiah, in its lowest aspect, abutting upon the Qliphoth.

3. It is Atziluth, however, which is considered the natural sphere of the Sephiroth as such, and for this reason it is called the World of Emanations. It is here, and here only, that God acts directly and not through His ministers. In Briah He acts through the mediation of the Archangels, in Yetzirah through the Angelic Orders, and in Assiah through those centres which I have named the Mundane Chakras—the planets, elements, and signs of the Zodiac.

4. We have, then, in these four sets of symbols a complete system of notation for expressing the mode of function of any given power at any given level, and this system of notation is the basis of ceremonial magic with its Names of Power, and also of talismanic magic and the Tarot system of divination. It is for this reason that it is said of the "barbarous names of evocation" that not so much as a letter may be changed, for these names are formulæ based on the Hebrew alphabet, which is the sacred language of the West as Sanskrit is the sacred language of the East.   In Hebrew, moreover, each letter is also a number, so the Names are numerical formulæ; a most intricate system of metaphysical mathematics, called Gematria, is based on this principle.   There are aspects of Gematria which I, at the present stage of my knowledge at any rate, consider debased and idle, being the accretions of superstition, but the basic idea of the system of cosmic mathematics un-questionably enshrines great truths and contains great possi-bilities.   Using this system, it is possible to unravel the relationships of all manner of cosmic factors if the correct Hebrew spelling of the Names of Power is known, for these Names were formulated in accordance with the principles of Gematria, and therefore Gematria supplies the key to them. But this aspect of our subject, fascinating as it is, we cannot enter upon now.

5. In the Archetypal World of Atziluth there are assigned to the Ten Sephiroth ten forms of the Divine Name.   Anyone who has read the Bible cannot fail to have observed that God is referred to under divers titles, as the Lord, as the Lord God, as the Father, and by several other appellations.   Now these are not literary devices to avoid needless repetition, but are exact metaphysical terms, and according to the Name used we know the aspect of Divine force in question and the plane on which it is functioning.

6. In the world of Briah it is held that the mighty Arch-angels carry out the mandates of God and give them expression, and assigned to the Sephirothic Spheres on the Tree in this World are the names of these ten mighty spirits.

7. In Yetzirah it is the choirs of angels, innumerable in their concourse, who carry out the Divine commands; and these also are assigned to their Sephirothic Spheres, thus enabling us to know their mode and level of function.

8. In Assiah, as we have already noted, certain natural centres of force are given similar correspondences. We will consider all these associations when we come to study the Sephiroth in detail.

9. In the symbolic rendering of the Ten Holy Sephiroth in the Four Worlds there is another important set of factors to be considered, and these are the four colour scales classified by Crowley as the King scale, assigned to the Atziluthic World; the Queen scale, assigned to the Briatic World; the Emperor scale, assigned to the Yetziratic World; and the Empress scale, assigned to the Assiatic World.

10. This fourfold classification has a far-reaching significance in all Qabalistic matters, and also in Western magic, which is largely based upon the Qabalah. It is said to be under the presidency of the Four Letters of Tetragrammaton, the Sacred Name popularly rendered as Jehovah. In Hebrew, which has no vowels in its alphabet, this word is spelt Yhvh, or, according to the Hebrew names of these letters, Yod, Hé, Vav, Hé. The vowels are indicated in Hebrew by points inserted in and under the square letters of the script, which is written from right to left. These vowel-points were only introduced at a comparatively recent date, and the older Hebrew scripts are unpointed so that the reader cannot see the pronunciation of any proper name for himself, but needs to have it communicated to him by someone who knows it. The true mystical pronunciation of the Tetragrammaton is said to be one of the arcana of the Mysteries.

11. To the Four Letters of the Name are allotted any fourfold mystical classification, and by means of their correspondences we can trace all manner of relationships, and these are very important in practical occultism, as will be seen later.

12. Four important fourfold divisions find a place under

them, thus enabling us to see their relationships among themselves.   These are the Four Worlds of the Qabalists; the four
elements of the alchemists; the fourfold classification of the
signs of the Zodiac and the planets into triplicities, employed
by the astrologers; and the four suits of the Tarot pack used in
divination.   This fourfold classification resembles the Rosetta
Stone which gave the key to the Egyptian hieroglyphs, for
on it were inscriptions in Egyptian and Greek; Greek being
known, it was possible to work out the meaning of the corresponding Egyptian hieroglyphs.   It is the method of arranging all these sets of factors on the Tree which gives the real
esoteric clue to each of these systems of practical occultism.
Without this key they have no philosophical basis and become
matters of rule of thumb and superstition.   It is for this
reason that the initiated occultist will have nothing to do with
the uninitiated fortune-teller, for he knows that, lacking this
key, his system is valueless.   Hence the vital importance of the
Tree in Western occultism.   It is our basis, our standard of
measurement, and our textbook.

13. To understand a Sephirah, then, we need to know firstly
its primary correspondences in the Four Worlds; its secondary
correspondences in the four systems of practical occultism
mentioned above; and, thirdly, any other correspondences we
can by any means gather together, in order that the testimony
of many witnesses may yield the truth.   Of this gathering of
correspondences there can be no end, for the whole cosmos on
all its planes corresponds in endless sequences.   We are constantly adding to our knowledge if we are good students of
occult science.   No better simile than that of the card-index
system could possibly have been found.

14. But yet again we must remind the reader in this connection that the Qabalah is as much a method of using the
mind as a system of knowledge.   If we have the knowledge
without having acquired the Qabalistic technique of mentation,
it is of little use to us.   In fact, we might go so far as to say that
it is not possible to acquire any great degree of knowledge until
this technique of the mind has been mastered; for it is not the

conscious mind to which the Tree appeals, but subconsciousness, for the logical method of the Qabalah is the logical
method of dream association; but in the case of the Qabalah
the dreamer is the racial subconsciousness, the oversoul of the
peoples, the Earth-spirit.   Into communion with this Earth-
soul the adept enters by means of meditation on the prescribed
symbols.   This is the real import of the Tree and its correspondences.

15. The highest of the Four Worlds, Atziluth, the plane of
pure Deity, is called by the Qabalists the Archetypal World.
It is also called, in the somewhat clumsy translation of Mac-
Gregor Mathers, the Intellectual World.   This term is misleading.   It is only intellectual as we commonly understand
the word as relating to the mind, the rational intellect, in so far
as it is the realm of archetypal ideas.   But these ideas are
entirely abstract, and are conceived by a function of consciousness quite outside the range of mind as we know it.
Therefore to call this level the Intellectual World is to mislead
the reader, unless at the same time we say that by intellect we
mean something quite different to what the dictionary means.
This is a poor way of expressing our ideas.   It is far better to
coin a new term with a precise meaning than to use an old one
in a misleading sense, especially as, in the case of Atziluth,
there is an excellent term already current, the term Archetypal,
which exactly describes it.

16. The Atziluthic World is said by the Qabalists to be
under the presidency of the Yod of the Sacred Name of Tetragrammaton.   We may justly deduce from this that in any other
fourfold system whatever is said to be also under the presidency of Yod will refer to the Atziluthic, or purely spiritual
aspect of that force or subject.   Among other associations
given by different authorities are the Wands suit of the Tarot
pack and the Element of Fire.   It will be apparent to anyone
who has any knowledge of occult matters that as soon as we
know the element to which a symbol is assigned, we know a
good deal, for it open' up all the ramifications of astrology for
us, and we can trace)ut its astrological affinities through the

triplicities of the Zodiac and the affinities of the planets with them.   As soon as we know what Zodiacal and planetary associations exist, we are in a position to explore the correlated symbolism of any pantheon, for all the gods and goddesses of all the systems that the human mind has ever invented have astrological associations.   The stories of their adventures are really parables of the workings of cosmic forces.   Through this maze of symbolism we could never hope to find our way unaided, but if we anchor the end of each chain of correspondences to its Sephirah, we have the clue we need.

17. All systems of esoteric thought, as well as all popular theologies, attribute the construction and presidency of the different parts of the manifested universe to the mediation of intelligent and purposive beings, working under the instruction of Deity.   Modern thought has tried to escape from the implications of this concept by reducing manifestation to a matter of mechanics; it has not succeeded, and there are signs that it is not far from the point when it will perceive mind as being at the root of form.

18. The concepts of the Ancient Wisdom may be crude from the standpoint of modern philosophy, but we are forced to admit that the causative force behind manifestation is more akin in its nature to mind than to matter.   To go a step further and personify the different types of force is a legitimate analogy, provided we realise that the entity which is the soul of the force may differ as much in kind and degree from our minds as our bodies differ in type and scale from the bodies of the planets.   We shall be nearer an understanding of nature if we look for mind in the background than if we refuse to admit that the visible universe has an invisible framework. The ether of the physicists is closer akin to mind than to matter; time and space, as understood by the modern philosopher, are more like modes of consciousness than linear measures.

19. The initiates of the Ancient Wisdom made no bones about their philosophy; they took each factor in Nature and personified it, gave it a name, and built up a symbolic figure

to represent it, just as British artists have by their collective efforts produced a standard Britannia, a female figure with shield charged with the Union Jack, a lion at her feet, a trident in her hand, a helmet on her head, and the sea in the background.   Analysing this figure as we would a Qabalistic symbol, we realise that these individual symbols in the complex glyph have each a significance.   The various crosses which make up the Union Jack refer to the four races united in the United Kingdom.   The helmet is that of Minerva, the trident is that of Neptune; the lion would need a chapter to himself to elucidate his symbolism.   In fact, an occult glyph is more akin to a coat of arms than anything else, and the person who builds up a glyph goes to work in the same way as a herald designing a coat of arms.   For in heraldry every symbol has its exact meaning, and these are combined into the coat of arms that represents the family and affiliations of the man who bears it. A magical figure is the coat of arms of the force it represents.

20. These magical figures are built up to represent the different modes of the manifestation of cosmic force in its different types and on its different levels.   They are given names, and the initiate thinks of them as persons, not troubling himself about their metaphysical foundations.   Consequently, for all practical purposes they are persons, for whatever they may be in actual fact, they have been personalised, and thought-forms have been built up on the astral plane to represent them. These, being charged with force, are of the nature of artificial elementals; but the force with which they are charged being cosmic, they are much more than what we ordinarily imply when we speak of artificial elementals, and we assign them to the angelic kingdom and call them angels or archangels according to their grade.   An angelic being, then, may be defined as a cosmic force whose apparent vehicle of manifestation to psychic consciousness is a form built up by the human imagination.   In practical occultism, these forms are built up with great care and the most elaborate attention to the details of the symbolism, and are used to evoke the force

required; anyone who has had experience of their use will agree that they are peculiarly effectual for the purposes for which they are designed. By holding the magical image in mind and vibrating the traditional name assigned thereto, remarkable phenomena are obtained.

21. As we have already noted, it is necessary to use the mental technique of the Qabalists in order to get any sense out of the Qabalah; this formulation of the image and vibration of the name is designed to put the student in touch with the forces behind each Sphere of the Tree, and when he comes into touch in this way his consciousness is illuminated and his nature energised by the force thus contacted, and he obtains remarkable illuminations from his contemplation of the symbols. These illuminations are not a generalised flooding of light, as in the case of the Christian mystic, but a specific energising and illumination according to the Sphere opened up; Hod gives understanding of sciences, Yesod understanding of life-force and its tidal modes of functioning. When Hod is contacted we become filled with enthusiasm and energy for research; when Yesod is contacted we enter deeply into psychic consciousness and touch the hidden life-forces of the earth and our own natures. These are matters of experience; those who have used the method know what it yields them. Whatever may be the rational foundations of the system, as an empirical method it yields results.

22. If we want to study a Sephirah—in other words, if we want to investigate the aspect of Nature to which it refers—we not only study it intellectually and meditate upon it, but we try to get into psychic and intuitive touch with its influence and Sphere. In order to accomplish this, we always start at the top and try to get into spiritual touch with the aspect of Deity which emanated that Sphere and manifests in it. If this is not done, the forces belonging to the Sphere on the elemental levels may get out of hand and cause difficulties. Starting under the presidency of the Divine Name, however, no evil can enter.

23. Having adored the Creator and Sustainer of All under

His Holy Name in the Sphere we are investigating, we next invoke the Archangel of the Sphere, the mighty spiritual being in whom we personify the forces that built up that level of evolution and continue to function in the corresponding aspect of Nature. We ask the blessing of the Archangel, and beg that he will bid the Order of Angels assigned to that Sphere that they shall be friendly and helpful towards us in the realm of nature in which they function. By the time we have done this, we shall be thoroughly tuned to the keynote of the Sphere we are investigating, and be ready to follow out the ramifications of the correspondences of that Sephirah and its cognate symbols.

24. Approached in this way, we shall find the association-chains far richer in symbolism than we have ever believed to be possible, for the subconscious mind has been stirred and one of its many chambers of imagery thrown open, to the exclusion of all the others. The association-chains that rise into consciousness should therefore be free from any admixture of extraneous ideas and true to type.

25. First we review in our minds all the possible symbols that we can recollect, and as these present themselves to consciousness we try and see their import and bearing upon the secrets of the Sphere under investigation. But we do not try too hard; for if we concentrate upon a symbol and strain at it, as it were, we shall close the meshes of the tenuous veil that shields the subconscious mind. In these investigations, half meditation, half reverie, we want to work on the borders of consciousness and subconsciousness so as to induce that which is subconscious to cross the threshold and come within our reach.

26. As we proceed thus, following out the ramifications of the association-chains, we shall find that a running comment of intuition accompanies the process, and after the experiment has been repeated two or three times we shall feel that we know that Sephirah in a peculiarly intimate way, that we feel at home there, that the feel of it is quite different to that of the other Sephiroth which we have not yet worked with.

We shall also find that some Sephiroth are more congenial to us than others, and that we get better results when working with them than we do with the uncongenial ones, where the association-chains keep on breaking and the doors of sub-consciousness resolutely refuse to open to our knocking. One pupil of mine could do excellent meditations on Binah—Saturn, and Tiphareth, the Redeemer, but did not get on at all well with Geburah—Severity—Mars.

27. I shall never forget my own experience with the first attempt I made at this method. I was working on the Thirty-second Path, the Path of Saturn, uniting Malkuth and Yesod, a very difficult and treacherous Path. In my horoscope Saturn is not well aspected, and I have often experienced his opposing influence in my affairs. But after I had succeeded in treading the Path of Saturn out into the indigo darkness of the Unseen until the Moon of Yesod rose in purple and silver over the horizon, I felt that I had received the initiation of Saturn, that he was no longer inimical to me, but a friend who, though candid and stern, was to be trusted to protect me from mistakes and rash judgments. I realised his function as the tester, and not the antagonist or avenger. I realised him as Time with his scythe, but knew also why he was called in Hebrew Shabbathai, rest, "for he giveth his beloved sleep." After that, the Thirty-second Path was open to me, not only on the Tree, but in life, for the forces and problems symbolised by that Path and its correspondences had become harmonised in my soul. From these two brief examples it will be seen that the meditations upon the Tree form a most practical and exact system of mystical development; and one that is pecul-iarly valuable in that it is equilibrated, for the different aspects of manifestation are, as it were, dissected out and dealt with in turn, nothing being neglected. By the time we have trodden all the Paths of the Tree we shall have learnt the lessons of Death and the Devil, as well as of the Angel and the High Priest.

CHAPTER X

THE PATHS UPON THE TREE

1. The *Sepher Yetzirah* refers to the Ten Sephiroth them-selves, as well as the lines connecting them, as Paths, and justly so, for they are all equally channels of Divine influence; but it is usual in practical working to consider the lines between the Sephiroth only as the Paths, and the Sephiroth themselves as Spheres upon the Tree. This is one of the many tricks and blinds to be found in the Qabalistic system, for if we think of the Paths as thirty-two in number, as they are given in the *Sepher Yetzirah*, we shall not be able to equate them with the twenty-two letters of the Hebrew alphabet which, with their numerical value and correspondences, form the key to the Paths.

2. Each Path is said to represent the equilibrium of the two Sephiroth it connects, and we have to study it in the light of our knowledge of these Sephiroth if we are to appreciate its significance. Certain symbols are also assigned to the Paths themselves. These are, as already noted, the twenty-two letters of the Hebrew alphabet; the signs of the Zodiac, the planets, and the elements. Now there are twelve signs in the Zodiac, seven planets, and four elements, making in all twenty-three symbols. How are these to be arranged on Twenty-two Paths? Here is another Qabalistic blind to puzzle the uninitiated. The answer is quite simple when it is known. Our consciousness being in the element of Earth, we do not need the symbol of earth in our calculations when we make contact with the Unseen, so we leave it out and then find our-selves with the correct set of correspondences. Malkuth is all the earth we need for practical purposes.

3. The third set of symbols to go upon the Paths are the twenty-two trumps or major arcana of the Tarot pack. With these three sets of symbols and the colours of the four colour scales, our major symbolism is complete; the minor symbolism consists of the innumerable ramifications of the correspondences through all systems and planes.

4. The Tree of Life, astrology, and the Tarot are not three mystical systems, but three aspects of one and the same system, and each is unintelligible without the others. It is only when we study astrology on the basis of the Tree that we have a philosophical system; equally does this apply to the Tarot system of divination, and the Tarot itself, with its comprehensive interpretations, gives the key to the Tree as applied to human life.

5. Astrology is so elusive because the uninitiated astrologer works on one plane only; but the initiated astrologer, with the Tree as his ground-plan, interprets on the four planes of the Four Worlds, and the effect of, shall we say, Saturn, is very different in Atziluth, where it is the Divine Mother, Binah, to what it is in Assiah.

6. All systems of divination and all systems of practical magic find their principles and philosophy based upon the Tree; whoever tries to use them without this key is like the foolhardy person who has a pharmacopœia of patent medicines and doses himself and his friends according to the descriptions given in the advertisements, wherein backache includes every disease which does not cause pain in front. The initiate who knows his Tree is like the scientific physician who understands the principles of physiology and the chemistry of drugs, and prescribes accordingly.

7. Various methods of attributing the Tarot cards have been worked out from traditional sources. In his little book, *The Key to the Tarot,* A. E. Waite gives the chief of these; but refrains from indicating which, in his opinion, is the correct one. In his valuable tabulation of esoteric symbolism, "777," Crowley has no such reticence, but gives the system as it is known among initiates. This is the method I propose to

follow in these pages, for I believe it to be the correct one, because the correspondences work out without discrepancies, a thing they do in none of the other systems.

8. According to this system, the four suits of the Tarot pack are assigned to the Four Worlds of the Qabalist and the four elements of the Alchemists. The suit of Wands is assigned to Atziluth and Fire. The suit of Cups to Briah and Water. The suit of Swords to Yetzirah and Air. The suit of Pentacles or Coins to Assiah and Earth.

9. The four aces are assigned to Kether, the first Sephirah; the four twos to Chokmah, the second Sephirah; and so on down the pack, the four tens being assigned to Malkuth. It will thus be seen that the cards of the four suits of the Tarot pack represent the action of the Divine Forces in each sphere and on each level of nature. Equally, if we know the significance of the Tarot cards we shall obtain much light on the nature of the Paths and Spheres to which they are assigned. Both these systems, the Tarot and the Tree, being of immemorial antiquity, their origins lost in the vistas of the ages, there is an enormous mass of symbolic correspondences accumulated around each of them. Every practical occultist who has ever worked with the Tree has added to this stock of associations, making the symbols live in the Astral by means of his operations. The Tree and its keys are infinite in their adaptability.

10. The four court-cards of the Tarot are called in modern packs, King, Queen, Knight, and Knave; but in the traditional packs they are, according to Crowley, arranged and symbolised differently. The King being a mounted figure, indicating the swift action of the Yod of Tetragrammaton in the sphere of the suit, and thus equating with the Knight of the modern pack. The Queen, as in the modern packs, is a seated figure, representing the steadfast forces of the Hé of Tetragrammaton; the Prince of the esoteric Tarot is a seated figure, corresponding to the Vav of Tetragrammaton; and the Princess, the Knave of the modern packs, corresponds to the Hé final of the Sacred Name.

11. The twenty-two trumps are arranged in various ways by various authorities, of which Mr Waite gives a selection, but in our system we will follow the order given by Crowley for reasons already discussed.

12. In these pages we propose to give the philosophical Tree of Life, and enough practical instruction to render it available for meditation purposes; but we do not propose to give the Practical Qabalah, which is used for magical purposes; because that can only properly be learnt and safely practised in a Temple of the Mysteries. Reference must be made to the Practical Qabalah, however, in order to render some of the concepts intelligible, but those who are rightfully in possession of its keys need have no fear that these keys will be revealed to the uninitiated in these pages, for I am quite alive to the consequences of so doing.

13. If, from the information here given, and as a result of pursuing the methods described herein, anyone is able to work out for himself the keys of the Practical Qabalah, as he well may, can any dispute that he is entitled to them?

14. The Tree is enormously valuable as a meditation glyph, quite apart from its use in magic. By meditations such as I have described in my account of my own experiences on the Thirty-second Path, it is possible to equilibrate the warring elements in one's own nature and bring them into harmonious balance. It is also possible to get into sympathetic rapport with the different aspects of Nature which these symbols represent when applied to the Macrocosm, even if these forces are not given a definite form in talismanic magic. The information that is obtained from the study of one's own horoscope is not to be accepted passively as the dispensation of Fate from which there is no appeal. We ought to realise that talismanic magic, or the less concentrated method of meditation upon the Tree, should be used to compensate all un-balanced force in the horoscope and bring all into equilibrium. Talismanic magic is to astrology what medical treatment is to medical diagnosis.

15. It is not possible for me to give any formulæ of practical

magic here; before such formulæ can be made use of it is necessary to have received the grades of initiation to which they belong. Without these grades the student is no better off than the person who tries to diagnose and treat his own complaints after reading a medical textbook. That delightful humorist, Jerome K. Jerome, has told us what happens in such a case. The unfortunate imagines that he has every disease described therein, except housemaid's knee, and cannot make up his mind as to the appropriate treatment, for everything he fancies is contra-indicated.

16. The ritual initiations of the Greater Mysteries of the Western Esoteric Tradition are based upon the principles of the Tree of Life. Each grade corresponds to a Sephirah and confers, or should confer, if the Order working them is worthy of the name, the powers of that sphere of nature. Likewise it opens up the Paths leading to that Sephirah, so that the initiate is said to be Lord of the Thirty-second Path when he has taken the initiation that corresponds to Yesod, or Lord of the Twenty-fourth, Twenty-fifth, and Twenty-sixth Paths when he has taken the initiation corresponding to Tiphareth, which constitutes him a full initiate. Beyond this lie the higher grades of adepthood.

17. The aim of each grade of initiation of the Greater Mysteries is to introduce the candidate to the Sphere of each Sephirah in turn, working from Malkuth up the Tree. The instructions given in each grade concern the symbolism and forces of the Sphere to which it refers and the Paths that equilibrate it. The sign and word of the grade are used when treading these Paths in the spirit-vision or projecting by them on the astral plane. Consequently the initiate is able to move with accuracy and certainty into whatsoever sphere of the Unseen he desires to penetrate, and to countercheck all beings he meets and all visions he sees, for he knows what the colours of the Paths are in all four scales, and he checks his vision by these. If he is working up the Thirty-second Path of Saturn, whose colours are all in the sombre hues of indigo, dark blue and black, he knows that something is amiss if a

scarlet-robed figure presents itself. Either that figure is illusive, or he himself has wandered off the Path.

18. To project the astral body along the Paths it is necessary for many reasons to hold the degrees of initiation to which they correspond; chief among which is that, unless one has received the grade, one will be unknown to guardians of the Paths, and they will be inimical rather than helpful, and do all in their power to turn the wanderer back. Secondly, if one should succeed in forcing one's way past the guardian, one still has no means of counterchecking the vision or knowing whether one is on or off the Path, and there are plenty of beings in the lower sphere who are only too ready to take advantage of presumptuous ignorance.

19. These considerations, however, need in no way discourage anyone who wishes to meditate upon the Paths and Spheres in the manner I have described; and in the course of his meditations he may so enter into the spirit of the Path that its guardian shall come to know him and make him welcome. He will then literally have initiated himself, and no one can deny his right to be there.

20. The Tree, considered from the initiatory standpoint, is the link between the microcosm, which is man, and the Macrocosm, which is God made manifest in Nature. A ritual initiation is the act of linking the microcosmic Sephirah, the chakra, with the Macrocosmic Sephirah; it is the introduction of a newcomer to the Sphere by those who are already there. They construct a symbolic representation of the Sphere on the physical plane in the furniture of the temple; they construct an astral replica of it by concentrated imagination; and by means of invocation they call down into this temple not made with hands the forces of the Sphere of the Sephirah they are working upon.

21. These forces stimulate the corresponding chakras of the initiate and wake them to activity in his aura. The process of self-initiation by the meditations I have described is slower than the processes of ritual initiation, but it is sure enough if persevered with by a suitable person, but one cannot teach a jelly-fish to sing by feeding it on canary-seed.

CHAPTER XI

1. As above, so below, man is a miniature macrocosm. All the factors that go to the make-up of the manifested universe are present in his nature. Hence, in his perfection, he is said to be higher than the angels. At the present time, however, the angels are fully evolved beings and man is not. Thus he is as much lower than the angels as a three-year-old child is less developed than a three-year-old dog.

2. Hitherto we have considered the Tree of Life as an epitome of the Macrocosm, the universe, and the use of its symbols to put us in touch with the different spheres of objective Nature. We will now consider it in relation to the subjective sphere of the nature of the individual.

3. The accepted correspondences, as given by Crowley (who, unfortunately, never gives his authorities, so we do not know when he is using MacGregor Mathers' system and when he is relying upon his independent researches), are based partly on the astrological attribution of the planets assigned to the different Sephiroth, and partly upon a crude anatomical scheme of the human form standing with its back to the Tree. This is too crude for our purposes, and probably represents the work of later generations of scribes; during the Middle Ages the Qabalah was rediscovered by European philosophers, and they grafted astrological and alchemical symbolism upon its system. Moreover, the Rabbis themselves used an extremely detailed set of anatomical metaphors, discussing in detail the significance of every hair on the head of God, and even the more intimate parts of His anatomy. Such references cannot be taken literally and applied to the human form.

78

4. The Sephiroth, individually and in their pattern of relationships, represent in relation to the Macrocosm the successive phases of evolution, and in relation to the Microcosm the different levels of consciousness and factors of character. That these levels of consciousness have some relation to the psychic centres of the physical body is a reasonable assumption, but we must not be crude and mediæval in the conclusions we draw. Occult anatomy and physiology have been worked out in detail in the Yoga science of the Hindus, and we can learn much from their teachings. The latest advances in physiology are pointing to the conclusion that the link between mind and matter is to be sought primarily in the endocrine system of ductless glands and only secondarily in the brain and central nervous system. We can learn much from this source of knowledge also, and piecing together all the information we can collect from every source, we may finally arrive by inductive reasoning at what the ancients learnt by means of the intuitive and deductive methods which they brought to such a high degree of perfection in their Mystery schools.

5. It is generally agreed that the chakras, or psychic centres described in Yoga literature, are not situated inside the organs with which they are associated, but in the auric envelope at spots roughly approximating thereto. We shall do well, therefore, not to associate the different Sephiroth with the limbs and other parts of our anatomy, but to regard the use of such analogies as metaphorical and look for the psychic principles which they may be held to represent.

6. Before proceeding to a detailed study of each Sephirah from this standpoint, it is very helpful to have a general survey of the Tree as a whole, because so much of the elucidation of the symbolism depends upon the relationship of one symbol to another in the pattern of the Tree. This chapter must needs be discursive and inconclusive, but it will enable the detailed study of the individual Sephiroth to be much more effectually carried out.

7. The first and most obvious division of the Tree is into

the three Pillars, and this immediately reminds us of the three channels of Prana described by the yogis, Ida, Pingala, and Shushumna; and the two principles, the Yin and the Yang of Chinese philosophy, and the Tao, or Way, which is the equilibrium between them. By the agreement of witnesses truth is established, and when we find three of the great metaphysical systems of the world in complete agreement we may conclude that we are dealing with established principles and should accept them as such.

8. The Central Pillar should, in my opinion, be taken to represent consciousness, and the two side pillars as the positive and negative factors of manifestation. It is noteworthy that in the Yoga system consciousness is extended when Kundalini rises through the central channel of the Shushumna, and that the Western magical operation of Rising on the Planes takes place up the Central Pillar of the Tree; that is to say, the symbolism employed to induce this extension of consciousness does not take the Sephiroth in their numerical order, commencing with Malkuth, but goes from Malkuth to Yesod, and Yesod to Tiphareth, by what is called the Path of the Arrow.

9. Malkuth, the Sphere of Earth, is taken by occultists as signifying brain-consciousness, as is proved by the fact that after any astral projection the ceremonial return is made to Malkuth and normal consciousness re-established therein.

10. Yesod, the Sphere of Levanah, the Moon, is taken as psychic consciousness, and also as the reproductive centre. Tiphareth is taken as the higher psychism, the true illuminated vision, and is associated with the highest grade of the initiation of the personality, as is evidenced by the fact that to it is assigned, in the system taken by Crowley from Mathers, the first of the grades of adepthood.

11. Daath, the mysterious, invisible Sephirah, which is never marked upon the Tree, is associated in the Western system with the nape of the neck, the point where the spine meets the skull, the spot at which the development of the brain from the notochord took place in our primeval ancestors.

Daath is usually held to represent the consciousness of another dimension, or the consciousness of another level or plane; it essentially represents the idea of change of key.

12. Kether is called the Crown. Now a crown is above the head, and Kether is generally held to represent a form of consciousness which is not achieved during incarnation. It is essentially outside the scheme of things so far as the planes of form are concerned. The spiritual experience associated with Kether is Union with God, and whoso achieves that experience is said to enter into the Light and come not forth again.

13. These Sephiroth unquestionably have their correlations in the chakras of the Hindu system, but the correspondences are given differently by different authorities. As the method of classification is different, the West using a fourfold system and the East a sevenfold system, correlation is not easy to obtain, and in my opinion it is better to look for first principles rather than obtain a tidy pattern of arrangement which does violence to the correspondences.

14. The only two writers known to me who have attempted this correlation are Crowley and General J. F. C. Fuller. General Fuller assigns the Muladhara Lotus to Malkuth, pointing out that its four petals correspond with the four elements. It is interesting to note that in the Queen scale of colour, as given by Crowley, the Sphere of Malkuth is represented as divided into four quarters, coloured respectively citrine, olive, russet, and black, to represent the four elements, and bearing the closest resemblance to the usual representations of the Four-petalled Lotus.

15. This Lotus is represented as situated in the perineum and is associated with the anus and the function of excretion. In column XXI of the table of correspondences given by Crowley in "777" he attributes the buttocks and anus of the Perfected Man to Malkuth. I consider that from every point of view the attribution of Fuller, who refers the Muladhara Lotus to Malkuth, is to be preferred to that of Crowley, who in column CXVIII refers it to Yesod, thus contradicting

himself. In the infantile mind, according to Freud, the functions of reproduction and excretion are confused, but I do not consider that this attribution is one that can be generally accepted or ought to be perpetuated.

16. Malkuth, viewed as the Muladhara Lotus, represents, we may take it, the end-result of the life processes, their final concretion in form, and their submission to the disintegrating influences of death in order that their substance may be utilised again. The form into which they have been organised by the slow processes of evolution has served its purpose, and the force must be set free; this is the spiritual significance of the processes of excretion, putrefaction, and decomposition.

17. The Svadisthana Chakra, the Six-petalled Lotus, at the base of the generative organs, is assigned by General Fuller to Yesod. This agrees with the Western tradition, which assigns Yesod to the reproductive organs of the Divine Man; its astrological correspondence with the Moon, Diana-Hecate, also agrees with this attribution. Crowley, though assigning Yesod to the phallus in column XXI of "777," assigns the Svadisthana Lotus to Hod, Mercury. It is difficult to understand this attribution, and as he does not give his authority, I consider it better to adhere to the principle of referring the levels of consciousness to the Central Pillar.

18. Tiphareth, by universal consent, represents the solar plexus and breast; it therefore seems reasonable to attribute to it the Manipura and Anahata Chakras, as Crowley does. Fuller attributes these chakras to Geburah and Chesed, but as these two Sephiroth find their equilibrium in Tiphareth, this attribution presents no difficulty and causes no discrepancy.

19. In the same way the Visuddhu Chakra, which in the Hindu system correlates with the larynx and is referred to Binah by Crowley, and the Ajna Chakra at the root of the nose, which correlates with the pineal gland and is referred to Chokmah by the same authority, may be taken as uniting for function in Daath, situated at the base of the skull.

20. The Sahasrara Chakra, the Thousand-petalled Lotus, situated above the head, is referred by Crowley to Kether, and

there can be little reason to quarrel with this attribution, for it is foreshadowed in the very name of the First Path, Kether, the Crown, which rests upon and above the head.

21. The two flanking pillars of Severity and Mercy can readily be seen as representing the positive and negative principles, and their respective Sephiroth as representing the modes of functioning of these forces upon the different levels.

22. The Pillar of Severity contains Binah, Geburah, and Hod, or Saturn, Mars, and Mercury. The Pillar of Mercy contains Chokmah, Chesed, and Netzach, or the Zodiac, Jupiter, and Venus. Chokmah and Binah, in the symbolism of the Qabalah, are represented by male and female figures and are the supernal Father and Mother, or in more philosophical language, the positive and negative principles of the universe, the Yang and the Yin, of which maleness and femaleness are but specialised aspects.

23. Chesed (Jupiter) and Geburah (Mars) are both represented in Qabalistic symbolism as crowned figures, the former a lawgiver upon his throne, and the latter a warrior king in his chariot. These are the constructive and destructive principles respectively. It is interesting to note that Binah, the supernal Mother, is also Saturn, the solidifier, who connects through his sickle with Death with his scythe, and Time with his hour-glass. In Binah we find the root of Form. It is said of Malkuth in the *Sepher Yetzirah* that it sitteth upon the throne of Binah—matter has its root in Binah—Saturn—Death; form is the destroyer of force. With this passive destroyer goes also the active destroyer, and we find Mars-Geburah immediately below it on the Pillar of Severity; thus is the force locked up in form set free by the destructive influence of Mars, the Siva aspect of the Godhead. Chokmah, the Zodiac, represents kinetic force; and Chesed, Jupiter, the benign king, represents organised force; and the two are synthesised in Tiphareth, the Christ-centre, the Redeemer and Equilibrator.

24. The next trinity, of Netzach, Hod, and Yesod, represents the magical and astral side of things. Netzach (Venus)

represents the higher aspects of the elemental forces, the Green Ray; and Hod (Mercury) represents the mind side of magic. The one is the mystic and the other the occult, and they synthesise in the elemental Yesod. This pair of Sephiroth should never be considered apart, any more than the upper pair of Geburah and Gedullah, which is another name for Chesed. This is indicated by the fact that the Qabalah attributes them respectively to the right and left arms and the left and right legs.

25. It will thus be seen that the three form-Sephiroth are in the Pillar of Severity, and the three force-Sephiroth in the Pillar of Mercy, and between them, in the Pillar of Equilibrium, are set the different levels of consciousness. The Pillar of Severity, with Binah at its head, is the female principle, the Pingala of the Hindus and the Yang of the Chinese; the Pillar of Mercy, with Chokmah at its head, is the Ida of the Hindus and the Yin of the Chinese; and the Pillar of Equilibrium is Shushumna and Tao.

CHAPTER XII

THE GODS UPON THE TREE

1. All students of comparative religion and its poor relation, folk-lore, are agreed that primitive man, observing and beginning to analyse the natural phenomena surrounding him, attributed them to the agency of beings akin to himself in nature and type, but transcending him in power. As he could not see them, he not unnaturally called them invisible; and as he could not see his own mind during life, or his friend's soul after death, he concluded that the beings that produced natural phenomena were of the same nature as the invisible but active mind and soul.

2. Now all this sounds very crude as it is put by the anthropologists, but that is only because when translating savage ideas they choose words that have crude associations. For instance, the standard translation of one of the chief scriptures of China refers to the venerable philosopher Lao Tse as "the Old Boy." This sounds comical to European ears, yet it is not so far removed from the words of another Scripture which has been fortunate enough to receive translation at the hands of those who reverenced it—"Except ye become as a little child——" I am not a sinologue, but I incline to the opinion that the translation "Eternal Child" would have been equally accurate and in better taste.

3. There is a saying in the Mysteries, "See that ye blaspheme not the Name by which another knoweth his God. For if ye do this in Allah, ye will do it in Adonai."

4. And after all, was primitive man so very far off the mark when he attributed the causation of natural phenomena to activities of the same nature as the thought-processes of the

human mind, but upon a higher arc? Is not that the point towards which both physics and metaphysics are gradually converging? Supposing we were to re-cast the statement of the savage philosopher and say, The essential nature of man is similar in type to that of his Creator, would we be held to have said anything either blasphemous or ridiculous?

5. We may personalise natural forces in terms of human consciousness; or we may abstract human consciousness in terms of natural forces; both are legitimate proceedings in occult metaphysics, and the process yields some very interesting clues and some very important practical applications. We must not, however, make the mistake of the ignorant, and say A is B when we mean A is of the same nature as B. But equally we may legitimately avail ourselves of the Hermetic axiom, "As above, so below," because if A and B are of the same nature, the laws governing A can be predicated concerning B. What is true of the drop is true of the ocean. Consequently, if we know anything concerning the nature of A, we may conclude that, allowing for the difference in scale, it will apply to B. This is the method of analogy used in the inductive science of the ancients, and provided it is counterchecked by observation and experiment, it can yield some very fruitful results and cut out many leagues of weary wandering in the dark.

6. The personification and deification of the natural forces was man's first crude and shrewd attempt to evolve a monistic theory of the universe and save himself from the destructive and crippling influence of an unresolved dualism. As age by age extended his knowledge and elaborated his intellectual processes, he read more and more significance into the first simple classifications. Nevertheless, he did not discard his original classifications, because they were fundamentally sound and represented actualities. He simply elaborated and extended them, and finally, when he fell on evil times, overlaid them with superstition.

7. We should not, therefore, regard the pagan pantheons as so many aberrations of the human mind; nor should we try

to understand them from the viewpoint of the uninstructed and uninitiated; we should try to find out what they must have meant to the highly intelligent and cultured high-priests of the cults in their heyday. Compare Mme David Neel and W. B. Seabrook on the subject of heathen rites with the reports of the average missionary. Seabrook shows us the spiritual significance of voodoo, and Mme David Neel shows us the metaphysical aspect of Thibetan magic. These things appear in one way to the sympathetic observer who wins the confidence of the exponents of these systems and succeeds in being received into their holy of holies as a friend, and who goes to learn instead of merely to observe and ridicule, and in another way to the "beef-fed zealot" who walks into the holy place in his dirty boots and gets stoned by the indignant worshippers.

8. In judging these things let us consider the form Christianity would present if approached in the same way. Unsympathetic observers would probably conclude that we worshipped a sheep, and the Holy Ghost would yield some spectacular interpretations. Let us credit other people with using metaphors if we do not expect to be taken literally ourselves. The outer form of the ancient pagan faiths is no cruder than Christianity in backward Latin countries, where Jesus Christ is represented in topper and tails and the Virgin Mary in lace-edged pantaloons. The inner form of the ancient faiths can compare very favourably with the best of our modern metaphysicians. After all, they produced Plato and Plotinus. The human mind does not change, and what is true of ourselves is probably true of the pagans. The Lamb of God which taketh away the sins of the world is only another version of the Bull of Mithra which does the same thing, the only difference being that the ancient initiate was literally "washed in blood" and the modern one takes it metaphorically. *Autres temps, autres mœurs.*

9. If we approach those whom we elect to call pagans, both ancient and modern, in a reverent and sympathetic spirit, knowing that Allah and Brahma and Amen Ra are but other

names for that which we worship as God, we shall learn a very great deal that was forgotten in Europe when the Gnosis was stamped out and its literature destroyed.

10. We shall find, however, that the pagan faiths present their teaching in a form that is not readily assimilable by the European mind, and that if we are to arrive at its significance we must re-state it in our own terms. We must correlate the metaphysical concept with the pagan symbol; then we shall be able to apply to the former the vast mass of mystical experience which generations of contemplatives and experimental psychologists have organised about the latter. And when we speak of experimental psychologists, we must not make the mistake of thinking that they are an exclusively modern product, because the priests of the ancient Mysteries, with their temple sleep and deliberately induced hypnogogic visions, were nothing more nor less than experimental psychologists, though their art has been lost, like many others of the ancient arts, and is only being laboriously recovered piecemeal in the more advanced circles of scientific thought.

11. The method used by the modern initiate for interpreting the language spoken by the ancient myths is a very simple and effectual one. He finds in the Qabalistic Tree of Life a link between the highly stylistic pagan systems and his own more rational methods; the Jew, Asiatic by blood and monotheistic by religion, has a foot in both worlds. Upon the Tree of Life with its Ten Holy Sephiroth the modern occultist bases both a metaphysic and a magic. He uses a philosophical conception of the Tree to interpret what it represents to his conscious mind, and he uses a magical and ceremonial application of its symbolism to link it up with his subconscious mind. The initiate, consequently, makes the best of both worlds, ancient and modern; for the modern world is all surface consciousness, and has forgotten and repressed the subconsciousness, to its own great hurt; and the ancient world was mainly subconsciousness, consciousness having been but recently evolved. When the two are linked

up and brought into polarised function they yield super-consciousness, which is the goal of the initiate.

12. Holding the foregoing conceptions in mind, let us now try to co-ordinate the ancient pantheons with the Spheres upon the Tree of Life. There are ten such Spheres, the Ten Holy Sephiroth, and between these we must distribute, according to type, the different gods and goddesses of whatever pantheon we wish to study; we are then in a position to interpret their significance in the light of what we already know concerning the principles represented by the Tree, and to add to our knowledge of the Tree all that is available concerning the significance of the ancient deities.

13. This is, obviously, of great intellectual value—but there is another value which does not so readily appear to the average man who has had no experience of Mystery-workings; the performance of a ceremonial rite symbolically representing the working of the force personified as a god, has a very marked and even drastic effect on the subconscious mind of any person who is at all susceptible to psychic influences. The ancients had brought these rites to a very high pitch of perfection, and when we moderns are trying to reconstruct the lost art of practical magic we can go to them with great profit. The whole philosophy of European magic is based upon the Tree, and no one can hope to understand it or use it intelligently who has not been trained in the Qabalistic methods. It is this lack of training which makes popular occultism so very apt to degenerate into the crudest superstition. "Your number in your name" becomes a different thing when we understand the mathematical Qabalah; fortunes in tea-cups are another matter when we understand the significance of the Magical Images and the method of their formulation and interpretation as a psychological device for penetrating the veil of the unconscious.

14. Broadly speaking, then, we sort out the gods and goddesses of all the pagan pantheons into the ten pigeon-holes of the Ten Holy Sephiroth, relying chiefly upon their astrological associations to guide us, because astrology is the

7

one universal language, for all people see the same planets. Space is referred to Kether, the Zodiac to Chokmah, the seven planets to the next seven Sephiroth, and Earth to Malkuth. Consequently, any god who has an analogy with Saturn will be referred to Binah, as will any goddess who might be termed the primordial mother, the Superior Eve, as distinguished from the Inferior Eve, the Bride of Microprosopos, Malkuth. The Supernal triangle of Kether, Chokmah, and Binah always refers to the Old Gods, which every pantheon recognises as the predecessors of those forms of godhead worshipped by the current faith. Thus Rhea and Kronos would be referred to Binah and Chokmah, and Jupiter to Chesed. All the corn goddesses refer to Malkuth, and all the lunar goddesses to Yesod. The war gods and destructive gods, or divine devils, refer to Geburah, and the goddesses of love to Netzach. The initiator gods of wisdom are referred to Hod, and the sacrificed gods and redeemers to Tiphareth. So great an authority as Richard Payne Knight, in his valuable book, *The Symbolic Language of Ancient Art and Mythology,* speaks of " the remarkable concurrence of the allegories, symbols, and titles of ancient mythology in favour of the mystic system of emanations." With this clue we sort out the pantheons, thus enabling ourselves to compare like with like and make the one illuminate the other.

15. In the system he gives in his book of correspondences, " 777," Crowley assigns the gods to the Paths as well as to the Sephiroth. This, in my opinion, is a mistake and leads to confusion. It is the Sephiroth alone that represent natural forces; the Paths are states of consciousness. The Sephiroth are objective and the Paths are subjective. It is for this reason that in the working glyph of the Tree used by initiates the Sephiroth are always represented in one Colour Scale and the Paths in another. Those who possess this glyph will know to what I refer.

16. The Paths themselves, in my opinion, should be regarded as under the direct presidency of the Holy Names governing their Sephirothic attributions only, and should not be confused

with other pantheons; for although we may go to other systems for intellectual enlightenment, we are unwise to attempt to mix the methods of practical working and unfoldment of consciousness.

17. For instance, the Seventeenth Path, between Tiphareth and Binah, is assigned by the *Sepher Yetzirah* to the Element of Air. We are far wiser to work it with the rite of the Element of Air and the Holy Names assigned thereto, and to approach it through the appropriate Tattva, rather than confuse the issue with the associations of the assorted collection of deities, Castor and Pollux, Janus, Apollo, Merti, and other incompatibles assigned to it by Crowley, whose correspondences present an inextricable tangle of associations.

18. The Sephiroth should be interpreted macrocosmically, and the Paths microcosmically; thus we shall find the clue to the Tree in both man and nature.

CHAPTER XIII

1. If among the readers who have followed these studies in the Qabalah thus far there are any of the more advanced students of Western occultism, they will no doubt have found much more that is familiar than is new or original. In working upon this storehouse of ancient knowledge we are in the position of excavators working on the site of a buried temple; we are digging up fragments rather than studying a coherent system; for the system, though coherent enough in its heyday, was broken and scattered and defaced by the persecutions of twenty centuries of unenlightened bigotry and spiritual jealousy.

2. More work has been done upon these scattered fragments than is generally realised, however. Mme Blavatsky gathered together a great mass of data and exposed it to the gaze of a public which understood it little better than the child gazing at the cases in a museum and marvelling at the queer things they contain. The scholarly work of G. R. S. Mead has given us much information concerning the Gnosis, the esoteric tradition of the Western world during the earlier centuries of our epoch; Mrs Atwood's monumental book has revealed the significance of the Alchemical symbolism to us. None of these, however, have expounded the Western Tradition as initiates of that Tradition, but have approached it from outside and either pieced together its fragments, or, as in the case of Mme Blavatsky, interpreted it by analogy in the light of the more familiar system of another Tradition.

3. Those who approached the study of the subject from the inside—that is to say, with the initiatory keys—and employed

it as a practical system for the exaltation of consciousness have, for the most part, maintained a secrecy which, though it might have been not only justifiable and even essential in the days when the Holy Inquisition rewarded such researches with the stake, is difficult to assign to any more creditable motive in our liberal age than a desire to create and maintain prestige. A very effectual "corner" in occult practice, if not in occult knowledge, has been established and maintained among English-speaking peoples for the last quarter of a century. A "corner" that effectually defeated the spiritual impulse which should have given rise to a renaissance of the Mysteries during the last quarter of the last century. Consequently, the earth being ripe for the sowing and the wheat not being broadcast therein, the four winds brought strange seeds to the waiting ground, and a tropical growth sprang up that, having no roots in racial tradition, withered away or developed strange forms.

4. The buried temple of our native tradition has in actuality been excavated in part at any rate, but the rescued fragments have not been made available for students according to the honourable traditions of European scholarship, but have been gathered together into private collections the keys whereof have rested in the pockets of individuals who have opened and closed the doors in an entirely arbitrary fashion. I have no doubt these pages will cause heart-burnings in certain quarters whose private collections they depreciate in value. But I have no doubt also that the innumerable students who essayed the Western Path in vain may find in these pages the keys to what was incomprehensible to them in the method, or perhaps, to be more accurate, the complete lack of method, in which they were trained. Speaking for myself, it took me ten years' work in the dark before I found the keys, and I only found these in the end because I was sufficiently psychic to pick up the Inner Plane contacts. I find it difficult to believe that any useful purpose is served by deliberately darkening counsel or by withholding from the student keys and explanations that are essential to his work. If the student is unworthy

to be trained, do not let us train him. If he is to be trained at all, let us train him properly.

5. In the following pages I have done my best to elucidate the principles governing the use of magical symbolism. The practical use of the ceremonial method is best attempted under the guidance of one who is already experienced in its use; to work alone or with equally inexperienced comrades is to run unnecessary risks, but there is no reason why anyone should not experiment with the meditative method.

6. In order to use the magical symbols effectually one has to make the contact of each individual symbol. It is of little use to make a list of symbols and proceed to the construction of a ritual. In magic, as in violin-playing, one has to "make one's notes"; one does not find them ready-made as on the piano. The student of the violin has to learn to make each individual note before he can play an air. So it is with any occult operation, we must know how to construct and contact the magical images before we can work with them.

7. The sets of symbols associated with each of the Thirty-two Paths are used by the initiate to build up the magical images; it is necessary that he should know these symbols not only in theory, but also in practice; that is to say, he must not only have them thoroughly well rooted in his memory, but must also have performed meditations upon them individually until he has penetrated their significance and experienced the force they represent. To know the vast range of symbols associated with each Path is, of course, the work of a lifetime, but the student must learn the key-symbols of each Path as the essential preliminary to his studies; he is then able to recognise all other symbol-forms as they come his way and assign them to their proper classification. His knowledge will thus develop under two aspects: firstly, the knowledge of the symbolism in its infinite ramifications; and secondly, the philosophy of the interpretation of that symbolism. Once he has mastered a working knowledge of the concepts of esoteric cosmogony and has the general scheme of symbolism assigned to each Sephirah well fixed in his memory, the student

is equipped with a card-index system and can commence filing, collecting the material for his files from every imaginable source in archæology, folk-lore, mystical religion, travellers' tales, and the speculations of ancient and modern philosophy and ultra-modern science.

8. The uninitiated inquirer may wonder how the enormous mass of data is kept sorted in the memory. To begin with, the serious student who uses the Tree as his meditation-method works at it regularly every day. Moreover, it will be found by experience that the assignation of symbols to each Sephirah has a peculiar logical basis, hidden somewhere deep in the subconscious mind, and the symbol-sequences are not nearly so difficult to remember as might be supposed, especially if they have been used for meditation. Some of the symbols refer to the concepts of esoteric philosophy, some to the methods of projecting consciousness in vision, and some to the composing of ceremonial. The student must remember, however, that the symbols will never yield their significance to conscious meditation alone, however correctly and completely they are known; they must be used as the initiates intended them to be used, to evoke images from the subconscious mind into conscious content.

9. One set of symbols is assigned to the Ten Holy Sephiroth themselves, and another set to the Twenty-two Paths that connect them. Some of the symbols, however, occur in both sets, and all of them interconnect through their astrological and numerical correlations. This sounds most perplexingly complex, but in actual practice it is far simpler than it sounds, because the work is not done with the conscious mind, but with the subconscious mind, and it matters very little in what manner the symbols are pitchforked into it, the strange dæmon that sits behind the censor sorts them out, picking that which it requires and rejecting all else, until finally a coherent pattern reappears in consciousness that only requires analysis to yield its significance after the same manner as a dream.

10. A vision evoked by the use of the Tree is, in fact, an

artificially produced waking dream, deliberately motived and consciously related to some chosen subject whereby not only the subconscious content, but also the superconscious perceptions are evoked and rendered intelligible to consciousness. In a spontaneous dream the symbols are drawn at random from experience; in the Qabalistic vision, however, the picture is evoked from a limited set of symbols to which consciousness is rigidly restricted by a highly trained habit of concentration. It is this peculiar power to turn the mind loose within determined limits which constitutes the technique of occult meditation, and it is only to be acquired by constant practice over a considerable period. It is this which constitutes the difference between the trained and the untrained occultist; the untrained person may be able to detach consciousness from the control of the directing personality and thus allow the images to rise, but he has no power to restrict and select what shall appear, and consequently anything may appear, including a varying proportion of subconscious content. The trained occultist, however, accustomed to use this method in his meditations, is able to swing instantly clear of the normal subconscious content unless it is disturbed by emotion, in which case he is liable to be entangled in its meshes; but even in this case his method is his protection, for he is immediately able to recognise confused symbolism in the images because he has a definite standard of comparison with which to compare them.

11. In studying the Tree the student should always think of each Sephirah under the threefold aspect we have already mentioned—of philosophy, psychism, and magic; to this end he should always think of it firstly as representing a certain factor in the evolution of the cosmos in the immemorial past of cosmic time, whether it remains in manifestation, has passed away, or has not yet arrived at the level of dense matter.

12. With this aspect of the Tree are also taken the curious cryptic texts of the *Sepher Yetzirah,* one to each Path. These most baffling utterances have a curious way of yielding sudden flashes of illumination to meditation and are by no means to

be rejected as rubbish, incomprehensible though they may appear at first sight.

13. Another source of illumination is to be found in the additional titles of the Sephiroth, each of which has anything from one to two or three dozen. These are graphic descriptive names applied to the various Sephiroth by the ancient Rabbis and found scattered through the Qabalistic literature, and they tell us a great many things. For instance, the titles "Concealed of the Concealed" and "Primordial Point" that are applied to Kether convey a good deal to those who know where to look for it.

14. We can also, once we are acquainted with the symbolism, assign to the various Sephiroth their equivalent gods in other systems, and when we look up the symbols, functions, cosmic concepts, and methods of worship assigned to these deities we get a fresh flood of illumination. By the use of a good mythological dictionary or an encyclopædia, Frazer's *Golden Bough*, and Mme Blavatsky's *Secret Doctrine* and *Isis Unveiled*, we can, by the mere application of diligence, read a great many riddles that at first appeared insoluble, and the exercise is a fascinating one. When used thus the Tree is peculiarly valuable, because its diagrammatic form causes things to be seen in relation to each other, thus causing them to throw light upon each other.

15. In order to manipulate the psychic aspect of the Tree and its Paths the occultist uses images, because it is by means of images and the names that evoke them that vision is formulated. He associates with each Sephirah a primary symbol, which is called its Magical Image. Secondly, he associates with it in his mind a geometrical form which, in various ways, embodies its characteristics, and when he composes symbols he uses that form as the basis. For instance, Geburah, Mars, the Fifth Sephirah, has assigned to it a pentagon or five-sided figure. Any symbol of Geburah, whether it be a talisman, an altar to Mars, or a mental picture of a symbol, would be in the form of a pentagon coloured in one of the colours of the Mars colour-scale.

16. The most important forms upon the Tree, however, are those associated with the four Names of Power assigned to each Sephirah; with these are associated four colours in which they are conceived to manifest in a symbolic form in each of the Four Worlds of the Qabalists. The highest of these is the God-name, which manifests in Atziluth, the plane of spirit, and is the supreme Name of Power of that Sephirothic Sphere and dominates all its aspects, whether cosmic, evolutionary, or subjective. It represents the idea underlying the development of manifestation in that Sphere; the idea that runs through all subsequent evolution and expresses itself in all ensuing effects and manifestations.

17. The second Name of Power is that of the Archangel of the Sphere, and represents the organised consciousness of the being through the activities of which the evolution of that phase was inaugurated and directed. Although these beings are represented pictorially as of human form, though etherealised, it must not be thought that life and consciousness as we know them in any way correspond to their nature. They are more akin in essence to natural forces, yet if we consider them simply as unintelligent energy we shall have no adequate concept of their nature, because they are essentially individualised, intelligent, and purposive. Both these ideas must enter into our concept, modifying each other, till finally we shall arrive at a realisation that differs very widely from anything to which Western thought is accustomed.

18. The third Name of Power denominates, not one being, but a whole class of beings, the choirs of angels as they are called by the rabbis, and these again represent intelligent natural forces.

19. The fourth denominates what we have called the Mundane Chakra, that is to say the celestial object which is looked upon as the product of the particular phase of evolution which took place under the presidency of that Sephirah and which represents it.

20. The third aspect under which we consider the Sephiroth is the magical aspect, and is essentially practical. To arrive

at this, we think of what may be experienced under the presidency of these different aspects of deity-manifestation, and what powers may be wielded by the magician when he has mastered their lessons.

21. Each Sephirah has assigned to it a virtue, which represents its ideal aspect, the gift which it brings to evolution; and a vice which is the result of the overplus of its qualities. For instance, Geburah, Mars, has for its virtues energy and courage, and for its vices cruelty and destructiveness. The student of astrology will at once recognise that the virtues and vices attributed to the various Sephiroth are derived from the characteristics of the planets associated with them, and will find that in this correspondence a whole new line of approach to astrology is opened up.

22. The spiritual experience as I prefer to call it, or occult power as Crowley calls it, is a profound realisation or vision of some aspect of cosmic science. This constitutes the essence of the initiation of the grade assigned to each Sephirah, for in the Greater Mysteries of the West the grades are associated with the Sephiroth.

23. The mediæval Qabalists also assigned a part of the body to each Sephirah, but this must not be taken too literally; the real key is to be found in the realisation that the different Sephiroth represent factors in consciousness, and if we take Geburah as the strong right arm, we must realise that it really means the dynamic will, the executive capacity, the destruction of the effete and unbalanced.

24. Each Sephirah and Path has assigned to it symbolic animals, plants, and precious stones. It is necessary that the student should know these for two reasons: firstly, they give some very important keys to the relations of the gods of the different pantheons to the Sephiroth; and secondly, they form part of the symbolism of the Astral Paths and serve as landmarks when travelling in the spirit-vision. For instance, if one saw a horse (Mars) or a jackal (Luna) in the sphere of Netzach (Venus), one would know that there was confusion of plane and the vision was not reliable. In her Sphere one

would expect to see her doves, and a spotted beast, such as a lynx or leopard.

25. It may be thought that the association of the symbolic beasts with the gods and goddesses in the old myths is entirely arbitrary and the fruit of the poetic imagination, which, like the wind, bloweth where it listeth. To this the occultist answers that the poetic imagination is not an arbitrary thing and refers the sceptic to the works of Dr Jung of Zurich, the famous psychiatrist, and to the essays of the Irish poet, "A.E.," in particular *Song and its Fountains*, wherein he analyses the nature of his own sources of inspiration. From the intrinsic nature of his poetry, and from many passing references in his works, I think we may be entitled to claim "A. E." as one of that band of students who have been nurtured on the mystical Qabalah. At any rate, what he has to say is sound Qabalistic doctrine and extremely illuminating to our present argument.

26. Dr Jung has a great deal to say concerning the myth-making faculty of the human mind, and the occultist knows it to be true. He knows also, however, that its implications are much farther reaching than psychology has yet suspected. The mind of poet or mystic, dwelling upon the great natural forces and factors of the manifested universe, has, by the creative use of the imagination, penetrated far more deeply into their secret causes and springs of being than has the scientist; it is not for nothing that the racial imagination, working thus, has come to associate certain animals with certain gods; a brief examination of the examples cited serves to show the basis of the association. The doves of Venus show her gentler aspect, and the cat-beasts her sinister beauty.

27. The association of plants with the different Paths rests upon a twofold basis. Firstly, there are plants traditionally associated with the legends of the gods, as is corn with Ceres and the vine with Dionysos; these we find associated with the Sephiroth, with which the functions of these gods are correlated—corn with Malkuth and the vine with Tiphareth, the Christ-centre, wherewith are associated all the Sacrificed Gods and the givers of illumination.

28. Plants are also associated with the Sephiroth in another way; the old doctrine of signatures assigned various plants to the presidency of various planets in a somewhat erratic fashion. In some cases there was a genuine association, in others it was arbitrary and superstitious. Old Culpeper and other ancient herbalists have a great deal to say on the subject, and some very interesting researches are being done on the Anthroposophical experimental farms.

29. In a similar way certain drugs are associated with the different Sephiroth; and here again we need to distinguish the superstitious from the mystical. The arbitrary attribution of drugs cannot always be justified by actual experiment, but we may safely say that whole classes of drugs could be regarded as under the presidency of certain Sephiroth because they partake of the nature of certain modes of activity which are classified under these Sephiroth. For instance, all aphrodisiacs could justly be assigned to Netzach (Venus), and all abortifacients to Yesod in her Hecate aspect; analgesics to Chesed (Mercy), and irritants and caustics to Geburah (Severity).

30. This opens up a very interesting aspect of the study of materia medica—the psychic and psychological aspect of drug activity. It was this aspect which was especially studied by the initiate-physicians such as Paracelsus, and it was the ignorant and superstitious abuse of this aspect by uninitiated physicians that led to the extraordinary aberrations of folk-medicine.

31. The occultist knows that there is a psychological aspect to every physiological action and function; he also knows that it is possible powerfully to reinforce the action of all drugs by the appropriate mental action, and that certain chemically inert substances lend themselves effectually to the transmission and storing of mental activities, just as other substances are effectual conductors or insulators of electricity.

32. This consideration brings us to the question of the association of certain precious stones and metals with the different Sephiroth, an association determined by both astrological and alchemical considerations. As is well known to

psychics, crystalline substances, metals, and certain liquids are the best media for conveying or storing subtle forces. Colour plays an important part in the visions induced by meditation on the various Sephiroth, and it is found by experience that a crystal of the appropriate colour is the best material out of which to make a talisman: a blood-red ruby for the fiery Martian forces of Geburah; an emerald for the Green Ray nature forces of Netzach.

33. Perfumes, especially incense, are also associated with the different Sephiroth. As has already been noted, certain spiritual experiences and certain modes of consciousness are assigned to each Sphere on the Tree; it is well known that nothing induces states of mind or stimulates psychic consciousness more effectually than odours. "Scents are surer than sights or sounds to make your heart-strings crack," says the most objective of poets, and the experience of practical occultists proves this to be true. There are certain aromatic substances associated by tradition with the different gods and goddesses, and these are most effectually potent to stimulate the mood which is in harmony with the function of that deity.

34. Magical weapons are also included in the long lists of symbols and substances associated with each Path. A magical weapon is an instrument of some sort which is used in the evocation of a particular force, or is the vehicle of its manifestation, such as the rod of the magician or the bowl of water or crystal sphere of the seer. The assignation of the magical weapons to the Paths tells us a good deal about the nature of the Paths, because we can deduce therefrom the kind of power that operates in the particular sphere in question.

35. As already noted, the various divinatory systems have their relations with the Tree and find their subtlest clues therein. The associations of astrology are readily traced through the symbolism of the planets and elements and their triplicities, houses, and rulership; geomancy links with the Tree *via* astrology; and the Tarot, the most satisfactory of all the systems of divination, rises from and finds its explanation in the Tree and nowhere else. That may seem a dogmatic

statement to the scholarly historian searching for traces of
the origin of those mysterious cards, and, may we add, most
lamentably failing to find it; but when it is realised that the
initiate works the Tarot and the Tree together, and that they
dovetail into each other at every imaginable angle, it will
be seen that such an array of correspondences could be neither
arbitrary nor fortuitous.

36. A most interesting and important aspect of the practical
work of the Tree concerns the manner in which ceremonial
and talismanic magic are used to compensate the findings of
the divinatory sciences. Each prick-symbol of geomancy,
each card of the Tarot, and each horoscopic factor have their
places assigned to them on the Paths of the Tree, and the
occultist with the necessary knowledge can put together a
ritual or design a talisman to compensate or reinforce each and
any of these.

37. It is for this reason that divination by the uninitiated is
apt to bring bad luck in its train, for it stirs the subtle forces
by concentrating the mind upon them, without compensating
that which is out of equilibrium by the appropriate magical
effort.

PART II

CHAPTER XIV

GENERAL CONSIDERATIONS

1. In Part I we considered the general scheme and method of using the Qabalistic Tree of Life. We now come to the detailed study of the individual Sephiroth. This study must necessarily be tentative, for a life's research could be given to the significance of the correspondences that spread in endless ramifications from every symbol associated with each Sephirah. But a start must be made, hence these tentative jottings; for I do not consider the following chapters on the individual Sephiroth worthy to be called anything better than this, even though they are the fruit of ten years' meditation on that marvellous composite symbol.

2. The Tables of Correspondences at the head of each section consist of a selection of the principal symbols and ideas associated with each Sephirah, and have no claim whatsoever to comprehensiveness. They contain, however, the more significant symbols, and are sufficient to enable the student to gain a sound philosophical grasp of the subject, and experiment for himself in the use of the Tree as a meditation symbol.

3. The references are taken chiefly from "777," by Aleister Crowley, who got them from the MacGregor Mathers MSS. Mathers, so far as I have been able to trace his references, for he gives no authorities, drew upon the work of Dr Dee and Sir Edward Kelly; Cornelius Agrippa; Raymond Lully and Pietro de Abana among the earlier writers. Among the moderns the same material is found scattered through the works of Knorr von Rosenroth; Wynn Westcott; Eliphas Levi; Mrs Atwood; Mme Blavatsky; Anna Kingsford;

Mabel Collins; Papus (Encausse); St Martin; Gerald Massey; G. R. S. Mead, and many others. To some of these it is probable he was indebted; others may have been indebted to him. Some of them were actually members of the Order of the Golden Dawn which he founded.

4. Other sources of information are Frazer's *Golden Bough*; the works of Wallis Budge; the writings of Drs Jung and Freud; the translations of Dr Jowett from the Greek; the Sacred Books of the East Series, the Loeb Classical Library; the translation of Plotinus by Stephen MacKenna; the translation of the Zohar issued by the Soncino Press; and last, but by no means the least valuable source of information, the Holy Bible. So much for occult secrecy!

5. It will be seen that the symbols assigned to each Sephirah are classified in regular order under certain headings. To understand the significance attached to these different sections by the occultist and the use he makes of them it is necessary to explain the method of classification in detail.

6. SECTION 1. *The Title assigned to the Sephirah.*—Its name is given first in Hebrew and then in English, and the Hebrew spelling appended. The accurate spelling of all proper names used in the Qabalah is vitally important because of the numerical value attached to them by the Qabalists and the use made of the significance of these numbers by those who work the numerological methods. I am neither a numerologist nor a mathematician, and I do not therefore propose to comment on that which lies outside the sphere of my knowledge. I merely give the data for the convenience of those who can appreciate its significance.

7. SECTION 2. *The Magical Image and the Symbols associated with each Sephirah.*—The magical image is the mental picture which the occultist builds up to represent the Sephirah, and its details yield many significant symbols to meditation. These images are so old, and have been built with such a wealth of magical working, that they are apt to build themselves up of their own accord during meditation upon the Sephiroth. In the course of my own work on the Qabalah I saw most of

8

them long before I had access to the tables that gave them. In practical working the initiated adept builds them up with detailed symbolism, and it is a very valuable magical exercise to practise the visualisation of the magical images in their fullest detail. Much of this detail can be gleaned from the accounts I give of each Sephirah, but readers who have any specialised knowledge of the Eastern or classical pantheons can elaborate these images to any extent, surrounding them with all the paraphernalia of the gods assigned to each station on the Tree; these can be identified through their astrological associations.

8. SECTION 3. *The Situation on the Tree.*—This throws an immense amount of light upon any meditation, for it reveals the equilibrium of the spiritual forces working in nature. For instance, Geburah (Mars) and Chesed or Gedulah (Jupiter) are opposite each other upon the Tree. The warrior king and the wise and benign lawgiver of peace balance each other. Geburah when unbalanced becomes cruelty and oppression, and Gedulah when unbalanced suffers evil to multiply.

9. SECTION 4. *The Yetziratic Text.*—This consists of the description of the Sphere or Path given in the *Sepher Yetzirah*, or *Book of Formations.* The translation I have used is that of Wynn Westcott.

10. These descriptions are exceedingly cryptic, but they will from time to time yield a flash of inspiration, and undoubtedly contain the essence of the Qabalistic philosophy.

11. SECTION 5. *Descriptive Titles.*—A catalogue of the names that have been applied to that particular Sephirah in the Rabbinical literature. These throw great light on the subject and are also useful to the student for purposes of reference when tracing out the ideas associated with a particular Sephirah.

12. SECTION 6. *The Names of Power assigned to each Sephirah.*—The God-name represents the most spiritual form of the force and is conceived of as representing the functioning of that force in the Kingdom of Atziluth, the highest of the Four Kingdoms of the Qabalists.

13. The Archangelic Names represent the functioning of the same force in Briah, the Kingdom of the higher mind, wherein are the archetypal ideas.

14. The Angelic Choirs correspond to the Kingdom of Yetzirah, or the Astral Plane, and the Mundane Chakras are the representatives of each force in the Kingdom of Assiah, or the Material Plane.

15. What I call in my tables the spiritual experience assigned to each Sephirah is called by Crowley the magical power. But whereas this term may be rightly assigned to the Twenty-two Paths, it is misleading when applied to the Sephiroth. I therefore have changed the term in relation to the Sephiroth themselves, but retained it in reference to the Paths for reasons which will presently be seen.

16. SECTION 7. *The Virtues and Vices assigned to each Sphere on the Tree.*—These indicate the qualities necessary in order to take the initiation of that grade, and the form that is taken by any unbalanced force in that sphere. In the highest grades of all, before form is developed, there is no corresponding vice.

17. SECTION 8. *Correspondence in Microcosm.*—The microcosm, which is man, corresponds with the Sephirothic macrocosm, and is important from many practical standpoints, especially that of spiritual healing and astrology.

18. SECTION 9. *The Four Suits of the Tarot Pack.*—The assignation of the Tarot cards to the Tree opens up immense ranges of practical importance and forms the philosophical basis of the divinatory art.

19. If the reader keeps these explanations in mind he will be able to follow the lines of reasoning and allusion developed in the elucidation of the symbolism assigned to each Sephirah.

20. There is an immense amount of work to be done in correlating the different polytheistic pantheons and the angelologies of Christian, Hebrew, and Mohammedan faiths with the classifications of the Tree. This has been done tentatively by Crowley, and is, I fancy, original work and not derived from Mathers. Its implications are not altogether

clear to me, and I doubt if I could subscribe to all of them. An immensely wide range of scholarship is necessary for the satisfactory accomplishment of this branch, a range of scholarship which I do not possess. I shall therefore content myself with touching upon such points as have come within the range of my knowledge and make no attempt in the present pages at an ordered classification.

21. SECTION 10. *The Flashing Colours.*—This is only of use to advanced students who possess the necessary keys.

CHAPTER XV

TITLE: Kether, the Crown. (Hebrew spelling: כתר: Kaph, Tau, Resh.)

MAGICAL IMAGE: An ancient bearded king seen in profile.

SITUATION ON THE TREE: At the head of the Pillar of Equilibrium in the Supernal Triangle.

YETZIRATIC TEXT: The First Path is called the Admirable or Hidden Intelligence because it is the Light giving the power of comprehension of the First Principle, which hath no beginning. And it is the Primal Glory, because no created being can attain to its essence.

TITLES GIVEN TO KETHER: Existence of Existences. Concealed of the Concealed. Ancient of Ancients. Ancient of Days. The Primordial Point. The Point within the Circle. The Most High. The Vast Countenance. The White Head. The Head which is not. Macroprosopos. Amen. Lux Occulta. Lux Interna. He. The Inscrutable Height.

GOD-NAME: Ehyeh

ARCHANGEL: Metatron. Angel of the Presence.

ORDER OF ANGELS: Holy living creatures. Chayyoth ha-Qodesh.

MUNDANE CHAKRA: Reshith ha-Gilgulim. Primum Mobile. First Swirlings.

SPIRITUAL EXPERIENCE: Union with God.

VIRTUE: Attainment. Completion of the Great Work.

VICE: ——

CORRESPONDENCE IN MICROCOSM: The Cranium. The Sah. Yechidah. The Divine Spark. The Thousand-petalled Lotus.

SYMBOLS: The point. The crown. The swastika.

TAROT CARDS: The four Aces.

    ACE OF WANDS: Root of the Powers of Fire.
    ACE OF CUPS: Root of the Powers of Water.
    ACE OF SWORDS: Root of the Powers of Air.
    ACE OF PENTACLES: Root of the Powers of Earth.

COLOUR IN ATZILUTH: Brilliance.
      ,,   BRIAH: Pure white brilliance.
      ,,   YETZIRAH: Pure white brilliance.
      ,,   ASSIAH: White, flecked gold.

I

1. Kether, the Crown, is placed at the head of the Middle Pillar of Equilibrium, and from it depend backwards the Negative Veils of Existence. I have already written concerning the use of these Negative Veils as a background to thought, so I will not repeat myself upon this point, but remind the reader that Kether, the First Manifest, represents the primal crystallisation into manifestation of that which was hitherto unmanifest and therefore unknowable by us. Concerning the root from which Kether springs we can know nothing; but concerning Kether itself we can know something. It may be for us at our stage of development the Great Unknown, but it is not the Great Unknowable. The mind of the magus must compass it in his higher visions. In my own experiences with the operation known as Rising on the Planes, which consists in carrying consciousness up the Middle Pillar by means of concentration on the successive symbols and the Paths, Kether, on the one occasion when I touched its fringe, appeared as a blinding white light, in which all thought went completely blank.

2. In Kether there is no form but only pure being, whatever that may be. It is, one might say, a latency only one degree removed from non-existence. Such concepts must necessarily be vague, and I am ill-equipped to give them such definiteness as they might possess, but I am quite satisfied that we should recognise grades of becoming, and that the crude differentiation of Being and Non-being does not represent the facts. With manifested existence there come into being the pairs of opposites; but in Kether there is no division into the pairs of opposites, which must wait for their manifestation till Chokmah and Binah are emanated.

3. Kether, then, is the One, and existed before there was

any reflection of itself to serve it for an image in consciousness and set up polarity. We must believe that it transcended all known laws of manifestation by existing alone, without reaction. But when we speak of Kether it must be remembered that we do not mean a person, but a state of existence, and this state of existing substance must have been utterly inert, pure being without activity, until the activity began which emanated Chokmah.

4. The human mind, knowing no other mode of existence than that of form and activity, has the greatest difficulty in obtaining any adequate concept of an entirely formless state of passivity which is nevertheless most distinctly not nonbeing. Yet this effort must be made if we are to understand cosmic philosophy in its fundamentals. We must not draw the Veils of Negative Existence in front of Kether or we shall condemn ourselves to a perpetual unresolved duality; God and the Devil will for ever war in our cosmos, and there can be no finality to their conflict. We must train the mind to conceive the state of pure being without attributes or activities; we may think of it as the blinding white light, undifferentiated into rays by the prism of form; or we may think of it as the darkness of interstellar space, which is nothing, yet contains the potentialities of all things. These symbols, dwelt upon by the inner eye, are a greater aid to the understanding of Kether than any amount of exact philosophical definitions. We cannot define Kether; we can only indicate it.

5. It is a continual surprise and illumination to discover the extraordinary significance of the hints contained in the tables of correspondences, and the manner in which they lead the mind on from concept to concept when pondered upon. The First Sephirah is called the Crown, be it noted, not the head. Now the Crown is something superimposed upon the head, and this gives us a clear hint that Kether is of our cosmos, but not in it. We also find its microcosmic correspondence in the Thousand-petalled Lotus, the Sahamsara Chakra, which is in the aura immediately above the head. This, I think, teaches

us clearly that the innermost spiritual essence of anything, whether man or world, is never in actual manifestation, but is always the underlying, behind-standing basis or root whence all springs, belonging in fact to a different dimension, a different order of being. It is this concept of the different types of existence which is fundamental to esoteric philosophy, and must always be borne in mind when considering the invisible kingdoms of the magician, or operative occultist.

6. In the Vedantan philosophy Kether would undoubtedly equate with Parabrahmâ, Chokmah with Brahman, and Binah with Mulaprakriti. In the other great systems of human thought Kether equates with their primary concept and may be taken as the Father of the Gods. If for them the universe originated in space, then Kether is the Sky God. If it originated in water, Kether is the primordial ocean. Always we find in connection with Kether the sense of formlessness and timelessness. The gods of Kether are terrible gods which eat their children, for Kether, although the parent of all, reabsorbs the universe back into itself at the end of an epoch of evolution.

7. Kether is the abyss whence all arose, and back into which it will fall at the end of its epoch. Therefore in exoteric myths associated with Kether we find the implication of non-existence. In esoteric concepts, however, we learn that such a concept is erroneous. Kether is the intensest form of existence, pure being unlimited by form or reaction; but it is existence of another type than that to which we are accustomed, and therefore it appears to us as non-existence because it conforms to none of the requirements we are accustomed to think of as determining existence. This concept of other modes of existence is implicit in our philosophy and must ever be borne in mind, for it is the key to Kether, and Kether is the key to the Tree of Life.

8. The Yetziratic Text descriptive of Kether, like all the sayings of the *Sepher Yetzirah*, is a hidden saying. It calls Kether the Hidden Intelligence, and this appellation is confirmed by several other of the titles given to Kether in Qabalistic literature. It is the Concealed of the Concealed, the

Inscrutable Height, the Head which is not. Here again we get confirmation of the idea that the crown is above the head of the Celestial Man, Adam Kadmon; that pure being stands behind manifestation and is not absorbed into it, but rather emanates or projects it. As we express ourselves in our works, so does Kether express itself in manifestation. But a man's works do not constitute his personality, but are the expression of its natural activity. So it is with Kether; its mode of existence is not manifested, but is the cause of manifestation.

II

9. We have hitherto considered Kether in Atziluth, that is to say as its essential and primal essence. We must now consider Kether as it appears in the three other Kingdoms distinguished by the Qabalists.

10. Each Kingdom or plane of manifestation has its primary form; matter, for instance, is in all probability primarily electric, and this is expressed by the esotericists as the etheric sub-plane which lies behind the four elemental planes of Earth, Air, Fire, and Water; or in other words, the four conditions of dense matter, solid, liquid, gaseous, and etheric.

11. The Qabalists conceive of the Tree as existing in each of the four Kingdoms of Atziluth, pure spirit; Briah, archetypal mind; Yetzirah, astral picture-consciousness; and Assiah, the material world in both its dense and subtler aspects. The operations of the forces of each Sephirah are represented in each world under the presidency of a Divine Name, or Word of Power, and these words give the keys to the operations of practical occultism upon the planes. The God-name represents the action of the Sephirah in the world of Atziluth, pure spirit; when the occultist invokes the forces of a Sephirah by the God-name, it means that he desires to contact its most abstract essence, that, he is seeking the spiritual principle underlying and conditioning that particular mode of manifestation. It is a maxim of White Occultism that every operation should commence with the invocation of the God-name

of the Sphere in which the operation is to take place. This
ensures that the operation shall be in harmony with cosmic
law. The balance of natural force is not lightly to be overset.
It is essential to the safety of the magician that he should
conduct his operations in accordance with cosmic law; therefore he must seek to understand the spiritual principle involved
in every problem and work it out accordingly. Every operation, therefore, must have its final unification or resolution in
Ehyeh, the God-name of Kether in Atziluth.

12. The invocation of Deity under the name of Ehyeh, that
is to say the affirmation of pure being, eternal, unchanging,
without attributes or activities, underlying, maintaining, and
conditioning all, is the primary formula of all magical working.
It is only when the mind is imbued with the realisation of this
endless unchanging being of the utmost concentration and
intensity that it can have any realisation of limitless power.
Energy derived from any other source is a limited and partial
energy. In Kether alone is the pure source of all energy.
The operations of the magician that aim at the concentrating of
energy (and what operations do not?) must always start with
Kether, because here we touch the upwelling force arising
from the Great Unmanifest, the reservoir of limitless power.
It is through Kether, from the Great Unmanifest hidden
behind the Veils of Negative Existence, that power is drawn.
If we draw power from any specialised sphere of nature, we
are, as it were, robbing Peter to pay Paul. The power has
come from somewhere, and gone somewhere, and it has to be
accounted for at the final reckoning. It is for this reason that
it has been held that the magician pays in suffering for what he
wins by magical means. This is true if his operation is performed in any of the lower spheres of nature; but if it starts in
the Kether of Atziluth, he is drawing unmanifest force into
manifestation; he is adding to the resources of the universe,
and provided he keeps the forces in equilibrium, there need be
no untoward reaction and no payment in suffering for the use
of the magical powers.

13. This is a point of tremendous practical importance.

Students have been taught that the Three Supernals, Kether, Chokmah, and Binah, are beyond the range of practical working so long as we are in incarnation. True, they are beyond the range of brain consciousness, but they are the essential basis of all magical calculations, and if we do not work from this basis we have no cosmic foundation, but are poised between heaven and earth and find no place of rest or security, but must ever maintain the magical stresses that keep the astral forms in being.

14. The great difference between Christian Science and the cruder forms of New Thought and Auto-suggestion is that it starts all its workings in the Divine Life; and utterly irrational though its attempts to philosophise its system may be, its methods are empirically sound. The occultist, and especially the practitioner of ceremonial magic, if uninstructed in this discipline, tends to start his operation without any reference to cosmic law or spiritual principle; consequently the astral images he forms are like foreign bodies in the organism of the Celestial Man, or Macrocosm, and all the forces of nature are spontaneously directed towards the elimination of the foreign substance and the restoration of the normal equilibrium of stresses. Nature fights the magician tooth and nail; consequently, whosoever has resorted to unconsecrated magic may never lay down his sword, but must always be on the defensive in order to maintain that which he has won. But the adept who starts his work in the Kether of Atziluth, that is to say in spiritual principle, and works that principle downwards to its expression on the planes of form, employing power drawn from the Unmanifest for this purpose, has made his operation a part of the cosmic process, and Nature is with him instead of against him.

15. We cannot hope to understand the nature of Kether in Atziluth, but we can open our consciousness to its influence; and its influence is very powerful and gives a strange sense of eternity and immortality. We may know when the invocation of Eheieh in its pure white brilliance has been effectual, because we shall find ourselves realising with complete conviction the

utter impermanence and insignificance of the planes of form and the supreme importance of the One Life which conditions all form as clay in the hands of the potter.

16. Meditation upon Kether gives us an intuitive realisation that the issue of an operation does not matter in the very least. "Let the dirt play with the dirt if it pleases the dirt." Once that realisation has been obtained we have lordship over the astral images and can turn them this way and that as it pleases us. It is only when the operator cares nothing for the outcome of the operation on the physical plane that he attains to this complete lordship over the astral images. He is concerned simply and solely with the handling of forces and the bringing of them through into manifestation in form; but he does not care what form the forces may ultimately assume, he leaves that to them; for they will assuredly assume the form that is most consonant with their nature, and thus be truer to cosmic law than any design which his limited knowledge could assign to them. This is the real key to all magical operations, and their sole justification, for we may not turn the universe round and about to suit our whim or convenience, but are only justified in the deliberate work of magic when we work with the great tide of evolving life in order to bring ourselves into fullness of life, whatever form that experience or manifestation may take. "I am come that they might have life, and that they might have it more abundantly," said Our Lord, and that should be the word of the magician. Life, and life alone, should be his word, and not any specialised manifestation of it as Wisdom, Power, nor even Love.

17. Those who have followed the preceding discussion point by point may now be able to see some significance in the cryptic words of the Yetziratic Text assigned to Kether. The words "Hidden Intelligence" convey a hint of the unmanifest nature of the existence of Kether, which is confirmed by the statement that "No created being can attain to its essence"; that is to say, no being using as its vehicle of consciousness any organism of the planes of form. When, however, consciousness has been exalted to the point where it

transcends thought, it receives from the " Primal Glory " the " power of comprehension of the First Principle "; or in other words, " Then shall we know even as we are known. "

III

18. Ehyeh, I Am That I Am, pure being, is the God-name of Kether, and its magical image is an ancient bearded king seen in profile. The *Zohar* says of this ancient bearded king that he is all right side; we do not see the magical image of Kether full-face, that is to say complete, but only partially. There is an aspect which must ever be hidden from us, like the hidden side of the moon. This side of Kether is the side that is towards the Unmanifest, which the nature of our manifested consciousness prevents us from comprehending, and which must ever be a sealed book to us. But accepting this limitation we may gaze in contemplation upon the aspect of Kether, the profile of the ancient bearded king, presented to us reflected downwards into form.

19. Ancient is this king, the Ancient of Ancients, the Ancient of Days, for he was from the beginning, when countenance beheld not countenance. A king he is, because he rules all things according to his supreme and unquestioned will. In other words, it is the nature of Kether that conditions all things, because all things are evolved from it. Bearded he is, because in the curious symbolism of the rabbis every hair of his beard has significance.

20. The manifestation of the forces of Kether in Briah, the world of archetypal mind, is said to be through the archangel Metatron, the Prince of Countenances, who tradition avers was the teacher of Moses. The *Sepher Yetzirah* says of the Tenth Path, Malkuth, that "it causes an influence to flow from the Prince of Countenances, the archangel of Kether, and is the source of illumination of all the lights of the universe." Thus plainly do we learn that not only does spirit flow out into manifestation in matter, but matter by its own energy draws spirit into manifestation, an important point for the practitioner of magic, for it teaches him that he is justified

in his operations and that man is not required to wait upon the word of the Lord, but may call upon God to hear him.

21. The angels of Kether, operating in the Yetziratic world, are the Chayyoth ha-Qodesh, Holy Living Creatures, and their name carries the mind to the Chariot Vision of Ezekiel and the Four Holy Creatures before the Throne. The fact that the four aces of the Tarot, assigned to Kether, are regarded as representing the roots of the four elements of Earth, Air, Fire, and Water further bears out this association. We may look, then, to Kether as the fountain-head of the elements. This concept clears up many occult and metaphysical difficulties that occur if we limit their operation to the astral plane and regard elementals as little better than devils, as some schools of transcendental thought appear to do.

22. The whole question of the angels, archons, and elementals is a very vexed and very important one in occultism, because its practical application to magic is immediate. Christian thought can tolerate with an effort the idea of archangels, but the ministering spirits, the messengers who are flames of fire, and the heavenly builders, are alien to its theology; God, alone and in an instant, made the heavens and earth. The Great Architect of the universe is also the bricklayer. Not so does esoteric science. The initiate knows the legions of spiritual beings who are agents of God's will and the vehicles of creative activity. It is through these that he works, by the grace of their ruling archangel. But an archangel cannot be conjured by any spell, however potent. Rather is it that when we effect an operation of the Sphere of a particular Sephirah, the archangel works through us for the fulfilment of its mission. The art of the magician therefore lies in aligning himself with cosmic force in order that the operation he desires to perform may come about as a part of the working of cosmic activities. If he be truly purified and dedicated, this will be the case with all his desires; and if he be not truly purified and dedicated, he is no adept, and his word is not a word of power.

23. It is interesting to note that in the World of Assiah the

title of the Sphere of Kether is Reshith ha-Gilgulim, or First
Swirlings, thus indicating that the rabbis were acquainted
with the Nebular Theory before science was acquainted with
the telescope. The manner in which the ancients deduced
the basic facts of cosmogony by purely intuitive means and
the use of the method of correspondences, centuries before
the invention and perfection of the instruments of precision
which enabled modern man to make the same discoveries
from another angle, must be a matter of perpetual amazement
to anyone who comes to the traditional philosophy unbiased.

24. As above, so below. The microcosm corresponds to
the macrocosm, and we must therefore seek in man the Kether
above the head which shines with a pure white brilliance in
Adam Kadmon, the Heavenly Man. The rabbis call it the
Yechidah, the Divine Spark; the Egyptians call it the Sah;
the Hindus call it the Thousand-petalled Lotus. But under
all these names we have the same idea—the nucleus of pure
spirit which emanates but does not indwell its many manifestations upon the planes of form.

25. It is said that never while in incarnation can we rise
to the consciousness of Kether in Atziluth and retain the
physical vehicle intact against our return. Even as Enoch
walked with God and was not, so the man that has the vision
of Kether is disrupted so far as the vehicle of incarnation
is concerned. Why this must be is readily discerned when
we remember that we cannot enter into a mode of consciousness save by reproducing it in ourselves, just as music means
nothing to us unless the heart sings with it. If therefore we
reproduce in ourselves the mode of being of that which has
neither form nor activities, it follows that we must free ourselves from form and activity. If we succeed in doing so,
that which is held together by the form-mode of consciousness
will fall apart and return to its elements. Thus dissolved,
it cannot be reassembled by returning consciousness. Therefore
when we aspire to the Vision of Kether in Atziluth we must
be prepared to enter into the Light and come not forth again.

26. This does not imply that Nirvana is annihilation, as an

ignorant rendering of Eastern philosophy has taught European thought; but it does imply a complete change of mode or dimension. What we shall be when we find ourselves ranked with the Holy Living Creatures, we do not know, and none who achieved the vision of Kether in Atziluth have returned to tell us; but tradition avers that there are those who have done so, and that they are intimately concerned with the evolution of humanity and are the prototypes of those supermen concerning whom all races have a tradition; a tradition which, unfortunately, of recent years has been cheapened and debased by pseudo-occult teaching. Whatever these beings may or may not be, it is safe to say that they have neither astral form nor human personality, but are as flames in the fire which is God. The state of the soul which has attained Nirvana may best be likened to a wheel that has lost its rim and whose spokes have become rays that penetrate and interpenetrate the whole creation; a centre of radiation to whose influence no limit is set save that of its own dynamism, and which maintains its identity as a nucleus of energy.

27. The Spiritual Experience assigned to Kether is said to be Union with God. This is the end and aim of all mystical experience, and if we look for any other goal we are as those who build a house in the world of illusion. Anything that holds him back from the straight path to this goal is felt by the mystic to be a bond that binds, and as such to be broken. All that holds consciousness to form, all desires other than the one desire—these are to him evils, and from the standpoint of his philosophy he is right, and to act otherwise would invalidate his technique.

28. But this is not the only test which the mystic has to face; it is required of him that he shall fufil the requirements of the planes of form before he is free to commence his withdrawal and escape from form. There is a Left-hand Path that leads to Kether, the Kether of the Qliphoth, which is the Kingdom of Chaos. If he embarks upon the Mystic Path prematurely it is thither he goes, and not to the Kingdom of Light. To the man who is naturally of the Mystic Path the

discipline of form is uncongenial, and it is the subtlest of temptations to abandon the struggle with the life of form that resists his mastery and retreat back up the planes before the nadir has been rounded and the lessons of form have been learnt.   Form is the matrix in which the fluidic consciousness is held till it acquires an organisation proof against dispersal; till it becomes a nucleus of individuality differentiated out of the amorphous sea of pure being.   If the matrix be broken too soon, before the fluidic consciousness had become set as an organised system of stresses stereotyped by repetition, consciousness settles back again into formlessness, even as the clay returns to mud if freed from the supporting restraint of the mould before it has set.   If there is a mystic whose mysticism produces mundane incapacity or any form of dissociation of consciousness, we know that the mould had been broken too soon for him, and he must return to the discipline of form until its lesson has been learnt and his consciousness has attained a coherent and cohesive organisation that not even Nirvana can disrupt.   Let him hew wood and carry water in the service of the Temple if he will, but let him not profane its holy place with his pathologies and immaturities.

29. The virtue assigned to Kether is that of Attainment, the Completion of the Great Work, to use a term borrowed from the alchemists.   Without completion there can be no attainment, and without attainment no completion.   Good intentions weigh light in the scale of cosmic justice; it is by our completed work that we are known.   True, we have all eternity in which to complete it, but complete it we must, even to the final Yod.   There is no mercy in perfect justice save that which gives us leave to try again.

30. Kether, viewed from the standpoint of form, is the crown of the kingdom of oblivion.   Unless we have realisation of the nature of the life of the pure white light we shall have little temptation to strive for the Crown which is not of this order of being at all; and if we have this realisation, then are we free from the bondage of manifestation and can speak to all forms as one having authority.

CHAPTER XVI

CHOKMAH, THE SECOND SEPHIRAH

TITLE: Chokmah, Wisdom. (Hebrew spelling: חכמה:
Cheth, Kaph, Mem, Hé.)

MAGICAL IMAGE: A bearded male figure.

SITUATION ON THE TREE: At the head of the Pillar of Mercy
in the Supernal Triangle.

YETZIRATIC TEXT: The Second Path is called the Illuminating
Intelligence. It is the Crown of Creation, the Splendour
of Unity, equalling it. It is exalted above every head,
and is named by Qabalists the Second Glory.

TITLES GIVEN TO CHOKMAH: Power of Yetzirah. Av. Abba.
The Supernal Father. Tetragrammaton. Yod of Tetragrammaton.

GOD-NAME: Jehovah.

ARCHANGEL: Raziel, Secret, or Herald, of God.

ORDER OF ANGELS: Ophannim, wheels.

MUNDANE CHAKRA: Mazzaloth, the Zodiac.

SPIRITUAL EXPERIENCE: The Vision of God face to face.

VIRTUE: Devotion.

VICE: ——

CORRESPONDENCE IN MICROCOSM: The left side of the face.

SYMBOLS: The Lingam. The Phallus. The Yod of Tetragrammaton. The Inner Robe of Glory. The Standing-
stone. The Tower. The Uplifted Rod of Power.
The Straight Line.

TAROT CARDS: The four Twos.
       TWO OF WANDS: Dominion.
       TWO OF CUPS: Love.
       TWO OF SWORDS: Peace restored.
       TWO OF PENTACLES: Harmonious change.

COLOUR IN AZILUTH: Pure soft blue.
      ,,   BRIAH: Grey.
      ,,   YETZIRAH: Pearl-grey, iridescent.
      ,,   ASSIAH: White flecked with red, blue, and yellow.

I

1. Every phase of evolution commences by being in a state of unstable force and proceeds through organisation to equilibrium. Equilibrium having been achieved, no further development is possible without once more oversetting the stability and passing through a phase of contending forces. As we have already seen, Kether is the Point formulated in the Void. According to Euclid's definition, a point has position but no dimensions. If, however, a point may be conceived of as extending through space, it becomes a line. The nature of the organisation and evolution of the Three Supernals is so remote from our experience that we can only conceive of them symbolically; but if we conceive of the Primordial Point which is Kether as being extended into the line which is Chokmah, we shall have as adequate a symbolic representation as we may hope to achieve at our present state of understanding.

2. This forth-flowing energy, represented by the straight line or the uplifted rod of power, is essentially dynamic. It is, in fact, the primary dynamism, for we cannot conceive the crystallisation of Kether in space as a dynamic process; it partakes rather of a staticism—of the limiting of the formless and free in the bonds of form, tenuous as that form may be in our eyes.

3. The limits of the organisation of such a form having been reached, the ever-inflowing force of the Unmanifest transcends its limitations, demanding fresh modes of development, establishing fresh relationships and stresses. It is this out-driving of unorganised, uncompensated force which is Chokmah, and because Chokmah is a dynamic Sephirah, ever out-flowing in boundless energy, we do well to look upon it as a channel for the passage of force rather than a receptacle for the storage of force.

4. Chokmah is not an organising Sephirah, but it is the Great Stimulator of the Universe. It is from Chokmah that Binah, the Third Sephirah, receives its influx of emanation, and Binah is the first of the organising, stabilising Sephiroth. It

is not possible to understand either of the paired Sephiroth without considering its mate; therefore in order to understand Chokmah we shall have to say something about Binah. Let it be noted, then, that Binah is assigned to the planet Saturn and is called the Superior Mother.

5. In Chokmah and Binah we have the archetypal Positive and Negative; the primordial Maleness and Femaleness, established while "countenance beheld not countenance" and manifestation was incipient. It is from these primary Pairs of Opposites that the Pillars of the Universe spring, between which is woven the web of Manifestation.

6. As we have already noted, the Tree of Life is a diagrammatic representation of the Universe on which the positive and negative, male and female aspects are represented by the two flanking Pillars of Mercy and Severity. It may seem strange to uninstructed thought that the title of Mercy should be given to the male or positive Pillar, and that of Severity to the female Pillar; but when it is realised that the dynamic male type of force is the stimulator of upbuilding and evolution, and that the female type of force is the builder of forms, it will be seen that the nomenclature is apt; for form, although it is the builder and organiser, is also the limiter; each form that is built must in turn be outgrown, lose its usefulness, and so become a hindrance to evolving life, and therefore the bringer-in of dissolution and decay, which lead on to death. The Father is the Giver of life; but the Mother is the Giver of death, because her womb is the gate of ingress to matter, and through her life is ensouled in form, and no form can be either infinite or eternal. Death is implicit in birth.

7. It is between these two polarising aspects of manifestation—the Supernal Father and the Supernal Mother—that the web of Life is woven; souls going back and forth between them like a weaver's shuttle. In our individual lives, in our physiological rhythms, and in the history of the rise and fall of nations, we observe the same rhythmic periodicity.

8. In these, the first paired Sephiroth, we have the key to sex—the pair of biological opposites, maleness and femaleness.

But the pairing of opposites does not only occur in type, it also occurs in time, and we have alternating epochs in our lives, in our physiological processes, and in the history of nations, during which activity and passivity, construction and destruction alternately prevail; the knowledge of the periodicity of these cycles is part of the secret, guarded, ancient wisdom of the initiates, and is worked out astrologically and Qabalistically.

9. The Magical Image of Chokmah and the symbols assigned to it bear out this idea. The Magical Image is that of a bearded male, bearded to indicate maturity; the father who has proved his manhood, not the untried virgin male. The symbolic language speaks plainly, and the lingam of the Hindus and the phallus of the Greeks are the male generative organ in their respective tongues. The standing-stone, the tower, and the uplifted rod all signify the same virile member at its most potent.

10. It must not be thought, however, that Chokmah is a phallic or sexual symbol and nothing else. It is primarily a dynamic or positive symbol, for maleness is a form of dynamic force, just as femaleness is a form of static, latent, or potential force, inert till stimulus be given. The whole is greater than the part, and Chokmah and Binah are wholes of which sex is a part. In understanding the relationship which sex has to polarising force as a whole, we find the key to the right understanding of sex, and we can assess against a cosmic standard the teachings of psychology and morality relating thereto. We can also see how it comes about that the subconscious mind of man can represent the sexes by so many and such diverse symbols, as the Freudians aver; and why sublimation of the sexual instinct is possible, as the moralists aver. Manifestation, then, is sexual insomuch as it takes place always in terms of the pairs of opposites; and sex is cosmic and spiritual because it has its roots in the Three Supernals. We must learn not to dissociate the airy flower from the earthy root, for the flower that is cut off from its root fades, and its seeds are barren; whereas the root, secure in mother earth, can produce flower after flower and bring their fruit to maturity. Nature is greater and truer than conventional morality, which is often

nothing but taboo and totemism. Happy the people whose morality embodies Nature's laws, for they shall lead harmonious lives and increase and multiply and possess the earth. Unhappy the people whose morality is a savage system of taboos designed to propitiate an imaginary Moloch of a deity, for they shall be sterile and sinful. Equally unhappy the people whose morality outrages the sanctity of natural process and in plucking the flower has no regard for the fruit, for they shall be diseased of body and corrupt of estate.

11. In Chokmah, then, we must see both the creative Word which said "Let there be light," and the lingam of Siva and the phallus adored by the Bacchantes. We must learn to recognise dynamic force, and revere it wherever we see it, for its God-name is Jehovah Tetragrammaton. We see it in the spread tail of the peacock and the iridescence of the neck of the dove; but we also hear it in the yowl of the tom-cat and smell it in the stench of the he-goat. Likewise we meet it in the colonising adventurers of the most virile epochs of our history, notably those of Elizabeth and Victoria—both women! We see it again in the man diligent in his toil, strenuous in his profession, in order that his home may be provided for. All these are types of Chokmah, whose additional title is Abba—Father. In all these manifestations let us see the father, the giver of life to the unborn as well as the male lusting after its mate; thus we shall get a truer perspective in matters of sex. The Victorian attitude, in its reaction against Restoration grossness, practically arrived at the standard of the most primitive tribes, who, travellers tell us, do not associate the union of the sexes with the production of offspring.

12. The colour of Chokmah is said to be grey; in its higher aspects, pearl-grey, iridescent. In this we see the veiling of the pure white light of Kether descending in its path of emanation towards Binah, whose colour is black.

13. The Mundane Chakra, or direct physical manifestation of Chokmah, is said to be the Zodiac, called in Hebrew Mazzaloth. We thus see that the ancient rabbis rightly understood the process of the evolution of our solar system.

14. The Yetziratic Text assigned to Chokmah is, as usual, exceedingly obscure in its wording; nevertheless we can gather from it certain illuminating hints. The Second Path, as it denominates Chokmah, it calls the Illuminating Intelligence. We have already referred to the creative Word which said "Let there be light." Among the symbols assigned to Chokmah in "777" (Mathers-Crowley system) is that of the Inner Robe of Glory, a gnostic term. These two ideas, taken together, lead on the imagination to the idea of the ensouling life, the illuminating spirit. It is the male force that implants the fecundating spark in the passive ovum on all planes and transforms its inert latency into the active up-building of growth and evolution. It is the dynamic force of life, which is spirit, that ensouls the clay of physical form and constitutes the Inner Robe of Glory that is worn by all beings in whom is the breath of life. Force embodied in form, and form ensouled by force, is signified by the Illuminating Intelligence and the Inner Robe of Glory.

15. The Yetziratic Text also calls Chokmah the Crown of Creation, thus implying that, like Kether, it is overshadowing and external to, rather than immanent and absorbed in, the manifested Universe. Actually it is the virile force of Chokmah which gives the impulse to manifestation, and thus is prior to manifestation itself. The Voice of the Logos was crying "Let there be light" long ere the waters were separated from the waters and the firmament appeared. This idea is further borne out in the phrase of the Yetziratic Text which speaks of Chokmah as the Splendour of Unity, equalling it, thus clearly indicating its affinity to Kether, Unity, rather than to the planes of dualistic form. The word splendour, as used here, clearly indicates an emanation, or shining forth, and teaches us to think of Chokmah as the emanating influence of pure being rather than as a thing in itself. This again leads us on to a truer apprehension of sex. Let it be made quite clear, however, that the sphere of Chokmah has nothing to do with fertility cults as such, save that maleness, dynamic force, is the primary life-giver and caller into manifestation. Though

the higher and lower manifestations of dynamic force are the same in essence, they are upon different levels; Priapus is not identical with Jehovah. Nevertheless, the root of Priapus is to be found in Jehovah, and the manifestation of God the Father is to be found in Priapus, as is indicated by the fact that the rabbis call Chokmah the Yod of Tetragrammaton, and Yod is identical with lingam in their phraseology.

16. It is curious that the *Sepher Yetzirah* says of two of the Sephiroth that they are exalted above every head—a contradictory statement; yet in the fact that it is made with regard to Chokmah and Malkuth there is illumination for us if we ponder its significance. Chokmah is the Supernal Father, Malkuth is the Inferior Mother, and the text which declares her exaltation above every head also says that she sitteth upon the throne of Binah, the Superior Mother, the negative counterpart of Chokmah. Now Chokmah is the most abstract form of force, and Malkuth is the densest form of matter; so in this statement we have a hint that each of this pair of extreme opposites is the supreme manifestation of its own type, and both are equally holy in their different ways.

17. We must distinguish between the fertility rite, the vitality rite, and the illumination or inspiration rite, which calls down the Pentecostal tongues of flame. The fertility cult aims at plain and simple reproduction, whether of flocks, fields, or wives; it belongs to Yesod, and has nothing whatever to do with the vitality cult, which belongs to Netzach, the sphere of Venus-Aphrodite. This concerns certain very important esoteric teaching on the subject of the vitalising or magnetic influences which the sexes have on each other, quite apart from physical intercourse, and will be dealt with when Netzach, the sphere of Venus, comes to be considered.

18. The Rite of Chokmah, if such it can be called, is concerned with the influx of cosmic energy. It is formless, being the pure impulse of dynamic creation; and being formless, the creation it gives rise to can assume any and every form; hence the possibility of sublimating creative force from its purely Priapic aspect.

19. So far as I know, there is no formal magical ceremony of any of the Three Supernals. They can only be contacted through participation in their essential nature. Kether, pure being, is contacted when we win to realisation of the nature of existence without parts, attributes or dimensions. This experience is aptly called the Trance of Annihilation, and those who experience it walk with God and are not, for God has taken them; therefore is the spiritual experience assigned to Kether that of Divine Union, of which it is said that those who experience it enter into the Light and come not forth again.

20. In order to contact Chokmah we must experience the rush of the dynamic cosmic energy in its pure form; an energy so tremendous that mortal man is fused into disruption by it. It is recorded that when Semele, mother of Dionysos, saw Zeus her divine lover in his god-form as the Thunderer, she was blasted and burnt, and gave birth to her divine son prematurely. The spiritual experience assigned to Chokmah is the Vision of God face to face; and God (Jehovah) said to Moses, "Thou canst not look upon my face and live."

21. But although the sight of the Divine Father blasts mortals as with fire, the Divine Son comes familiarly among them and can be invoked by the appropriate rites—Bacchanalia in the case of the Son of Zeus, and the Eucharist in the case of the Son of Jehovah. Thus we see that there is a lower form of manifestation, which " shews us the Father," but that this rite owes its validity solely to the fact that it derives its Illuminating Intelligence, its Inner Robe of Glory, from the Father, Chokmah.

II

22. The grade of initiation corresponding to Chokmah is said to be that of Magus, and the magical weapons assigned to that grade are the phallus and the Inner Robe of Glory. This teaches us that these symbols have a microcosmic or psychological significance as well as a macrocosmic or mystical one. The Inner Robe of Glory must surely signify the Inner Light

which lighteth every man that cometh into the world—the spiritual vision whereby the mystic discerns spiritual things, the subjective form of the Illuminating Intelligence referred to in the Yetziratic Text.

23. The phallus or lingam is given as one of the magical weapons of the initiate operating the grade of Chokmah; this tells us that a knowledge of the spiritual significance of sex and the cosmic significance of polarity concern this grade. Anyone who can see beneath the surface in things mystical and magical cannot fail to be aware of the fact that in the understanding of the tremendous and mysterious potency (which we call sex in one of its manifestations) lies the key to a very great deal. It is not for nothing that sexual imagery pervades the visions of the seer, from the *Song of Songs* to *The Interior Castle*.

24. It must not be thought from this that I advocate orgiastic rites as the Way of Initiation; but I may as well say plainly that without the right understanding of the esoteric aspect of sex, the Path is a blind alley. Freud spoke the truth to this generation when he pointed to sex as a key to psychopathology; he erred, in my opinion, when he made it the only key to the nine-chambered soul of man. As there can be no health of subconsciousness without harmony of sex-life, so there can be no positive or dynamic working upon the plane of superconsciousness unless the laws of polarity are understood and observed. To many mystics, seeking refuge from matter in spirit, this may be a hard saying, but experience will prove it a true one; therefore it must be said, though there may be few thanks for saying it.

25. The tremendous down-rush of the Chokmah-force invoked through the Divine Four-lettered Name comes from the macrocosmic Yod to the microcosmic Yod, and is then sublimated. Unless the subconscious mind is free from dissociations and repressions, and all the parts of the many-sided nature of man are co-ordinated and synchronised, reactions and pathological symptoms are the result of that down-rush. This does not mean that the invoker of Zeus is necessarily a

worshipper of Priapus, but it *does* mean that no man can sublimate a dissociation. When the channel is free from obstructions the down-rushing force can swing round the nadir and become an up-rushing force which can be directed to any sphere or turned into any channel that is desired; but, like it or not, it will be a down-rushing force before it is an up-rushing one, and unless our feet are firmly planted on elemental earth we shall be like bursting wine-skins.

26. Every practical occultist knows that Freud has spoken the truth, even though it is not the whole truth, but they are afraid to say so for fear of being accused of phallic worship and orgiastic practices. These things have their place, though it is not in the Temple of the Holy Spirit, and to deny them their place is a folly for which the Victorian age paid dearly in a rich harvest of psychopathology.

27. Whenever we are working dynamically upon any plane we are operating the Right-hand Pillar of the Tree and derive our primary energy from the Yod-force of Chokmah. In this connection we must refer to the fact that the microcosmic correspondence of Chokmah is given as the left side of the face. The macrocosmic and microcosmic correspondences play an important part in the practical workings. The Macrocosm, or Great Man, is, of course, the universe itself; and the microcosm is the individual man. It is said that man is the only being that has a fourfold nature exactly corresponding in its levels to the cosmos. The angels lack the lower planes, and the animals lack the higher planes.

28. The references to the microcosm should not, of course, be taken crudely as representing the parts of the physical body; the references are to the aura and the functions of the magnetic currents in the aura, and it must always be borne in mind, as the Swami Vivekananda points out, that what is on the right in the male is on the left in the female. In addition to this it must be remembered that what is positive on the physical plane is negative on the astral plane; it is positive again on the mental plane and negative on the spiritual plane, as is indicated in the twining black and white serpents of the Caduceus of Mercury.

If this Caduceus be placed upon the Tree when the Tree is marked off to represent the Four Worlds of the Qabalists, a glyph is formed which reveals the workings of the Law of Polarity in relation to the Planes. This is a very important glyph, and yields a great deal to meditation.

29. From this we learn that when the soul is in a female incarnation it will function negatively in Assiah and Briah, but positively in Yetzirah and Atziluth. In other words, a woman is physically and mentally negative, but psychically and spiritually positive, and the reverse holds good for a man. In initiates, however, there is a considerable degree of compensation, for each learns the technique of both positive and negative psychic methods. The Divine Spark, which is the nucleus of every living soul, is, of course, bi-sexual, containing the roots of both aspects, as does Kether, to which it corresponds. In the more highly evolved souls the compensating aspect is developed in some degree at least. The purely female woman and the purely male man prove to be oversexed as judged by civilised standards, and can only find an appropriate place in primitive societies, where fertility is the primary demand that society makes upon its women, and hunting and fighting are the constant occupation of the men.

30. This does not mean, however, that the physical functions of the sexes are perverted in the initiate, or that the configuration of the body is modified. Esoteric science teaches that the physical form and racial type which the soul assumes in each incarnation are determined by destiny, or Karma, and that the life has to be worked out and lived accordingly. It is inadvisable for us to play tricks with our type, racial or physical, and we should always accept it as the basis of our operations, and choose our methods accordingly. There are certain operations and certain offices in the lodge for which a male vehicle is more suitable than a female, and when practical work is on hand the officers in a ceremony are selected on type; but when the routine training of an initiate is in progress it is the custom to let everyone take turns at the different offices in

order that they may learn to handle the different types of force and so become equilibrated.

31. Benjamin Kidd, in his very stimulating book, *The Science of Power*, points out that the highest type of human being approximates to the infantile. We observe the enormous relative size of the head as compared with the body-weight in the infant, and that the secondary sexual characteristics are not present. We find the same tendency appearing in a modified form in the civilised adult. The highest type of man is not a hirsute gorilla, nor is the highest type of woman an exaggerated mammal. The tendency of evolution in civilisation is to an approximation of type between the sexes so far as the secondary sexual characteristics are concerned. What percentage of city-dwelling males could grow a really patriarchal beard? The primary sexual character, however, must be maintained unimpaired or the race speedily dies out, and we have no reason to believe that this is the case even among our most epicene moderns, who fill the divorce courts with abundant evidence of their overflowing philoprogenitiveness.

32. These things we can understand in the light that is thrown on them when they are "placed upon the Tree." The two Pillars, the positive under Chokmah and the negative under Binah, correspond respectively to the Ida and Pingala of the Yoga systems. These two magnetic currents, running in the aura parallel to the spine, are called the Sun and Moon currents. In a male incarnation we work predominantly with the Sun current, the fertiliser; in a female incarnation we work predominantly with the moon-forces. If we desire to work with the opposite type of force to that with which we are naturally endowed, we have to do so by using our natural mode as the basis of operations and, as it were, "cannoning off the cushion." The male who wants to use the moon-forces employs devices that enable him to get his natural sun-force reflected, and the female who wants to use the sun-forces employs a device whereby she is enabled to focus them upon herself and reflect them. On the physical plane the sexes mate, and the man begets a child upon the woman, thus

availing himself of her moon-powers. The woman, on the other hand, desiring creation and unable to compass it single-handed, entices the male through his desires till he bestows upon her his sun-force and she is impregnated.

33. In magical workings the man or woman who desires to work with the opposite type of force to that of their physical vehicle, and it is part of the routine of occult training that they should do so, shifts the level of consciousness on to a plane on which they find themselves of the requisite polarity, and works thereon. The priest of Osiris sometimes employs the elemental spirits to supplement his polarity, and the priestess of Isis invokes angelic influences.

34. Because manifestation takes place through the Pairs of Opposites, the principle of polarity is implicit not only in the macrocosm but also in the microcosm. By understanding it, and knowing how to avail ourselves of the potentialities it affords, we can raise our natural powers far above their normal; we can use our environment as a thrust-block; we can look for the potent Chokmah-force in books, in our racial tradition, in our religion, in our friends and associates; from all these we can receive the stimulus that fecundates us and makes us creative mentally, emotionally, and dynamically. We make our environment play Chokmah to our Binah. Equally, we can play Chokmah to its Binah. Upon the subtle planes polarity is not fixed, but is relative; that which is more force-ful than ourselves is positive towards us, and renders us negative towards itself; that which is less forceful than we are in any given aspect is negative towards us, and we can assume the positive rôle towards it. This fluidic, ever-fluctuating subtle polarity is one of the most important points in the practical workings; if we understand it and avail ourselves of it, we can do some very remarkable things and put our lives and our relations with our environment on an altogether different basis.

35. We must learn to know when we can function as Chokmah and beget deeds upon the world; and when we had best function as Binah, and make our environment fertilise us

so that we become productive. We must never forget that self-fertilisation involves sterility in a few generations, and that we must ever and again be fertilised by the medium in which we are working. There must be an interplay of polarity between us and whatever we have set out to do, and we must always be on the alert to find polarising influences, whether in tradition, or in books, or in fellow-workers in the same field, or even in the very opposition and antagonism of enemies; for there is just as much polarising force in a hearty hatred as there is in love, if we know how to use it. We must have stimulus if we are to create anything, even a useful life well lived. Chokmah is the cosmic stimulus. Whatever stimulates is assigned to Chokmah in the classification of the Tree. Sedatives are assigned to Binah. We shall obtain further insight into this principle of cosmic polarity as we study Binah, the Third Sephirah, for it is hardly possible to understand the implications of Chokmah without reference to its polarising opposite, with which it always functions. We will, therefore, carry no further our study of polarity at the present time, but conclude our examination of Chokmah by reference to the cards attributed to it in the Tarot pack, and resume our research into this most significant subject when Binah has afforded us further data.

III

36. As was noted in the chapter upon Kether, the four suits of the Tarot pack are assigned to the four elements, and we saw that the four aces represented the roots of the powers of these elements. The four twos are assigned to Chokmah, and represent the polarised functioning of these elements in harmonised balance; therefore a two is always a card of harmony.

37. The two of Wands, which is assigned to the element of Fire, is called the Lord of Dominion. The wand is essentially a male phallic symbol, and is attributed to Chokmah, so we may take this card as meaning polarisation; the positive that has found its mate in the negative, and is in equilibrium. There

is no antagonism or resistance to the Lord of Dominion, but a contented land accepts his rule; Binah, fulfilled, accepts her mate.

38. The two of Cups (Water) is called the Lord of Love; and here again we have the concept of harmonious polarisation.

39. The two of Swords (Air) is called the Lord of Peace Restored, indicating that the disruptive force of Swords is in temporary equilibrium.

40. The two of Pentacles (Earth) is called the Lord of Harmonious Change. Here, as in Swords, we see a modification of the essential nature of the elemental force by its polarising opposite, thus inducing equilibrium. The disruptive force of Swords is restored to peace, and the inertia and resistance of Earth becomes, when polarised by the influence of Chokmah, a balanced rhythm.

41. These four cards indicate the Chokmah-force in polarity, that is to say the essential balance of power as it manifests in the Four Worlds of the Qabalists. When they appear in a divination they indicate power in equilibrium. They do not indicate a dynamic force, as might be expected where Chokmah is concerned; because Chokmah, being one of the Supernals, its force is positive upon the subtle planes, and consequently negative upon the planes of form. The negative aspect of a dynamic force is represented by equilibrium, polarity. The negative aspect of a negative potency is represented by destruction, as is shown in the glyph of Kali, the terrible wife of Siva, girdled with skulls and dancing upon the body of her husband.

42. This concept gives us a key to another of the many problems of the Tree—the relative polarity of the Sephiroth. As has previously been explained, each Sephirah is negative in its relation with those above it, from which it receives the influx of the emanations, and positive in relation to those beneath it, which proceed from it, and to which it therefore acts as emanator. Certain of the paired Sephiroth are, however, more definitely positive or more definitely negative in their nature. For instance, Chokmah is a positive Positive,

and Binah is a positive Negative. Chesed is a negative Positive, and Geburah a negative Negative. Netzach (Venus) and Hod (Mercury) are said to be hermaphroditic. Yesod (Luna) is a positive Negative, and Malkuth (Earth) is a negative Negative. Neither Kether nor Tiphareth are predominantly male or female. In Kether the Pairs of Opposites are latent and have not yet declared themselves; in Tiphareth they are in perfect equilibrium.

43. There are two ways in which transmutation can be effected on the Tree; and these are indicated by two of the glyphs which are superimposed upon the Sephiroth; one of these is the Glyph of the Three Pillars, and the other is the Glyph of the Lightning Flash. The Pillars have been already described; the Lightning Flash simply indicates the order of emanation of the Sephiroth, zigzagging from Chokmah to Binah and from Binah to Chesed, backwards and forwards across the Tree. If transmutation takes place according to the Lightning Flash, the force changes its type; if according to the Pillars, it remains of the same type, but on a higher or lower arc as the case may be.

44. This sounds very complex and abstract, but examples will soon serve to show it to be simple and practical when understood. Take the problem of the sublimation of sex-force, which besets the psychotherapists, concerning which they talk so glibly and say so little. In Malkuth, which in the microcosm is the physical body, sex-force is in terms of ovum and spermatozoon; in Yesod, which is the etheric double, it is in terms of magnetic force, concerning which nothing is known to orthodox psychology, but concerning which we shall have a good deal to say under the heading of the appropriate Sephirah. Hod and Netzach are on the astral plane, and in Hod we find that the sex-force is expressed in visual images, and in Netzach in another and altogether subtler type of magnetism popularly referred to as "It." In Tiphareth, the Christ-centre, the force becomes spiritual inspiration, illumination, the influx from the higher consciousness. If it is positive in type, it becomes the Dionysiac inspiration, a divine

inebriation; and if it is negative, it becomes the impersonal, all-harmonising Christ-love.

45. When the transmutation is worked upon the Pillars we are impressed by the truth of the ironical French phrase —*Plus ça change, plus c'est la même chose*. Chokmah, pure dynamism, pure stimulus without formed expression, in Chesed becomes the upbuilding, organising aspect of evolution; anabolism, as distinguished from the katabolism of Geburah. In Chesed the Chokmah force becomes that peculiarly subtle form of magnetism which gives power of leadership and is the root of greatness. Equally, on the Left-hand Pillar, the force-restraining Binah becomes the form-destroying Geburah, and again the maker of magical images, Mercury-Hermes-Thoth.

46. From time to time the symbols of occult science have leaked out into popular knowledge, but the uninitiated have not understood the method of arranging these symbols in their pattern as the Tree, nor of applying to them the alchemical principles of transmutation and distillation wherein lie the real secrets of their use.

CHAPTER XVII

BINAH, THE THIRD SEPHIRAH

TITLE: Binah, Understanding. (Hebrew spelling: בינה :
Beth, Yod, Nun, Hé.)

MAGICAL IMAGE: A mature woman. A matron.

SITUATION ON THE TREE: At the head of the Pillar of
Severity in the Supernal Triangle.

YETZIRATIC TEXT: The Third Intelligence is called the
Sanctifying Intelligence, the Foundation of Primordial
Wisdom; it is also called the Creator of Faith, and its
roots are in Amen. It is the parent of faith, whence
faith emanates.

TITLES GIVEN TO BINAH: Ama, the dark sterile Mother.
Aima, the bright fertile Mother. Kursiya, the Throne.
Marah, the Great Sea.

GOD-NAME: Jehovah Elohim.

ARCHANGEL: Tzaphkiel. Beholder, or Eye, of God.

ORDER OF ANGELS: Er 'elim, Thrones.

MUNDANE CHAKRA: Shabbathai, Saturn.

SPIRITUAL EXPERIENCE: Vision of Sorrow.

VIRTUE: Silence.

VICE: Avarice.

CORRESPONDENCE IN MICROCOSM: The right side of the face.

SYMBOLS: The Yoni. The Kteis. The Vesica Piscis. The
cup or chalice. The Outer Robe of Concealment.

TAROT CARDS: The four Threes.
THREE OF WANDS: Established Strength.
THREE OF CUPS: Abundance.
THREE OF SWORDS: Sorrow.
THREE OF PENTACLES: Material works.

COLOUR IN ATZILUTH: Crimson.
„   „   BRIAH: Black.
„   „   YETZIRAH: Dark brown.
„   „   ASSIAH: Grey flecked pink.

139

I

1. Binah is the third member of the Supernal Triangle, and the task of its elucidation will be both extended and simplified because we can study it in the light of Chokmah, which balances it on the opposing Pillar of the Tree. It is never possible to understand a Sephirah if we consider it apart from its position on the Tree, because this position indicates its cosmic relationships; we see it in perspective, as it were, and can deduce whence it comes and whither it goes; what influences have gone to its making, and what it contributes to the scheme of things entire.

2. Binah represents the female potency of the universe, even as Chokmah represents the male. As already noted, they are Positive and Negative; Force and Form. Each heads its Pillar, Chokmah at the head of the Pillar of Mercy, and Binah at the head of the Pillar of Severity. It may be thought that this is an unnatural distribution; that the Supernal Mother should preside over the mercies, and the male force of the universe over the severities. But we must not sentimentalise these things. We are dealing with cosmic principles, not personalities; and even the symbols under which they are presented give us insight if we have eyes to see. Freud would not have quarrelled with the attribution of Binah to the head of the Pillar of Severity, for he has a great deal to say about the image of the Terrible Mother.

3. Kether, Ehyeh, I Am, is pure being, all-potential but non-active; when a flowing-forth of activity takes place from it, we call that activity Chokmah; it is this descending stream of pure activity which is the dynamic force of the universe, and all dynamic force belongs to this category.

4. It must be remembered that the Sephiroth are states, not places. Wherever there is a state of pure, unconditioned being, without parts or activities, it is referred to Kether. Thus into these ten pigeon-holes of our metaphysical card-index system we can sort our ideas of the whole of the manifested universe without the necessity of removing any object

from its place in nature as it appears to our understanding. In other words, wherever we see pure energy functioning, we know that the underlying force is that of Chokmah; this enables us to see the intrinsic identity in type of all manner of phenomena which at first sight appear entirely unrelated; for we learn by the Qabalistic method to refer them according to their type to the different Sephiroth, thus enabling ourselves to link them up with all manner of cognate ideas according to the system of correspondences explained on a previous page. This is the method of the subconscious mind, which it pursues automatically; the occultist trains his conscious mind in the use of the same method. Incidentally we may note that whenever individuals are working directly off the subconscious, as occurs in artistic genius, in lunacy, and in dream or trance, this method is used.

5. It may seem strange to the reader that this digression concerning Chokmah should be included under the heading of Binah, but it is only in the light of its polarity with Chokmah that Binah can be understood; and equally, we shall have a great deal more to add to our explanation of Chokmah now that we have got Binah to compare it with. Each of the Pairs of Opposites throws light on the other and is incomprehensible alone.

6. But to return to Binah. The Qabalists state that it is emanated by Chokmah. Let us translate this statement into other terms. It is an occult maxim, which is, I believe, confirmed by the researches of Einstein, though I have not the knowledge necessary to correlate his findings with the esoteric doctrines, that force never moves in a straight line, but always in a curve vast as the universe, and therefore eventually returns whence it issued forth, but upon a higher arc, for the universe has progressed since it started. It follows, then, that force proceeding thus, dividing and redividing and moving at tangential angles, will eventually arrive at a state of interlocking stresses and some manner of stability; a stability which tends to be overset in course of time as fresh forces are emanated into manifestation and introduce new factors with which adjustment has to be made.

7. It is this state of stability, which is arrived at by the inter-acting forces when they act and react and come to a standstill, which is the basis of form, as is exemplified in the atom, which is nothing more nor less than a constellation of electrons, each of which is a vortex, or whirlpool. The stability thus achieved, which, be it noted, is a condition and not a thing in itself, is what Qabalists call Binah, the Third Sephirah. Wherever there is a state of interacting stresses which have achieved stability, the Qabalists refer the condition to Binah. For instance, the atom, being for all practical purposes the stable unit of the physical plane, is a manifestation of the Binah type of force. All social organisations on which the dead hand of unprogressiveness weighs heavily, such as the Chinese civilisa-tion before the revolution, or our older universities, are said to be under the influence of Binah. To Binah are attributed the Greek God Kronos (who is none other than Father Time) and the Roman God Saturn. It will be observed the import-ance attached to time, in other words to age, in these Binah institutions; only grey hairs are venerable; ability alone carries little weight. That is to say, only those who are con-genial to Kronos can succeed in such an environment.

8. Binah, the Great Mother, sometimes also called Marah, the Great Sea, is, of course, the Mother of All Living. She is the archetypal womb through which life comes into mani-festation. Whatsoever provides a form to serve life as a vehicle is of Her. It must be remembered, however, that life confined in a form, although it is enabled thereby to organise and so evolve, is much less free than it was when it was un-limited (though also unorganised) on its own plane. Involve-ment in a form is therefore the beginning of the death of life. It is a straitening and a limiting; a binding and a constricting. Form checks life, thwarts it, and yet enables it to organise. Seen from the point of view of free-moving force, incarceration in a form is extinction. Form disciplines force with a merciless severity.

9. The disembodied spirit is immortal; there is nothing of it that can grow old or die. But the embodied spirit sees death

on the horizon as soon as its day dawns. We can see then how terrible must the Great Mother appear as She binds free-moving force into the discipline of form. She is death to the dynamic activity of Chokmah; the Chokmah-force dies as it issues into Binah. Form is the discipline of force; therefore is Binah the head of the Pillar of Severity.

10. We may conceive that the first Cosmic Night set in, the first Pralaya, or sinking of manifestation to rest, when the Supernal Triangle found stability and equilibrium of force with the emanation and organisation of Binah. All was dynamic before; all was forthrushing and expansion; but with the coming into manifestation of the Binah aspect there was an interlocking and stabilising, and the old dynamic free flow was no more.

11. That such an interlocking and consequent stabilisation was inevitable in a universe whose lines of force ever move in curves is a foregone conclusion. And we can see, if we observe how the Binah-state was the inevitable outcome of the Chokmah-state in a curvilinear universe, that time must move through epochs in which either Binah or Chokmah predominate. Before the lines of force had completed their circuit of the manifested universe and begun to return upon themselves and interlace, all was Chokmah, and dynamism was unrestricted. After Binah and Chokmah, as the first Pairs of Opposites, had found equilibrium, all was Binah, and stability was immovable. But Kether, the Great Emanator, continues to make manifest the Great Unmanifest; force flows in upon the universe, and the sum of force is increased. This inflowing force oversets the equilibrium that is arrived at when Chokmah and Binah have acted, reacted, and come to a stop. Action and reaction commence again, and the Chokmah-phase, a phase in which dynamic force predominates, supervenes upon the static condition which is Binah, and the cycle proceeds once more; equilibrium between the Pairs of Opposites being arrived at in a more complex form—on a higher arc, as it is called from the evolutionary point of view—only to be overset again as the ever-emanating Kether weighs down the balance

in favour of the kinetic principle as opposed to the static principle.

12. It will thus be seen that if Kether, the source of all being, is conceived of as the highest good, as it inevitably must be, and the nature of Kether is kinetic, and its influence is for ever inclined towards Chokmah, it inevitably follows that Binah, the opposite of Chokmah, the perpetual opposer of the dynamic impulses, will be regarded as the enemy of God, the evil one. Saturn-Satan is an easy transition; and so is Time-Death-Devil. Implicit in the ascetic religions such as Christianity and Buddhism is the idea that woman is the root of all evil, because she is the influence which holds men to a life of form by their desires. Matter is regarded by them as the antinomy of spirit in an eternal, unresolved duality. Christianity is ready enough to recognise the heretical nature of this belief when it is presented to it in the form of Antinomianism; but it does not realise that its own teaching and practice are equally antinomian when it regards matter as the enemy of spirit, and as such to be abrogated and overcome. This unhappy belief has caused as much human suffering in Christian countries as war and pestilence.

13. The Qabalah teaches a wiser doctrine. To it, all the Sephiroth are holy, Malkuth equally with Kether, and Geburah the destroyer with Chesed the preserver. It recognises that rhythm is the basis of life, not a steady forward progress. If we understood this better, how much suffering we should save ourselves, for we should watch the Chokmah and Binah phases succeeding each other, both in our own lives and the lives of nations, and would realise the deep significance of Shakespeare's words when he says:

"There is a tide in the affairs of men
Which taken at the flood leads on to fortune."

14. Binah is the primordial root of matter, but the full development of matter is not found till we arrive at Malkuth, the material universe. We shall see repeatedly in the course of our studies that the Three Supernals have their specialised

expressions on a lower arc in one or another of the six Sephiroth
which form Microprosopos.   It is repeatedly said of these
that they have their roots in or are reflections of the higher
triad, and these hints have a deep significance.   Binah links
with Malkuth as the root with the fruit.   This is indicated in
the Yetziratic text of Malkuth, in which it says: "She sitteth
upon the throne of Binah."   It is for this reason that a hard
and fast attribution of the gods of other pantheons to the
different Sephiroth is impracticable.   Aspects of Isis are to be
found in Binah, Netzach, Yesod, and Malkuth.   Aspects of
Osiris are to be found in Chokmah, Chesed, and Tiphareth.
This comes out clearly in Greek mythology, wherein the
different gods and goddesses are given descriptive titles.   For
instance, Diana, the moon-goddess, the virgin huntress, was
worshipped at Ephesus as the Many-breasted; Venus, the
goddess of female beauty and of love, had a temple where she
was worshipped as the Bearded Venus.   These things teach
us some important truths.   They teach us to look for the
principle behind the multiform manifestation, and to realise
that it assumes different forms on different levels.   Life is not
quite so simple as the uninformed would like to believe.

II

15. The meaning of the Hebrew names of the second and
third Sephiroth are Wisdom and Understanding, and these are
curiously balanced one against the other as if the distinction
were of primary importance.   Wisdom suggests to our minds
the idea of accumulated knowledge, of the infinite series of
images in the memory; but Understanding conveys to us the
idea of a penetration into their significance, a power to perceive
their essence and interrelation, which is not necessarily implicit
in wisdom, taken as intellectual knowledge.   Thus we get a
concept of an extended series, a chain of associated ideas, in relation to Chokmah, which at once correlates with the Chokmah
symbol of a straight line.   But in regard to Understanding we
get the idea of synthesis, of the perception of significances

which comes when ideas are related one to another, and superimposed, metaphorically speaking, one upon another, in evolutionary series from the dense to the subtle. Thus does the idea of the binding-together Binah-principle come once again to our minds.

16. These are subtle ways of mind-working, and may appear foolishness to those unaccustomed to the initiate's method of using his mind; but the psycho-analyst understands them and appreciates them at their true significance; and so likewise does the poet when he constructs his cloud-capped towers of imagery.

17. The Yetziratic Text stresses the idea of faith, the faith that rests on understanding, whose parent is Binah. This is the only place where faith may rightly rest. A cynic defined faith as the power of believing what you know isn't true; and this appears to be a fairly accurate definition for the manifestations of faith as they appear in many uninstructed minds, the fruit of the discipline of sects unenlightened by mystical consciousness. But in the light of that consciousness we may define faith as the conscious result of superconscious experience which has not been translated into terms of brain-consciousness, and of which, therefore, the normal personality is not directly aware, though it nevertheless feels, possibly with great intensity, the effects, and its emotional reactions are fundamentally and permanently modified thereby.

18. In the light of this definition we can see how the roots of faith may indeed rest in Binah, Understanding, the synthetic principle of consciousness. For there is a form aspect to consciousness as well as to substance, and that aspect we shall consider in detail when we come to the study of Hod, the basal Sephirah of Binah's Pillar of Severity. Thus we see yet again how the Sephiroth link up among themselves, and the illumination that comes from observing their interrelationships.

19. The statement that the roots of Binah are in Amen refers to Kether, for one of the titles of Kether is Amen. This clearly declares that although Chokmah emanates Binah, we must not pause there when seeking origins, but move back

to the fount of all as it rises from the Unmanifest behind the Veils of Negative Existence. This concept is brought out very clearly by the Yetziratic Text of Chesed, wherein it says, speaking of spiritual forces: "They emanate one from another by virtue of the primordial emanation, the highest crown, Kether."

20. We must not be misled or confused in this respect by the fact that the Yetziratic Text of Geburah declares that Binah, Understanding, emanates from the primordial depths of Chokmah, Wisdom. Binah is in Kether as well as Chokmah, "but after another manner." In pure being, formless and partless though it is, are the possibilities of both force and form; for where there is a positive pole, there is necessarily the correlative aspect of a negative pole. Kether is for ever in a state of becoming. In fact, I have been told by a Jewish Qabalist that the real translation of Ehyeh, the God-name of Kether, is "I will be," not "I am." This constant becoming cannot remain static, it must overflow into activity; and that activity cannot for ever remain uncorrelated within itself ; it must organise; some manner of adjustment of interlocking stresses must be arrived at; thus we have the potentiality of both Chokmah and Binah implicit in Kether; for be it said yet again that the Holy Sephiroth are not things, but states, and that all manifested things exist in one or another of these states, and contain an admixture of these factors in their make-up, so that the whole of the manifested universe can be sorted out into its appropriate pigeon-holes in our minds when the glyph of the Tree is established there. Indeed, when once that glyph is clearly formulated and well established, the mind uses it automatically, and the complex phenomena of objective existence sort themselves out in our understanding. It is for this reason that the student of occultism who is working in an initiatory school is made to learn the principal correspondences of the Ten Holy Sephiroth off by heart, instead of being allowed to depend upon tables of reference. It has often been objected that this is an intolerable waste of time and energy, and that reference to the tables of correspondences,

such as Crowley's "777," is quite as good. But experience proves that this is not the case, and that the esotericist who sets himself to this discipline and rehearses them daily, as the Catholic tells his rosary, is amply repaid by the subsequent illumination he receives as his mind automatically sorts out the innumerable changes and chances of mundane life on to the Tree, thus revealing their spiritual significance. It must always be borne in mind that the use of the Tree of Life is not merely an intellectual exercise; it is a creative art in the literal meaning of the words, and faculties have to be developed in the mind even as manual skill is acquired by sculptor or musician.

21. The Yetziratic Text specifically refers to Binah as the Sanctifying Intelligence. Sanctification conveys the idea of that which is holy. The Virgin Mary is held to be intimately associated with Binah, the Great Mother; and from this attribution the mind is led on to the idea of that which brings forth the All but retains its virginity; in other words, whose creativeness does not involve it in the life of its creation, but which remains apart and behind as the basis of manifestation, the root-substance whence matter arises. For although matter is held to have its roots in Binah, yet matter as we know it is of a very different order of being to the Supernal Sephirah in which its essence lies. Binah, the primordial formative influence, the parent of all form, is behind and beyond manifesting substance; in other words, is ever-virgin. It is this formative influence underlying all form-building, this tendency for curving lines of force to correlate and achieve stability, which is Binah.

22. These two basal Sephiroth of the Supernal Triad are especially referred to as the Father and Mother, Abba and Ama, and their magical images are those of the bearded male and the matron, thus representing, not the sex attraction of Netzach and Yesod, who are represented as maiden and youth, but the mature beings who have mated and reproduced. We must always distinguish between magnetic sex attraction and reproduction; they are by no means one and the same thing; nor

are they even different levels or aspects of the same thing. Herein is an important occult truth which we will consider in detail in due course.

23. Chokmah and Binah, then, represent essential maleness and femaleness in their creative aspects. They are not phallic images as such, but in them is the root of all life-force. We shall never understand the deeper aspects of esotericism unless we realise what phallicism really means. It most emphatically does not mean the orgies in the temples of Aphrodite that disgraced the decadence of the pagan faiths of the ancients and brought about their downfall; it means that everything rests upon the principle of the stimulation of the inert yet all-potential by the dynamic principle which derives its energy direct from the source of all energy. In this concept lie tremendous keys of knowledge; it is one of the most important points in the Mysteries. It is obvious that sex represents one aspect of this factor; it is equally obvious that there are many other applications of it which are not sexual. We must not allow any preconceived concept of what constitutes sex, or a conventional attitude towards this great and vital subject, to frighten us away from the great principle of the stimulation or fecundation of the inert all-potential by the active principle. Whosoever is thus inhibited is unfit for the Mysteries, over whose portal was written the words, "Know thyself."

24. Such knowledge does not lead to impurity, for impurity implies a loss of control that permits forces to override the bounds that Nature has set them. Whoso has not control of his own instincts and passions is no more fitted for the Mysteries than he who inhibits and dissociates them. Let it be clearly realised, however, that the Mysteries do not teach asceticism or celibacy as a requirement of achievement, because they do not regard spirit and matter as an unreconcilable pair of antinomies, but rather as different levels of the same thing. Purity does not consist in emasculation, but in keeping the different forces to their proper levels and in their proper places, and not allowing one to invade another. It teaches that frigidity and impotence are just as much imperfections,

and therefore pathologies of sex, as is uncontrolled lust that destroys its object and debases itself.

25. Every relationship of manifested existence involves the Binah and Chokmah principles, and because sex is such a perfect representation of these it was used as such by the ancients, who were not troubled by our timidities on the subject, and took their metaphors from the subject of reproduction as freely as we take ours from the Bible. For to them reproduction was a sacred process, and they referred to it, not with ribaldry, but with reverence. If we want to understand them, we must approach their teaching on the subject of the life-source and life-force in the same spirit in which they approached it, and no one whose eyes are not blinded by prejudice, or who does not stand in the shadow thrown by his own unsolved problems, can fail to realise that our present-day attitude towards life would be both saner and sweeter for a leavening of pagan common sense and discernment.

26. The principles of maleness and femaleness as manifested in Chokmah and Binah represent more than mere positivity and negativity, activity and passivity. Chokmah, the All-begetter, is a vehicle of primal force, the immediate manifestation of Kether. It is, in fact, Kether in action; for the different Sephiroth do not represent different things, but different functions of the same thing, *i.e.* pure force welling up into manifestation from the Great Unmanifest which is behind the Negative Veils of Existence. Chokmah is pure force, even as the expansion of petrol as it explodes in the combustion-chamber of an engine is pure force. But just as this expansive force would expand and be lost if there were no engine to transmit its power, so the undirected energy of Chokmah would radiate into space and be lost if there were nothing to receive its impulse and utilise it. Chokmah explodes like petrol; Binah is the combustion-chamber; Gedulah and Geburah are the back and forth strokes of the piston.

27. Now the expansive force given off by petrol is pure energy, but it will not drive a car. The constrictive organisation of Binah is potentially capable of driving a car, but it

cannot do so unless set in motion by the expansion of the stored-up energy of petrol-vapour.   Binah is all-potential, but inert.   Chokmah is pure energy, limitless and tireless, but incapable of doing anything except radiate off into space if left to its own devices.   But when Chokmah acts upon Binah, its energy is gathered up and set to work.   When Binah receives the impulse of Chokmah, all her latent capacities are energised.   Briefly, Chokmah supplies the energy, and Binah supplies the machine.

III

28. Consider now the maleness and femaleness of this Pair of Supernal Opposites as reflected in the act of generation. The spermatozoa of the male are incapable of more than the briefest life; they are the simplest possible units of energy; once that energy is expended, they dissolve.   But the reproductive mechanism of the female, the womb that bears and the breasts that feed, are capable of bringing this handed-on life to independent life of its own; and yet all this elaborate machinery must lie inert till the stimulus of the Chokmah-force sets it in action.   The female reproductive unit is all-potential, but inert; the male reproductive unit is all-potent, but incapable of bringing to birth.

29. Most people think that because maleness and femaleness as they know them on the physical plane are fixed principles determined by structure, that the potent and the potential are rigidly bound to their respective mechanisms.   Now this is an error.   There is a continual alternation of polarity on every plane except the physical.   And indeed, among primitive types of animal life there is even an alternation of polarity on the physical plane.   Among higher types, and especially the vertebrates, polarity is fixed by the accident of birth, save in hermaphroditic anomalies, which cannot be regarded as other than pathological, and in which only one sex is ever functionally active, whatever the apparent development of the other aspect may be.   It is a knowledge of this continual interplay of polarity which is one of the most important secrets of the Mysteries.

It is in no sense homosexuality, which is a perverted and pathological expression of this fact that breaks out as a disorder of sexual feeling when the law of alternating polarity is not rightly understood.

30. Briefly, although his actual mode of reproduction on the physical plane is determined for every individual by the configuration of his body, his spiritual reactions are not so fixed, for the soul is bi-sexual; in other words, in every relation of life we are sometimes positive and sometimes negative, according to whether circumstances are stronger than we are, or we are stronger than circumstances. This is clearly indicated in the proverb, that the grey mare is sometimes the better horse. It also comes out clearly in the fact that Netzach (Venus-Aphrodite) is the basal Sephirah of Chokmah's Pillar. We thus get the female nature showing a different polarity on different levels, for in Netzach she is as positive and dynamic as she is static in Binah.

31. All this is not only bewildering intellectually, but also confusing morally, and even at the risk of being accused of fostering all manner of abnormalities, I must try to make the matter clear, for its practical implications are so far-reaching.

32. It has been said by the Rabbis that each Sephirah is negative in relation to the one above it by which it is emanated, and positive in relation to the one below it which it emanates. This gives us the key; we are negative in our relationships with that which is of a higher potential than we are; and we are positive in our relationships with that which has a lower potential. This is a relationship which is in a perpetual state of flux, and which varies at every separate point at which we make our innumerable contacts with our environment.

33. For the most part, the relationship between a man and a woman is not entirely satisfactory to either party, and they have either to put up with incomplete satisfaction in their relationship under the compulsion of religious or economic pressure, or supplement elsewhere their incompleteness, with as a rule a recurrence of the previous conditions when once the novelty has worn off. It is to be observed that under such

circumstances it is only in novelty that sexual satisfaction at its highest is to be found; and novelty is a thing which requires constantly to be renewed, with disastrous results to sexual economics.

34. The trouble is, that while the male gives the physical stimulus which leads to reproduction, he does not realise that on the inner planes he is by virtue of the law of reversed polarity, negative, and is dependent for his emotional completeness upon the stimulation given by the female. He is dependent upon her for emotional fertilisation, as is clearly shown in the case of any highly creative mind, such as Wagner or Shelley.

35. Marriage is not a matter of two halves, but of four quarters, uniting in balanced harmony of reciprocal fecundation. Binah and Chokmah are balanced by Hod and Netzach. There are goddesses as well as gods for man to worship. Boaz and Jakin are both pillars of the Temple, and only when united do they produce stability. A goddessless religion is half-way to atheism. In the word Elohim we find the true key. Elohim is translated "God" in both Authorised and Revised Versions of the Holy Scriptures. It really ought to be translated "God and Goddess," for it is a feminine noun with a masculine plural termination affixed. This is an incontrovertible fact, in its linguistic aspect at any rate, and it is to be presumed that the various authors of the books of the Bible knew what they meant, and did not use this peculiar and unique form without good reason. "And the spirit of the male and female conjoined principles moved upon the surface of the formless, and manifestation took place." If we want equilibrium instead of our present condition of unequal stresses, we must worship the Elohim, not Jehovah.

36. The worship of Jehovah instead of the Elohim is a potent influence in preventing us from "rising on the planes," that is to say from obtaining supernormal consciousness as part of our normal equipment; for we must be prepared to shift our polarity as we shift level, for what is positive on the physical plane becomes negative on the astral, and *vice versa*.

Also, as practical occult work always involves the use of more than one plane, either simultaneously, as in invocation and evocation, or in succession, as when we correlate the levels of consciousness after psychic work, the negative factor must always have its place in our work, both subjectively and objectively.

37. This again opens up new aspects of the subject. How many people realise that their own souls are literally bi-sexual within themselves, and that the different levels of consciousness act as male and female towards each other?

38. Freud declared that the sex life determines the type of the whole life. Probably, fundamentally, the life as a whole determines the type of the sex life; but for practical purposes his manner of putting it is true; for while it is not possible to straighten out a tangled sexual life by operating upon life as a whole—for instance, no amount of wealth or fame is any adequate compensation if this fundamental instinct be thwarted—it is quite possible to straighten out the whole life-pattern by disentangling the sex life. This is a matter of practical experience, and does not need to be reasoned from *a priori* grounds. No doubt it is for this reason, learned by practical experience of the workings of the human consciousness, that the ancients made phallicism such an important part of their rites. Actually, it is a very important factor in the ceremonial aspect of the worship of moderns also, but recognition of the significance of the symbols employed traditionally has been repressed from consciousness.

39. Freudian psychology supplies the key to phallicism and opens a door that leads into the Adytum of the Mysteries. There is no getting away from this fact in practical occultism, unpalatable as it may be to many; and it explains why so many magical enterprises are sterile.

40. These matters are highly recondite secrets of the Mysteries, of which we moderns have lost the keys; but the experience of the new psychology, and its allied art of psychiatry, has abundantly proved the soundness of the basis on which the ancients built when they made adoration of the

creative principle and of fertility an important part of their religious life.   It is a matter of well-established experience that the person who has dissociated his or her sexual feelings from consciousness can never get to grips with life on any level. This fact is the basis of modern psychotherapy.   In occult work the inhibited, repressed person tends to unbalanced forms of psychism and mediumship, and is totally useless for magical work in which power has to be directed and handled by the will.   This does not mean that either total repression or total expression is necessary for magical working, but it does most emphatically mean that the person who is cut off from his instincts, which are his roots in Mother Earth, and in whose consciousness in consequence there is a gap, cannot be an open channel through which power can be brought down the planes into manifestation on the physical level.

41. I shall no doubt be abused and misrepresented for my frankness in these matters; but if no one will come forward and bear the odium of speaking the truth, how is the way-faring man to find his way in the Mysteries?   Are we to maintain a Victorian attitude in the lodge which has every-where been abandoned outside it?   Someone must break these false gods made in the image of Mrs Grundy.   I am inclined to think, however, that any loss I may sustain on this account will be small, for it would not be possible to train or to co-operate with the kind of person who is thrown into a panic by plain speaking.   Do not let it be thought that I am inviting anyone to participate with me in phallic orgies, as it will probably be said that I am doing.   I am merely pointing out that the person who cannot see the significance of phallic worship from the psychological point of view has not got enough brains to be of very much use in the Mysteries.

IV

42. Having given considerable space to the elucidation of the Binah principle functioning in polarity with Chokmah, for not otherwise can it be understood, for it is essentially a prin-ciple of polarity, we can now consider the significance of the

symbolism assigned to the Third Sephirah. This falls into two divisions—the Great Mother aspect and the Saturn aspect, for both these attributions are given to Binah. She is the mighty Mother of All Living, and she is also the death principle; for the giver of life in form is also the giver of death, for form must die when its use is outworn. Upon the planes of form, death and birth are the two sides of the same coin.

43. The mother aspect of Binah finds expression in the title of Marah, the Sea, which is given her. It is a curious fact that Venus-Aphrodite is represented as being born of the sea-foam, and the Virgin Mary is called by Catholics Stella Maris, Star of the Sea. The word Marah, which is the root of Mary, also means bitter, and the spiritual experience attributed to Binah is the Vision of Sorrow. A vision which calls to mind the picture of the Virgin weeping at the foot of the Cross, her heart pierced by seven swords. We also recall the teaching of the Buddha that life is sorrow. The idea of subjection to sorrow and death is implicit in the idea of the descent of life to the planes of form.

44. The Yetziratic Text of Malkuth, already referred to, speaks of the Throne of Binah. One of the titles given to the Third Sephirah is Khorsia, the Throne; and the angels assigned to this Sephirah are called the Aralim, which also means thrones. Now a throne essentially suggests the idea of a stable basis, a firm foundation, upon which the wielder of power takes his seat and cannot be moved. It is, in fact, a thrust-block which takes the back-pressure of a force as the shoulder takes the kick of a rifle. The great guns used for long-distance ranging have to be bedded in a mass of concrete in order that they may resist this back pressure of the charge that drives the shell forwards; for it is obvious that the pressure on the breech of the gun must equal the pressure on the base of the shell when the gun goes off. This is a truth which our idealising religious tendencies are inclined to ignore, with a consequent weakening and invalidating of their teaching. Binah, Marah, matter, is the thrust-block which gives dynamic life-force its secure basis.

45. Out of the resistance to spiritual force, as we have already noted, comes the idea of implicit evil, which is so unjust to Binah. This comes out very clearly when we consider the ideas that rise up in association with Saturn-Kronos. There is something sinister about Saturn. He is the Greater Malefic of the astrologers, and anyone who finds a square to Saturn in their horoscope regards it as a heavy affliction. Saturn is the resister; but, being a resister, he is also a stabiliser and tester who does not allow us to trust our weight to that which will not bear it. It is an illuminating point that the Thirty-second Path, which leads from Malkuth to Yesod and is the first Path trodden by the soul striving upwards, is assigned to Saturn. He is the god of the most ancient form of matter. The Greek myth of Kronos, which is simply the Greek name for the same principle, looks upon him as one of the Old Gods; that is to say, the Gods that made the Gods. He was the father of Jupiter-Zeus, who was saved from him by a cunning device of his mother, for Saturn had an unpleasant habit of eating his children. In this myth we get again the idea of the bringer into life as the giver of death. As we have already noted, Saturn with his reaping-hook readily becomes Death with his scythe. It is very interesting to note the re-entrant curves of these chains of associated ideas in connection with each Sephirah, for we cannot but see how the same images crop up again and again in every train of ideas that we pursue, even when we start from ideas as apparently divergent as the mother, the sea, and time.

46. To each planet is assigned a virtue and a vice; in other words, each planet may be, in the words of the astrologers, well or badly aspected, well or ill dignified. We cannot go through life without noting that every type of character has the vices of its virtues; that is to say, its virtues, carried to extremes, becomes vices. So it is with the seven planetary Sephiroth; they have their good and bad aspects according to the proportions in which they are represented; when there is lack of equilibrium owing to the unbalanced force of a particular Sephirah, we experience the evil influences of that

Sephirah; for instance, Saturn ate his children! Death began to destroy life before it had fulfilled its function. No Sephirah, therefore, is wholly and solely evil, not even Geburah, which is destruction personified. They are all equally indispensable to the scheme of things as a whole, and their relative good or evil influence depends on their being where they are wanted, in the right proportions, neither too much nor too little. Too little of the influence of a given Sephirah leads to unbalance on the part of its opposite number. Too much becomes a positively evil influence — a poisonous overdose.

47. The virtue of Binah is said to be Silence, and its vice Avarice. Here again we see the Saturn influence making itself felt. Keats speaks of "grey-haired Saturn, quiet as a stone," and in these few words the poet conjures up a magical image of the primordial age and silence of the Saturnian influence. Saturn is indeed one of the Old Gods and is concerned with the mineral aspect of earth. He is throned upon the most ancient rocks where no plant grows.

48. It is this silence which has ever been held to be an especially desirable virtue in women. Be that as it may, and no doubt her tongue is her most dangerous weapon, silence indicates receptivity. If we are silent, we can listen, and so learn; but if we are talking, the gates of entrance to the mind are closed. It is the resistance and receptivity of Binah which are her chief powers. And out of these virtues comes the vice which is constituted by their overplus, the avarice which denies too much and would withhold even that which is needful. When this prevails, we need the generous Gedulah-Geburah, Jupiter-Mars influence to slay the old god, the slayer of his children, and reign in his stead.

49. The magical symbols of Binah are said to be the yoni and the Outer Robe of Concealment, the latter is a gnostic term and the former an Indian one, meaning the genitals of the female, the negative correspondence of the phallus of the male. The less well-known term Kteis is the European equivalent. In Hindu religious symbols the yoni and lingam appear with

the greatest frequency, for the idea of life-force and fertility is a prime mover in their faith.

50. The idea of fertility is the main motif in the aspects of Binah that manifest in the world of Assiah, the material level. Life not only enters into matter for discipline, but it also issues thence triumphantly, increased and multiplied. The fertility aspect, balancing the Time-Death-Limitation aspect, is essential to our concept of Binah. Time-Death puts his sickle to the wheat of Ceres, and both are Binah symbols.

51. The idea of the Outer Robe of Concealment clearly suggests matter; and the shrouding herein of the Inner Robe of Glory of the life-principle. How clearly do these two ideas, taken together, convey to us the concept of the body ensouled by the spirit; its Inner Robe of Spiritual Glory concealed from all eyes by the outer covering of dense matter. Again and again, as we meditate upon these mysteries, do we find illumination from the apparently fortuitous collection of symbols assigned to each Sephirah. We have seen already in our study that no symbol stands alone, and that any penetration on the part of the intuition and the imagination serves to reveal long lines of interlacing connections between them.

52. The four Threes of the Tarot pack are the cards assigned to Binah, and indeed the number three is intimately associated with the idea of manifestation in matter. The two opposing forces find expression in a third, the equilibrium between them, which manifests on a lower plane than its parents. The triangle is one of the symbols assigned to Saturn as the god of densest matter, and the triangle of art, as it is called, is used in magical ceremonies when it is the intention to evoke a spirit to visible appearance on the plane of matter; for other modes of manifestation the circle is used.

53. The Three of Wands is called the Lord of Established Strength. Here again we have the idea of power in equilibrium, which is so characteristic of Binah. Wands, be it remembered, represent the dynamic Yod force. This force, when in the sphere of Binah, ceases to be dynamic and becomes consolidated.

54. Cups are essentially the female force, for the cup or chalice is one of the symbols of Binah and is intimately allied with the yoni in esoteric symbolism. The three of Cups is, therefore, at home in Binah, for the two sets of symbolism reinforce each other. The three of Cups, which is aptly named Abundance, represents the fertility of Binah in her Ceres aspect.

55. The Three of Swords, however, is called Sorrow, and its symbol in the Tarot pack is a heart pierced by three swords. Our readers will recall the reference to the sword-pierced heart of the Virgin Mary in Catholic symbolism, and Mary equates with Marah, bitter, the Sea. *Ave, Maria, stella maris!*

56. Swords are, of course, Geburah cards, and as such represent the destructive aspect of Binah as Kali, the wife of Siva, the Hindu goddess of destruction.

57. Pentacles are cards of Earth, and as such are congenial to Binah, form. The three of Pentacles, therefore, is Lord of Material Works, or activity on the plane of form.

58. It will be observed that, just as the planets have their influence reinforced when they are in those signs of the Zodiac which are called their own houses, so the Tarot cards, when the significance of the Sephirah coincides with the spirit of the suit, represent the active aspect of the influence; and when the Sephirah and the suit represent different influences, the card is malefic. For instance, the fiery Sword card is a card of evil omen when it finds itself in the sphere of influence of Binah.

59. And finally to sum up. I have written of Binah at this length because with her is completed the Supernal Triad and the first of the Pairs of Opposites. She represents not only herself but also the functioning partners, for it is impossible to understand any unit on the Tree save by reference to those other units with which it interacts and equilibrates. Chokmah without Binah, and Binah without Chokmah, are incomprehensible, for the pair are the functional unit, and not either of them separately.

CHAPTER XVIII

CHESED, THE FOURTH SEPHIRAH

TITLE: Chesed, Mercy. (Hebrew spelling: חסד: Cheth, Samech, Daleth.)

MAGICAL IMAGE: A mighty crowned and throned king.

SITUATION ON THE TREE: In the centre of the Pillar of Mercy.

YETZIRATIC TEXT: The Fourth Path is called the Cohesive or Receptive Intelligence because it contains all the Holy Powers, and from it emanate all the spiritual virtues with the most exalted essences. They emanate one from another by virtue of the Primordial Emanation, the Highest Crown, Kether.

TITLES GIVEN TO CHESED: Gedullah. Love. Majesty.

GOD-NAME: El.

ARCHANGEL: Tzadkiel. Benevolence of God.

ORDER OF ANGELS: Chashmallim, Brilliant Ones.

MUNDANE CHAKRA: Tzedek, Jupiter.

SPIRITUAL EXPERIENCE: Vision of Love.

VIRTUE: Obedience.

VICE: Bigotry. Hypocrisy. Gluttony. Tyranny.

CORRESPONDENCE IN THE MICROCOSM: The left arm.

SYMBOLS: The solid figure. Tetrahedron. Pyramid. Equal-armed Cross. Orb. Wand. Sceptre. Crook.

TAROT CARDS: The four Fours.

> FOUR OF WANDS: Perfected work.
> FOUR OF CUPS: Pleasure.
> FOUR OF SWORDS: Rest from strife.
> FOUR OF PENTACLES: Earthly power.

COLOUR IN ATZILUTH: Deep violet.

„ „ BRIAH: Blue.

„ „ YETZIRAH: Deep purple.

„ „ ASSIAH: Deep azure, flecked yellow.

I

1. Between the Three Supernals and the next pair of balancing Sephiroth upon the Tree there is a great gulf fixed

which is called by mystics the Abyss.   The next six Sephiroth, Chesed, Geburah, Tiphareth, Netzach, Hod, and Yesod, constitute what Qabalists call Microprosopos, the Lesser Countenance, Adam Kadmon, the King.   The Queen, the Bride of the King, is Malkuth, the Physical Plane.   We have, then, the Father (Kether), the King, and the Bride, and in this configuration of the Tree there is profound symbolism and great practical importance in both philosophy and magic.

2. The Abyss, the gulf fixed between Macroprosopos and Microprosopos, marks a demarcation in the nature of being, in the type of existence prevailing upon the two levels.   It is in the Abyss that Daath, the Invisible Sephirah, has its station, and it might aptly be named the Sephirah of Becoming.   It is also called Understanding, which might be further interpreted as Perception, Apprehension, Consciousness.

3. These two types of existence, Macroprosopos and Microprosopos, serve to indicate the potential and the actual. Actual manifestation, as our finite minds can conceive it, begins with Microprosopos; and the first aspect of Microprosopos to come into being is Chesed, the Fourth Sephirah, situated immediately below Chokmah, the Father, in the Pillar of Mercy, of which it is the central Sephirah.   It is balanced across the Tree by Geburah, Severity; and this pair, Geburah and Gedulah, form "the Power and the Glory" of the final invocation of the Lord's Prayer; the "Kingdom" being, of course, Malkuth.

4. As we have already seen, we can learn much from the position of a Sephirah in the pattern of the Tree; and from the position of Chesed on the Pillar of Mercy we see that it is Chokmah upon a lower arc.   It is emanated by Binah, a passive Sephirah, and emanates Geburah, a katabolic Sephirah, whose Mundane Chakra is Mars with all his warlike symbolism, who is Saturn upon a lower arc.

5. From these things we can learn a great deal about Chesed. It is the loving father, the protector and preserver, just as Chokmah is the All-begetter.   It continues the work of Chokmah, organising and preserving that which the All-

Father has begotten. It balances with mercy the severity of Geburah. It is anabolic, or upbuilding, in contra-distinction to the katabolism, or down-breaking of Geburah.

6. These two aspects are very well expressed in the Magical Images assigned to these two Sephiroth. These Magical Images are both kings; that of Chesed a king on his throne, and that of Geburah a king in his chariot; in other words, the rulers of the kingdom in peace and in war; the one a lawgiver and the other a warrior.

7. The analogy of physiology gives us a clear understanding of the significance of these two Sephiroth. Metabolism consists of anabolism, or the ingesting and assimilating of food and its building up into tissue, and katabolism, or the breaking down of tissue in active work and the output of energy. The by-products of katabolism are the fatigue-poisons which have to be eliminated from the blood by rest. The life-process is an everlasting upbuilding and down-breaking, and Gedullah and Geburah (another name for Chesed) represent these two processes in the Macrocosm.

8. Chesed, being the first Sephirah of Microprosopos, or the manifested universe, represents the formulation of the archetypal idea, the concretion of the abstract. When the abstract principle that forms the root of some new activity is formulating in our minds, we are operating in the sphere of Chesed. Let an example serve to make this clear. Supposing an explorer is looking out from a mountain over a newly discovered country and sees that the inland plains lying behind the coastal ranges are fertile, and that a river flows through these plains and makes its way to the sea through a gap in the mountain chain. He thinks of the agricultural wealth of the plains, transport down the river, and a harbour on the estuary, for he knows that the scour of the river will have made a channel by which ships can come in. In his mind's eye he sees the wharfs and the warehouses, the stores and the dwellings. He wonders whether the mountains contain minerals, and pictures a railway line alongside the river and branch lines up the valleys. He sees the colonists coming in, and the need

for a church, a hospital, a gaol, and the ubiquitous saloon.
His imagination maps out the main street of the township, and
he determines to stake corner lots that he may prosper with
the prosperity of the new settlement.   All this he sees while
virgin forest covers the coastal belt and blocks the mountain
passes.   But because he knows that the plains are fertile and
that the river has come through the mountains, he sees in terms
of first principles all the development that follows.   While his
mind is working thus, he is functioning in the sphere of
Chesed whether he knows it or not; and all those who can
also function in terms of Chesed and think ahead as he does,
seeing the thing that must arise from given causes long before
the first line is drawn on the plan or the first brick laid in the
trench, are able to possess themselves of the valuable land
where the wharfs must be built and the main street must run.

9.   All the creative work of the world is done thus, by minds
working in terms of Chesed the King seated upon his throne,
holding sceptre and orb, ruling and guiding his people.

10. By contrast with this we observe the people whose
minds cannot function above the level of Malkuth, the Bride
of the King.   They are the folk who cannot see the wood for
trees.   They think in terms of detail, lacking any synthetic
principle.   Their logic is never able to reach back to origins
but is always materialistic.   They are never able to discern
subtle causes, and are the victims of what they call the caprices
of chance.   They are unable to discern subtle conditions, nor
can they work out the line that primary impulses will follow,
or can be made to follow, when these are coming down, or
being brought down, into manifestation.

11. The occultist who does not possess the initiation of
Chesed will be limited in his function to the sphere of Yesod,
the plane of Maya, illusion.   For him the astral images reflected in the magic mirror of subconsciousness will be
actualities ; he will make no attempt to translate them into
terms of a higher plane and learn what they really represent.
He will have made himself a dwelling in the sphere of illusion,
and he will be deluded by the phantasms of his own uncon-

scious projection. If he were able to function in terms of Chesed, he would perceive the underlying archetypal ideas of which these magical images are but the shadows and symbolic representations. He then becomes a master in the treasure-house of images instead of being hallucinated by them. He can use the images as a mathematician uses algebraic symbols. He works magic as an initiated adept and not as a magician.

12. The mystic functioning in the Christ-centre of Tiphareth, if he lacks the keys of Chesed, will also be hallucinated, but in a different and more subtle way. Upon this level he will read the magical images truly enough, referring them to that which they represent and giving them no values save as tokens, as St Theresa has so clearly shown in her *Interior Castle*. He will fall into the error, however, of thinking that the images he perceives and the experiences he undergoes are the direct and personal dealings of God with his soul, instead of realising that they are stages on the Path. He will find a personal Saviour in the God-man instead of in the regenerative influence of the Christ-force. He will worship Jesus of Nazareth as God the Father, thus confounding the Persons.

13. Chesed, then, is the sphere of the formulation of the archetypal idea; the apprehension by consciousness of an abstract concept which is subsequently brought down the planes and concreted in the light of experience of the con-cretion of analogous abstract ideas. Equally, in its macro-cosmic aspect, it represents a corresponding phase in the process of creation. Materialistic science believes that the only abstract concepts are those formulated by the mind of man. Esoteric science teaches that the Divine Mind formu-lated archetypal ideas in order that substance might take form, and that without such archetypal ideas substance was formless and void, primordial slime awaiting the breath of life to organise into crystal and cell. The latest researches in physics have revealed that every substance, without exception, has a crystalline structure, and the lines of tension that the psychic perceives as etheric stresses have been revealed by the X-rays.

14. A very important and very imperfectly understood part in the Mysteries is played by those beings who are generally called the Masters. Different schools define the term differently, and some include living adepts of a high grade among the Masters; but we consider that it is advisable to make a distinction between the incarnate and disincarnate Elder Brethren because their mission and mode of function are entirely different. The title of Master should therefore be given only to those who are free from the wheel of birth and death. In the terminology of the Western Esoteric Tradition the grade of Adeptus Exemptus is assigned to Chesed, the term Exemptus, or exempt, indicating that freedom from karma which liberates from the Wheel. I am fully aware that others may attach a different significance to the title, and that there are persons in incarnation who hold this grade. To these I reply that such persons, if the grade be a functioning one and not a mere empty honour, are karma-free and will not reincarnate. Such persons might justly be termed Masters, for their consciousness is of the grade of a Master, but as it is so necessary to make the distinction between incarnate and discarnate adepts, it is better to qualify the classification by this minor distinction than to allow to humans a prestige which human nature is not fitted to bear. As long as an adept is incarnated he will be liable to human frailties in some degree, and to the limitations imposed by old age and physical health. It is not until he is free from the Wheel, and functions as pure consciousness, that he will escape from human bondage to heredity and environment; therefore the same reliance cannot be placed in him that can be placed in the true, discarnate Masters.

15. A very important part of the work of the Masters is the concretion of the abstract ideas conceived by the Logoidal consciousness. The Logos, Whose meditation gives birth to worlds and Whose unfolding consciousness is evolution, conceives archetypal ideas out of the substance of the Unmanifest —to use a metaphor where definition is impossible. These ideas remain within the Cosmic consciousness of the Logos

like the seed within the flower, because there is no soil therein
for their germination.   The Logoidal consciousness, as pure
being, cannot upon Its own plane provide the formative aspect
necessary for manifestation.   It is taught in the esoteric
traditions that the Masters, discarnate consciousnesses disciplined by form but now formless, in their meditations upon
the Godhead are able to perceive telepathically these archetypal ideas in the mind of God, and by realising the practical
application of them to the planes of form and the line this
development will follow, produce concrete images in their
own consciousness which serve to bring the abstract archetypal
ideas down to the first of the planes of form, called by the
Qabalists, Briah.

16. This, then, is the work that the Masters perform in their
special sphere, the sphere of the organising, upbuilding, constructive Chesed on the Pillar of Mercy.   The work of the
Dark Masters, who are quite different from the Black Adepts,
is performed in the corresponding sphere of Geburah, on the
Pillar of Severity, which will be considered in due course.
The point of contact between the Masters and their human
disciples is in Hod, the Sephirah of ceremonial magic, as is
indicated by the Yetziratic Text, which declares that from
Gedulah, the Fourth Sephirah emanates the essence of Hod.
These hints given in the Yetziratic Texts concerning the
relations between the individual Sephiroth are very important
in practical occultism.   Hod, then, may be taken as representing Chokmah and Chesed upon a lower arc, even as Netzach
represents Binah and Geburah.   This will be explained in
detail when these Sephiroth are dealt with, but it must be
referred to briefly now in order to make the function of
Chesed intelligible.

17. We have now reached a point in the scheme of the Tree
where the type of activity comes within the range of human
consciousness.   In our study of the preceding Sephiroth we
were formulating metaphysical concepts.   These concepts,
although remote from immediate application to the life of
form, are exceedingly important, for unless they are at the

basis of our understanding of esoteric science we shall fall into superstition and use magic as magicians, not as adepts; in other words, we shall be unable to transcend the bondage of the planes of form and will be hallucinated and fall under the domination of the phantoms evoked by the magical imagination, instead of using them as the beads on the abacus of our calculations, which is as if the engineer used the slide-rule as if it were a foot-rule.

18. Chesed, then, reflects into Hod through the Christ-centre of Tiphareth, just as Geburah reflects into Netzach. This teaches us a great deal, for it indicates that for consciousness to rise from form to force, and for force to descend to form, it must pass through the Centre of Equilibrium and Redemption, to which are assigned the Mysteries of the Crucifixion.

19. It is to the Sphere of Chesed that the exalted consciousness of the adept rises in his occult meditations; it is here that he receives the inspirations which he works out on the planes of form. It is here that he meets the Masters as spiritual influences contacted telepathically, without any intermingling of personality. This is the true, and the highest, mode of contact with the Masters, contact with them as mind to mind in their own sphere of exalted consciousness. When the Masters are seen clairvoyantly as robed beings, the colours of whose robes indicate their ray, they are being perceived reflected into the sphere of Yesod, which is the kingdom of phantasms and hallucinations. We are treading on precarious ground when we have to meet the Masters here. It is here that the anthropomorphic form is given to the spiritual inspiration which so misleads those psychics who cannot rise to Chesed. It is thus that the announcement of a spiritual impulse flowing out upon the world gets interpreted as the coming of a World Teacher.

II

20. As we come down the Tree into those spheres more within the range of our comprehension than the

Three Supernals, we find the symbols associated with each Sephirah becoming more and more eloquent as they speak to our experience instead of causing us to reason by analogy.

21. The magical image representing Chesed is a mighty throned and crowned king; throned because he is seated in stability in a kingdom at peace, not going forth in his chariot to war, as is suggested by the magical image of Geburah. The additional titles of Chesed—Majesty, Love—bear out this concept of the benignant king, the father of his people; and the situation of Chesed in the centre of the Pillar of Mercy further bears out the idea of stability and ordered and merciful law, governing for the good of the governed. The title of the angelic host associated with Chesed—the Chashmallim, or Brilliant Ones—enhances the idea of the royal splendour of Gedullah, which is an alternative title frequently used for Chesed. The Mundane Chakra assigned to Chesed—Jupiter, the great benignity of astrology—confirms the whole chain of associations.

22. Upon the microcosmic, or subjective, side we find that the virtue assigned to this sphere of experience is that of obedience. It is only through the virtue of obedience that the subject can profit by the wise rule of Chesed. We have to sacrifice much of our independence and egoism in order to share in the amenities of organised social life. From this sacrifice and restriction there is no escape. In this sphere no more than in any other is it possible to eat one's cake and have it. There is no such thing as liberty if liberty is to be interpreted as unrestricted self-will. The force of gravity resists us, if nothing else. Liberty might be defined as the right to choose one's master, for a ruler one must have in all organised corporate life, else there is chaos. It is effectual and inspiring leadership that is the crying need of the world at the present time, and country after country is seeking and finding the ruler who approximates most closely to its national ideal, and is falling in as one man behind him. It is the benign, organising, ordering Jupiter influence that is the only medicine for

the world's sickness; as this comes to bear, the nations will recover their emotional poise and physical health.

23. Conversely, the vices assigned to Chesed—bigotry, hypocrisy, gluttony, and tyranny—are all social vices. Bigotry refuses to move with the times or see another point of view, both fatal vices in racial relationships. Hypocrisy implies that we do not give ourselves whole-heartedly to the corporate life, but, like Ananias, keep back a part of the price. Gluttony exposes us to the temptation of taking more than our fair share of the common store, and is but another name for selfishness. And tyranny is that wrong use of authority which arises where there are taints of cruelty and vanity in the nature.

24. The correspondence in the microcosm is given as the left arm, which indicates a less dynamic mode of the functioning of power than that of the right hand which grasps the sword in the magical image of Geburah. The left hand holds the orb, which signifies the earth itself, and shows that all is held secure in the firm grasp of the ruler. Chesed, in fact, denotes firmness rather than dynamic strength and energy.

25. The mystical number of Chesed is said to be four, and this is often represented as a four-sided figure, or tetrahedron. A talisman of Jupiter is always set up on such a figure. Another symbol of Chesed is the solid figure as understood in geometry. The reason for this is easily seen if one considers the geometrical figures assigned to the Sephiroth which have already been studied. The point is assigned to Kether; the line to Chokmah; the two-dimensional plane to Binah; consequently the three-dimensional solid naturally falls to Chesed.

26. But more is signified in this connection than a mere random series of symbols. The solid essentially represents manifestation as it is known to our three-dimensional consciousness. We cannot conceive of one- or two-dimensional existence save mathematically or symbolically. Chesed, as we have already noted, is the first of the manifested Sephiroth; therefore how naturally does the symbol of the solid figure

come into line with the rest of its symbolism. The solid figure used for the purpose of symbolising Chesed is usually the pyramid, which is a four-sided figure, consisting of three faces and a base, thus expressing the numerological quality of Chesed.

27. There are many different aspects of the cross as a significant Mystery symbol, besides the Calvary Cross of the Christian Mystery, and each of these crosses represents different modes of the functioning of spiritual power, just as do the different forms of the Holy Names of God. The form of cross associated with Chesed is the equal-armed cross, which is symbolic of the four elements in equilibrium, and implies the ruling of nature by a synthesising influence which brings all things into balanced harmony.

28. The orb, wand, sceptre, and crook, all assigned to this Sephirah, express so perfectly the different aspects of the benign royal power of Chesed that they are in no need of elucidation.

29. The four Tarot cards that are placed on Chesed when the pack is set up for a divination carry out the ruling idea in the correspondence. The Four of Wands symbolises Perfected Work, thus representing admirably the achievement of the king in peace-time in his well-governed kingdom. The Four of Cups is called the Lord of Pleasure, and is in keeping with the title of Splendour assigned to Chesed and with the brilliancy of its angelic host. The Four of Swords indicates Rest from Strife, and agrees perfectly with the significance of the seated ruler. The Four of Pentacles is the Lord of Earthly Power, a symbolism so obvious that it needs no elucidation.

30. The consideration of the Yetziratic Text has been left to the last in this study, in order that the sequence of the symbolism, unfolding in such ordered relationship, might not be broken in upon. Moreover, this text contains so much significance that it is best studied when we are as fully equipped as possible with the cognate symbolism. Much that relates to the teaching contained in this text, however, has already been studied as it came up for examination in relation to the

preceding Sephiroth. I will not repeat this at length, but content myself with referring the student to those pages where the matters are dealt with in detail, thus avoiding needless repetition which otherwise is bound to occur in the study of such a subject as the Tree of Life, where different symbols represent the same potency upon different levels of manifestation or under different aspects.

31. "The Fourth Path is called the Cohesive Intelligence." How clearly can we see the meaning of these words when we have learnt to look upon Chesed through the symbol of the king seated upon his throne, organising the resources and prosperity of his kingdom, and causing all things to be drawn together into an ordered whole for the common good.

32. It is also called the Receptive Intelligence in the Yetziratic Text, and this is borne out in the symbol of the left arm, which is assigned to this Sephirah in the microcosm.

33. Chesed "Contains all the Holy Powers, and from it emanate all the spiritual virtues with the most exalted Essences." The teaching implicit in this statement has already been elucidated in the previous exegesis under the concept of archetypal ideas.

34. "They emanate one from another by virtue of the primordial emanation, the Highest Crown, Kether." These concepts have already been dealt with in relation to the Second Sephirah, Chokmah, when the overflowing of force from Sphere to Sphere was considered.

CHAPTER XIX

GEBURAH, THE FIFTH SEPHIRAH

TITLE: Geburah, Strength, Severity. (Hebrew spelling: גבורה : Gimel, Beth, Vav, Resh, Hé.)

MAGICAL IMAGE: A mighty warrior in his chariot.

SITUATION ON THE TREE: In the centre of the Pillar of Severity.

YETZIRATIC TEXT: The Fifth Path is called the Radical Intelligence because it resembles Unity, uniting itself to Binah, Understanding, which emanates from the primordial depths of Chokmah, Wisdom.

TITLES GIVEN TO GEBURAH: Din: Justice. Pachad: Fear.

GOD-NAMES: Elohim Gibbor

ARCHANGEL: Chamael. Burner of God.

ORDER OF ANGELS: Seraphim, Fiery Serpents.

MUNDANE CHAKRA Ma'adim, Mars.

SPIRITUAL EXPERIENCE: Vision of Power.

VIRTUE: Energy. Courage.

VICE: Cruelty. Destruction.

CORRESPONDENCE IN THE MICROCOSM: The right arm.

SYMBOLS: The Pentagon. The Five-petalled Tudor Rose. The Sword. The Spear. The Scourge. The Chain.

TAROT CARDS: The four Fives.

> FIVE OF WANDS: Strife.
> FIVE OF CUPS: Loss in pleasure.
> FIVE OF SWORDS: Defeat.
> FIVE OF PENTACLES: Earthly trouble.

COLOUR IN ATZILUTH: Orange.
„ „ BRIAH: Scarlet red.
„ „ YETZIRAH: Bright scarlet.
„ „ ASSIAH: Red, flecked with black.

I

1. One of the least understood things in Christian philosophy is the problem of evil; and one of the things least

adequately dealt with in the Christian ethic is the problem of force, or severity, as contrasted with mercy and mildness. Consequently Geburah, the Fifth Sephirah, which has for additional titles Din (Justice) and Pachad (Fear), is one of the least understood of all the Sephiroth, and is therefore one of the most important. Were it not that the Qabalistic doctrine explicitly lays it down that all the Ten Sephiroth are holy, there are many who would be inclined to look upon Geburah as the evil aspect of the Tree of Life. Indeed, the planet Mars, whose sphere is the Mundane Chakra of Geburah, is called in astrology an infortune.

2. Those, however, who are instructed beyond the crude pretty-pretty of a wish-fulfilling philosophy know that Geburah is by no means the Enemy or Adversary described in Scripture, but the king in his chariot going forth to war, whose strong right arm protects his people with the sword of righteousness and ensures that justice shall be done. Chesed, the king on his throne, the father of his people in times of peace, may win our love; but it is Geburah, the king in his chariot going forth to war, who commands our respect. Sufficient justice has not been done to the part played by the sentiment of respect in the emotion of love. We have a kind of love for the person who can put the fear of God into us, should occasion arise, which is of quite a different quality, is far more steadfast and permanent, and, curiously enough, far more emotionally satisfying, than the love with which no tinge of awe is mingled. It is Geburah that supplies the element of awe, of the fear of the Lord which is the beginning of wisdom, and of a general wholesome respect which helps us to keep to the straight and narrow way and calls forth our better nature, because we know our sins will find us out.

3. This is a factor to which the Christian ethic, as popularly understood, does not give sufficient weight; and because the general tone of Christian society is biassed against the holy Fifth Sephirah, it will be necessary to consider its place in relation to the Tree and the part it plays in both spiritual and social life in considerable detail; for it is ill-understood, and

this absence of understanding of the Geburah-factor is the cause of many of our difficulties in modern life.

4. Geburah holds the central position on the Pillar of Severity; it therefore represents the katabolic, or down-breaking aspect of force. Katabolism, be it remembered, is that aspect of metabolism, or the life-process, which is concerned with the release of force in activity. It has been said that good is that which is constructive, which builds up, and evil is that which is destructive, which breaks down. How false this philosophy is we see when we try to classify, according to this principle, a cancer and a disinfectant. In the deeper, more philosophical teaching of the Mysteries we recognise that good and evil are not things in themselves, but conditions. Evil is simply misplaced force; misplaced in time, if it is out of date, or so far ahead of its day as to be impracticable. Misplaced in space, if it turns up in the wrong place, like the burning coal on the hearth-rug or the bath-water through the drawing-room ceiling. Misplaced in proportion, if an excess of love makes us silly and sentimental, or a lack of love makes us cruel and destructive. It is in such things as these that evil lies, not in a personal Devil who acts as Adversary.

5. Geburah the Destroyer, the Lord of Fear and Severity, is therefore as necessary to the equilibrium of the Tree as Chesed, the Lord of Love, and Netzach, the Lady of Beauty. Geburah is the Celestial Surgeon; he is the knight in shining armour, the dragon-slayer; beautiful as a bridegroom in his strength to the maiden in distress, though, no doubt, the dragon might have preferred a little more love.

6. The initiations of the infortunes, Saturn, Mars, and the deceptive lunar Yesod, are just as necessary to the evolution and balanced development of the soul as are the Mysteries of the Crucifixion assigned to Tiphareth. It is the one-sidedness of Christianity which is its bane, and is responsible for so much that is unsound and pathological in both our national and our private lives. But, equally, we must not forget that Christianity came as a corrective to a pagan world that was sick unto death

with its own toxins. We need what Christianity has to give; but also, unfortunately, we cannot do without that which it lacks. Let us now consider the astringent, corrective influence of Geburah.

7. Dynamic energy is as necessary to the welfare of society as meekness, charity, and patience. We must never forget that the eliminatory diet, which will restore health in disease, will produce disease in health. We must never exalt the qualities which are necessary to compensate an overplus of force into ends in themselves and the means of salvation. Too much charity is the handiwork of a fool; too much patience is the hall-mark of a coward. What we need is a just and wise balance which makes for health, happiness, and sanity all round, and the frank realisation that sacrifices are necessary to obtain it. You cannot eat your cake and have it in the spiritual sphere any better than anywhere else.

8. Geburah is the sacrificial priest of the Mysteries. Now sacrifice does not mean giving up something that is dear to you because a jealous God will brook no rival interests in His devotees and is flattered by your pain. It means the deliberate and open-eyed choice of a greater good in preference to a lesser good, as the athlete prefers the fatigue of exercise to the ease of the sloth that puts him out of condition. Coal burned in a furnace is sacrificed to the god of steam-power. Sacrifice is really the transmutation of force; the latent energy in the coal offered up on the sacrificial altar of the furnace is transmuted into the dynamic energy of steam by means of the appropriate machinery.

9. There is both psychological and cosmic machinery available in connection with every act of sacrifice which converts it into spiritual energy; and this spiritual energy can be applied to other mechanisms and re-appear on the planes of form as an entirely different type of force to that as which it started.

10. For instance, a man may sacrifice his emotions to his career; or a woman may sacrifice her career to her emotions. If the cut is clean, and there is no repining, an immense amount

of psychic energy is released for use in the chosen channel.
But if the lesser desire is merely inhibited and denied expression
and not really laid upon the altar of sacrifice as a deliberate
free-will offering, the unfortunate victim has made the worst
of both worlds. It is here that we need Geburah to come like
the priest that takes the sacrifice from our hands, even if it be
our first-born, and offers it up to God with the quick, clean,
merciful stroke. For Geburah in the microcosm, which is
the soul of man, is the courage and resolution that frees us
from the taint of self-pity.

11. How badly do we need the Spartan virtues of Geburah
in this age of sentimentality and the neuroses. How many
break-downs would be saved if this Celestial Surgeon were
permitted to make the clean cut that has a chance to heal, and
so avoid the deadly compromise and irresolution that is like
an open wound and so often goes septic.

12. And again, if there were no strong hand at the service
of good in the world, evil would multiply. Though it is not
well to quench smoking flax when the flax is making an
effort, it is equally evil to put up with the smouldering when
what it really wants is the use of the poker. There is a place
where patience becomes weakness and wastes the time of
better men, and when mercy becomes folly and exposes the
innocent to danger. The policy of non-resistance to evil can
only be pursued satisfactorily in a well-policed society; it has
never been tried with success under frontier conditions. For
Nature, red in tooth and claw, wears the colour of Geburah;
whereas the compensatory civilisation is of Chesed, Mercy,
which modifies the unrestricted force and mutual destructiveness of all that is in the Geburah phase of its development.
But, equally, we must remember that civilisation rests upon
Nature as a building rests upon its foundations, wherein is
concealed the sanitation so necessary to health.

13. Whenever there is anything that has outlived its usefulness, Geburah must wield the pruning-knife; wherever
there is selfishness, it must find itself impaled on the spear-
point of Geburah; wherever there is violence against the

weak, or the merciless use of strength, it is the sword of
Geburah, not the orb of Chesed, that is the most effectual
counteractant; wherever there is sloth and dishonesty,
Geburah's sacred scourge is needed; and where there is a
removal of the landmarks set for our neighbour's protection,
it is the chain of Geburah that must restrain.

14. These things are as necessary to the health of society
and of the individual as brotherly love, and a good deal rarer,
used medicinally and not vengefully, in our sentimental age.
Someone has got to cry "Halt" to the aggressor, and "Move
on" to those who are blocking the way, and that someone is
functioning as a priest in the sphere of the holy Fifth Sephirah.

II

15. If we watch life we shall see that rhythm, not stability,
is its vital principle. Such stability as manifesting existence
achieves is the stability of a man on a bicycle, balanced between two opposing pulls; he can fall over to the right, or he
can fall over to the left, and he keeps his balance by means of
his momentum.

16. In the life of individuals, in the development of any
transaction, in the tone of any disciplined or highly organised
group-mind, we see the constant alternation of the Geburah
and Gedulah influences in a rhythmic swing from one side to
the other. Anyone who is responsible for the disciplining of
an organised group knows the constant need for tightening
and slackening the reins; for stimulating and steadying.
There is a sense of the need to pay out line as the group surges
forward with an impulse of interest and keenness, followed
by the need to take up the slack as the impulse spends itself.
If the slack is not taken up with a firm hand, the group tangles
itself in the loops and waxes insubordinate. The wise
handler of humans knows when the reaction has spent itself,
and the moment has come to crack the whip of Geburah over
the team and make it jump into the collar again as the new
dynamic impulse surges up; but he also knows that he must

not crack it too soon, while the team is having a breather, or one of the less stable units will get a leg over the traces.

17. Especially do we see the alternating rhythms of Geburah and Gedulah in national life.   I venture to prophesy that the nation is passing out of a Gedulah phase and entering a Geburah one.   Everywhere we see a mercy, that has been overstrained by the imperfections of human nature, being abrogated in favour of a severity which shall restore the balance of even-handed justice and prevent evil from multi-plying.   Police work is being reorganised; judges are giving stiffer sentences; penal reform has had a set-back; the humanitarian no longer has the last word.   The group-soul of the race is entering upon a Geburah phase, and has lost patience with its sub-standard units.

18. For the next cycle the tendency will be to push the unfit into the discard and concentrate on bringing the fit to their finest development.   Geburah will be the senior partner, and any mitigations of severity that Gedulah proposes will have to pass the scrutiny of even-handed justice.   This is a very necessary reform, for towards the end of a phase extremes tend to develop, and the humanitarianism of Gedulah has been abused and made ridiculous, and its refinement has become finicking and lost touch with actualities.

19. When a new phase comes in on a group-mind scale, it is upon the least enlightened, the most crowd-minded that its influence is strongest; the cultured always tend to stand aside from extremes.   We see this clearly indicated in the line taken by the various types of journalism.   Popular journalism is cry-ing out for the free use of the cat as a punishment for crime; for the repudiation of debts and international agreements; for, in fact, a general slashing around with the sword of Geburah. There is on every hand a growing tendency to stand no non-sense from anybody; a tendency which makes negotiations exceedingly difficult to carry on, for Geburah is at his worst as a negotiator, his one contribution to the discussion being that of the Greek soldier who took his sword and cut the knot.

20. Now the initiate, knowing that phase succeeds phase in

rhythmic alternation, does not take any phase too seriously, nor think that it is either the end of the world or the millenium. He knows that it will run its course, being at first a valuable and necessary corrective, and in the end running to extremes; but provided there is sufficient vision among the illuminati of a race, the people will not perish, for the very fact of extremes being arrived at indicates the end of the swing, and the pendulum will normally reverse its motion and start coming back towards the centre of stability. It is only when vision is completely lost to a people that the pendulum is allowed to fly off its hook into self-destruction. Rome did it; Carthage did it; more recently Russia has done it. But even when social organisation breaks down and the pendulum has gone off into space, the principle of rhythm is inherent in all manifesting existence, and re-establishes itself as soon as any sort of organisation begins to arise out of the wreckage.

21. The great weakness of Christianity lies in the fact that it ignores rhythm. It balances God with Devil instead of Vishnu with Siva. Its dualisms are antagonistic instead of equilibrating, and therefore can never issue in the functional third in which power is in equilibrium. Its God is the same yesterday, to-day, and for ever, and does not evolve with an evolving creation, but indulges in one special creative act and rests on His laurels. The whole of human experience, the whole of human knowledge, is against the likelihood of such a concept being true.

22. The Christian concept being static, not dynamic, it does not see that because a thing is good, its opposite is not necessarily evil. It has no sense of proportion because it has no realisation of the principle of equilibrium in space and rhythm in time. Consequently, for the Christian ideal the part is all too often greater than the whole. Meekness, mercy, purity and love are made the ideal of Christian character, and as Nietzsche truly points out, these are slave virtues. There should be room in our ideal for the virtues of the ruler and leader—courage, energy, justice and integrity. Christianity has nothing to tell us about the dynamic virtues; con-

sequently those who get the world's work done cannot follow the Christian ideal because of its limitations and inapplicability to their problems. They can measure right and wrong against no standard save their own self-respect. The result is the ridiculous spectacle of a civilisation, committed to a one-sided ideal, being forced to keep its ideals and its honour in separate compartments.

23. We need Geburah's realism to balance Gedulah's idealism quite as much as we need to temper justice with mercy. Experience in the handling of children soon teaches us that the child that is never checked is a spoilt child; that the youth who lacks the spur of competition is apt to be a slack youth, for it is only the few who will work for work's sake. And so it is with nations. The monopoly, lacking the spur of competition, has always proved itself to be ineffectual; the non-competitive professions always suffer from intellectual obesity.

24. Geburah is the dynamic element in life that drives through and over obstacles. The character which is lacking in Martian aspects never gets to grips with life. Those who have had to depend on a non-Geburah bread-winner know that love is not a complete solution of life's problems. We must learn to love and trust the mailed warrior with the sword as well as Divine Love which gives us the cup of cold water and says, "Come unto me all ye that are weary and heavy laden."

25. When we have learnt to kiss the rod and realise the value of astringent experiences we have taken the first of the Geburah initiations; and when we have learnt to lose our lives in order to find them, we have taken the second. There is a certain type of courage which does not fear dissolution, for it knows that all spiritual principles are indestructible, and so long as the archetypes persist, anything can be rebuilt. Geburah is only destructive to that which is temporal; it is the servant of that which is eternal; for when by the acid activity of Geburah all that is impermanent has been eaten away, the eternal and incorporeal realities shine forth in all their glory, every line revealed.

26. Geburah is the best friend we can have if we are honest.

Sincerity has no need to fear his activities; indeed, it is the greatest protection we can have against the insincerity of others, for there is nothing to equal the Geburah-influence for "de-bunking" both persons and viewpoints.

27. Geburah and Gedulah must work together; never the one without the other. We must adore the God of Battles as well as the God of Love in order that the combative element in the universe may not break from its allegiance to the One God, I Am That I Am. The sword must not be cursed as an instrument of the Devil, but blessed and dedicated in order that it may never be unsheathed in an unrighteous cause. It must not be cast aside in an impracticable pacifism, but placed at God's service; so that when the command goes forth that the evil thing shall not be suffered any longer, the mighty Khamael, Archangel of Geburah, may lead the Seraphim into battle, not in destructive rage, but temperately and impersonally in God's service in order that evil may be cleared up and good prevail.

III

28. So much has already been said concerning the nature of Geburah that a great deal does not remain to say in the analysis of the attribution.

29. The Yetziratic Text tells us that the Fifth Path is called the Radical Intelligence because it resembles Unity. Now Unity is one of the titles applied to Kether; therefore we may say that Geburah is akin to Kether on a lower arc. There are several Sephiroth which are thus referred to in the *Sepher Yetzirah*, and these references are very important when arriving at an understanding of their nature. Chokmah is spoken of as the Splendour of Unity, equalling it. Of Binah it is said that its roots are in Amen, which is also a title of Kether.

30. Geburah is a highly dynamic Sephirah, and its energy overflowing into the world of form and energising it bears a close analogy to the overflowing force of Kether, which is the basis of all manifestation.

31. It is also said of Geburah in the Yetziratic Text that it unites itself to Binah, Understanding. When we recall that in astrology Saturn, the Mundane Chakra of Binah, and Mars, the Mundane Chakra of Geburah, are called the Greater and Lesser Infortunes, we see that there must be more than a superficial connection between the two.

32. Binah is called the bringer-in of death because it is the giver of form to primordial force, thus rendering it static; Geburah is called the Destroyer because the fiery Mars-force breaks down forms and destroys them. Thus we see that Binah is perpetually binding force into form, and Geburah perpetually breaking up and destroying all forms with its disruptive energy.

33. But equally we must see that it is only when the protecting, preserving influence of Chesed is in abeyance that the destructive influences of Geburah are able to work upon the forms built up by Binah, for the path of the Emanations between Binah and Geburah is *via* Chesed. Geburah is the essential corrective of Binah, without which Binah would bind all creation into rigidity. Binah, in its turn, as is pointed out in the Yetziratic Text, emanates from the primordial depths of Chokmah, Wisdom. Thus we see that there is a dynamic aspect even to Binah. No Sephirah is wholly of one kind of force, for each emanates from a Sephirah of the opposite type of polarity to itself, and in its turn emanates a Sephirah of opposite polarity. What we really have in the Lightning Flash is successive phases in the development of a single force; and because these emanate, but do not supersede each other, they remain as planes of manifestation and types of organisation.

34. These successive phases and planes of manifestation might be likened to the successive reaches of a river. It starts as a mountain stream; in the next reach is a series of rapids and waterfalls; then come water-meadows and placidity; and finally the great waterway between docks bearing shipping. The different reaches of the river remain constant; the type of water in each is constant; clear and sparkling in the upper reaches, loaded with alluvia among the water-meadows, and

fouled with grime below the docks. But at the same time, the water itself is not constant, for it does not stagnate on any reach, for they are all in unbroken communication the one with the other; they "emanate" each other, to use the language of the Qabalah. But the water changes its nature as it progresses because something is added to it by the experiences it undergoes in each reach; alluvial soil from the water-meadows; city grime from the docks.

35. So the primordial emanation of Kether becomes modified in each Sephirotic "reach" of the cosmic river; the "reaches," or Sephirotic Spheres, remain constant; the emanations flow on, undergoing modification in each Sphere.

36. The titles assigned to Geburah of Strength, Justice, Severity, and Fear speak for themselves and indicate the dual aspects of this Sephirah. Now that we are coming down the Tree into the planes of form we see more and more clearly that every Sephirah is two-sided, and that its overplus tends to unbalanced force.

37. The Magical Image of a mighty warrior in his chariot, crowned and armed, indicates the dynamic nature of the Geburah-force. The Mundane Chakra of the fiery Mars expresses even more fully the same idea.

38. The Spiritual Experience that is conveyed by initiation into the Sphere of Geburah is the Vision of Power. It is only when a man has received this that be becomes an Adeptus Major. The right handling of power is one of the greatest tests that can be imposed on any human being. Up to this point in his progress up the grades an initiate learns the lessons of discipline, control, and stability; he acquires, in fact, what Nietzsche calls slave-morality—a very necessary discipline for unregenerate human nature, so proud in its own conceit. With the grade of Adeptus Major, however, he must acquire the virtues of the superman, and learn to wield power instead of to submit to it. But even so, he is not a law unto himself, for he is the servant of the power he wields and must carry out its purposes, not serve his own. Though no longer responsible to his fellow-men he is still responsible to the

Creator of heaven and earth, and will be required to give an account of his stewardship.

39. Great freedom is his; but also great strain. He can speak the word of power that unlooses the wind, but he must be prepared to ride the ensuing whirlwind. This is a thing that the amateur magician does not always realise.

40. The energy and courage which are the virtues of Mars, and the cruelty and destruction which are his vices when these qualities run to excess, call for no comment, for they are self-explanatory.

41. The symbols assigned to Mars-Geburah need some elucidation, however, as their significance is not in all cases apparent at first sight.

42. Figures with a varying number of sides are assigned to the different planets, and in ceremonial or talismanic magic are used as the outline of any form associated with a planetary force. To Saturn, the oldest planet, the first to develop in evolutionary time, is assigned the simplest two-dimensional figure—the triangle. The balanced stability of Chesed gets the four-sided figure, the square; and to the third planetary Sephirah, Mars, is assigned the five-sided figure, and five is looked upon in the Qabalistic system as the number of Mars. Consequently the Pentagon, the five-sided figure, is the symbol of Mars, and any altar to Mars should be pentagonal or five-sided, likewise any talisman. The five-petalled Tudor rose, which is another symbol of Mars, requires more explanation; but when we remember the intimate association between Mars and Venus in mythology, and that the rose is the flower of Venus, we get a clue to the significance of the symbolism. The lines of force, crossing over on the Tree, go from Geburah-Mars to Netzach-Venus through Tiphareth, the Place of the Redeemer, the centre of equilibrium, in the same way that Chesed and Hod connect up, as is clearly indicated in the Yetziratic Text, which says of Hod that it has its root in the hidden places of Gedulah, the Fourth Sephirah.

43. Realising, then, the intimate relationship between the diagonal pairs that form the four corners of the central square

of the Tree, we understand the linked relationship indicated by the form of the rose with its five petals.

44. The sword, the spear, the scourge, and the chain are all such characteristic weapons of Mars that no comment is called for.

45. The four Fives of the Tarot pack are all evil cards, each according to its type. In fact, the whole suit of Swords, which is under the presidency of Mars, represents contentiousness; for its best aspects are "Rest from strife" and "Success after struggle," and where a Sword card is associated with a Sephirah whose Mundane Chakra is one of the astrological infortunes, the result is disastrous, and we find the Lords of Defeat and Ruin in this suit.

46. Our ability to take the Geburah initiation depends upon our ability to handle the Martian forces, and this is determined by the degree of self-discipline and stability we have attained in our own natures.

47. Geburah is the most dynamic and forceful of all the Sephiroth, but it is also the most highly disciplined. Indeed, the military discipline, presided over by the god of War, is a synonym for the sternest kind of control that can be imposed upon human beings. The discipline of Geburah must exactly equate with its energy; in other words, the brakes of a car must bear a relationship to its horse-power if it is to be safe on the road. It is this tremendous Geburah discipline which is one of the testing-points of the Mysteries. We speak of an iron discipline, and iron is the metal of Mars.

48. The initiate of Geburah is a very dynamic and forceful person, but he is also a very controlled person. His characteristic virtues are an even temper and patience under provocation. It is well known on the sports field, which is the play-aspect of the god of War, that a loss of temper gives the game away. Every boxer knows that if he gets angry and starts fighting instead of boxing, the odds are against him. The initiate of Mars is essentially the Happy Warrior, the initiate who has passed through the grade of Tiphareth and gained equilibrium.

49. He fights without malice; he spares the weak and

wounded; he does not set out to destroy the law but to see
to it that it is properly fulfilled.   He is the corrector of the
balance, and as such is always the defender of the weak and
oppressed.   He is never a god that is found on the side of
the large armies, although he says, "With the froward I will
show myself froward."   He takes that two-headed giant of
the Qliphoth, Te'omiel, the Dual Contending Forces, knocks
his heads together and says, "A plague on both your houses!
Keep God's peace or it will be the worse for you."

50. When a soul is at that stage of development when the
only way it can learn is by experience, Geburah sees that it
shall not be disappointed when it goes about looking for
trouble.   Geburah is the Great Initiator of the swollen-
headed.

CHAPTER XX

TIPHARETH, THE SIXTH SEPHIRAH

TITLE: Tiphareth, Beauty. (Hebrew spelling: תפארת : Tav,
Pé, Aleph, Resh, Tav.)

MAGICAL IMAGE: A majestic king. A child. A sacrificed
god.

SITUATION ON THE TREE: In the centre of the Pillar of
Equilibrium.

YETZIRATIC TEXT: The Sixth Path is called the Mediating
Intelligence, because in it are multiplied the influxes of the
Emanations; for it causes that influence to flow into all
the reservoirs of the blessings with which they themselves
are united.

TITLES GIVEN TO TIPHARETH: Zeir Anpin, the Lesser
Countenance. Melekh, the King. Adam. The Son.
The Man.

GOD-NAME: Tetragrammaton Eloah Va Daath.

ARCHANGEL: Raphael. Healing of God.

ORDER OF ANGELS: Melachim, Kings.

MUNDANE CHAKRA: Shemesh, the Sun.

SPIRITUAL EXPERIENCE: Vision of the harmony of things.
Mysteries of the Crucifixion.

VIRTUE: Devotion to the Great Work.

VICE: Pride.

CORRESPONDENCE IN THE MICROCOSM: The breast.

SYMBOLS: The Lamen. The Rose Cross. The Calvary Cross.
The truncated pyramid. The cube.

TAROT CARDS: The four Sixes.

        SIX OF WANDS: Victory.

        SIX OF CUPS: Joy.

        SIX OF SWORDS: Earned success.

        SIX OF PENTACLES: Material success.

COLOUR IN ATZILUTH: Clear rose-pink.

    ,,   ,,   BRIAH: Yellow.

    ,,   ,,   YETZIRAH: Rich salmon-pink.

    ,,   ,,   ASSIAH: Golden amber.

I

1. There are three important keys to the nature of Tiphareth. Firstly, it is the centre of equilibrium of the whole Tree, being in the middle of the Central Pillar; secondly, it is Kether on a lower arc and Yesod on a higher arc; thirdly, it is the point of transmutation between the planes of force and the planes of form. The titles that are bestowed on it in Qabalistic nomenclature bear this out. From the point of view of Kether it is a child; from the point of view of Malkuth it is a king; and from the point of view of the transmutation of force it is a sacrificed god.

2. Macrocosmically, that is to say from the Kether standpoint, Tiphareth is the equilibrium of Chesed and Geburah; microcosmically, that is to say from the point of view of transcendental psychology, it is the point where the types of consciousness characteristic of Kether and Yesod are brought to a focus. Hod and Netzach equally find their synthesis in Tiphareth.

3. The six Sephiroth, of which Tiphareth is the centre, are sometimes called Adam Kadmon, the archetypal man; in fact, Tiphareth cannot rightly be understood save as the central point of these six, wherein it rules as a king in his kingdom. It is these six which, for all practical purposes, constitute the archetypal kingdom which lies behind the kingdom of form in Malkuth and completely dominates and determines the passivities of matter.

4. When we have to consider a Sephirah in relation to its neighbours in order to interpret in the light of its position on the Tree, it is not possible to proceed with an entirely systematic and orderly exposition of the Qabalistic system, for we must of necessity forestall with partial explanations if our argument is to be comprehensible. We must therefore give some explanation of the three lower Sephiroth grouped around Tiphareth—Netzach, Hod, and Yesod.

5. Netzach is concerned with the Nature forces and elemental contacts; Hod with ceremonial magic and occult

knowledge; and Yesod with psychism and the etheric double. Tiphareth itself, supported by Geburah and Gedulah, represents seership, or the higher psychism of the individuality. Each Sephirah, of course, has its subjective and objective aspects—its factor in psychology and its plane in the universe.

6. The four Sephiroth below Tiphareth represent the personality or lower self; the four Sephiroth above Tiphareth are the Individuality, or higher self, and Kether is the Divine Spark, or nucleus of manifestation.

7. Tiphareth, therefore, must never be regarded as an isolated factor, but as a link, a focussing-point, a centre of transition or transmutation. The Central Pillar is always concerned with consciousness. The two side Pillars with the different modes of the operation of force on the different levels.

8. In Tiphareth we find the archetypal ideals brought to a focus and transmuted into archetypal ideas. It is, in fact, the Place of Incarnation. For this reason it is called the Child. And because incarnation of the god-ideal also implies the sacrificial disincarnation, to Tiphareth are assigned the Mysteries of the Crucifixion, and all the Sacrificed Gods are placed here when the Tree is applied to the pantheons. God the Father is assigned to Kether; but God the Son is assigned to Tiphareth for the reasons given above.

9. Exoteric religion goes no farther up the Tree than Tiphareth. It has no understanding of the mysteries of creation as represented by the symbolism of Kether, Chokmah, and Binah; nor of the modes of operation of the Dark and Bright Archangels as represented in the symbolism of Geburah and Gedulah; nor of the mysteries of consciousness and the transmutation of force as represented in the invisible Sephirah Daath, which has no symbolism.

10. In Tiphareth God is made manifest in form and dwells among us; *i.e.* comes within range of human consciousness. Tiphareth, the Son, "shows us" Kether, the Father.

11. In order that form may be stabilised, the component forces out of which it is built must be brought into equilibrium. Therefore do we find the idea of the Mediator, or

Redeemer, inherent in this Sephirah. When the Godhead its very Self manifests in form, that form must be perfectly equilibrated. One might with equal truth reverse the proposition and say that when the forces building a form are perfectly equilibrated, the Godhead its very Self is manifesting in that form according to its type. God is made manifest among us when the conditions permit of manifestation.

12. Having come through into manifestation on the planes of form in the Child aspect of Tiphareth, the incarnated god grows to manhood and becomes the Redeemer. In other words, having obtained incarnation by means of matter in a virgin state, *i.e.* Mary, Marah, the Sea, the Great Mother, Binah, a Supernal, as distinguished from the Inferior Mother, Malkuth, the developing God-manifestation, is for ever striving to bring the Kingdom of the six central Sephiroth into a state of equilibrium.

13. When the glyph of the Fall is represented upon the Tree it is interesting to note that the heads of the Great Serpent that rises out of Chaos only come as far as Daath and do not overpass it.

14. The Redeemer, then, manifests in Tiphareth, and is for ever striving to redeem His Kingdom by re-uniting it to the Supernals across the gulf made by the Fall, which separated the lower Sephiroth from the higher, and by bringing the diverse forces of the sixfold kingdom into equilibrium.

15. To this end are the incarnated gods sacrificed, dying for the people, in order that the tremendous emotional force set free by this act may compensate the unbalanced force of the Kingdom and thus redeem it or bring it into equilibrium.

16. It is this Sphere on the Tree that is called the Christ-centre, and it is here that the Christian religion has its focussing-point. The pantheistic faiths, such as the Greek and Egyptian, centre in Yesod; and the metaphysical faiths, such as the Buddhist and Confucian, aim at Kether. But as all religions worthy of the name have both an esoteric, or mystical, and an exoteric, or pantheistic, aspect, Christianity, although it is essentially a Tiphareth faith, has its mystical aspect centring in

Kether, and its magical aspect, as seen in popular continental Catholicism, centring in Yesod. Its evangelical aspect aims at a concentration on Tiphareth as Child and Sacrificed God, and ignores the aspect of the King in the centre of his Kingdom, surrounded by the five Holy Sephiroth of manifestation.

17. Hitherto we have considered the Tree from the macrocosmic point of view, seeing the different archetypes of manifesting force come into action and build the universe, and have but remotely approached them from the microcosmic point of view in their psychological aspect as factors in consciousness. But with Tiphareth our mode of approach changes, for from henceforward the archetypal forces are locked up in forms, and can only be approached from the point of view of their effect upon consciousness; in other words, our mode of approach must now be through the direct experience of the senses, though these senses are not of the physical plane only, but function in both Tiphareth and Yesod, each according to type. While we were on the higher levels we had to rely on metaphysical analogy and reasoning by deduction from first principles; now we are within the legitimate field of inductive science, and must submit ourselves to its discipline and express our findings in its terms; but at the same time we must maintain our link with the transcendentals through Tiphareth; this is achieved by expressing the symbolism of Tiphareth in terms of mystical experience. All mystical experiences of the type in which the vision ends in blinding light are assigned to Tiphareth; for the fading-out of form in the overwhelming influx of force characterises the transitional mode of consciousness of this Sphere on the Tree. Visions which maintain clearly outlined form throughout are characteristic of Yesod. Illuminations which have no form, such as those described by Plotinus, are rising towards Kether.

18. In Tiphareth also are gathered up and interpreted the operations of the nature magic of Netzach and the Hermetic magic of Hod. Both these operations are in terms of form, though form predominates in the operation of Hod to a greater degree than in those of Netzach. All the astral

visions of Yesod also must be translated into terms of meta-physics *via* the mystical experiences of Tiphareth.   If this translation is not made, we become hallucinated; for we think the reflections cast into the mirror of the subconscious mind and translated there into terms of brain-consciousness are the actual things of which they are really only the symbolic representations.

19. Kether is metaphysical; Yesod is psychic; and Tiphareth is essentially mystical; mystical being understood as a mode of mentation in which consciousness ceases to work in symbolic subconscious representations but apprehends by means of emotional reactions.

20. The different additional titles and symbolism assigned to the various Sephiroth, and especially the God-names thereof, give us a very important key for the unlocking of the mysteries of the Bible, which is essentially a Qabalistic book. According to the manner in which Deity is referred to, we know to what Sphere on the Tree the particular mode of manifestation should be assigned.   All references to the Son always refer to Tiphareth; all references to the Father refer to Kether; all references to the Holy Ghost refer to Yesod; and very deep mysteries are concealed here, for the Holy Ghost is the aspect of the Godhead that is worshipped in the occult lodges; the worship of pantheistic nature-forces and elemental operations take place under the presidency of God the Father; and the regenerative ethical aspect of religion, which is the exoteric aspect for this epoch, is under the presidency of God the Son in Tiphareth.

21. The initiate, however, transcends his epoch, and aims at uniting all three modes of adoration in his worship of Deity as a trinity in unity; the Son redeeming the pantheistic nature worship from debasement and making the transcen-dental Father comprehensible to human consciousness, for "whoso hath seen Me hath seen the Father."

22. Tiphareth, however, is not only the centre of the Sacrificed God, but also the centre of the Inebriating God, the Giver of Illumination.   Dionysos is assigned to this centre

as well as Osiris, for, as we have already seen, the Central Pillar is concerned with the modes of consciousness; and human consciousness, rising from Yesod by the Path of the Arrow, receives illumination in Tiphareth; therefore all the givers of illumination in the Pantheons are assigned to Tiphareth.

23. Illumination consists in the introduction of the mind to a higher mode of consciousness than that which is built up out of sensory experience. In illumination the mind changes gear, as it were. Unless, however, the new mode of consciousness is connected up with the old and translated into terms of finite thought, it remains as a flash of light so brilliant that it blinds. We do not see by means of the ray of light that shines upon us, but by means of the amount of that ray which is reflected from objects of our own dimension upon which it lights. Unless there are ideas in our minds which are illuminated by this higher mode of consciousness, our minds are merely overwhelmed, and the darkness is more intense to our eyes after that blinding experience of a high mode of consciousness than it was before. In fact, we do not so much change gear as throw the engine of our mind out of gear altogether. This, for the most part, is what so-called illumination amounts to. There is enough of a flash to convince us of the reality of super-physical existence, but not enough to teach us anything of its nature.

24. The importance of the Tiphareth stage in mystical experience lies in the fact that the incarnation of the Child takes place here; in other words, mystical experience gradually builds up a body of images and ideas that are lit up and made visible when illuminations take place.

25. This Child aspect of Tiphareth is also a very important one to us in such practical work of the Mysteries as is concerned with illumination. For we must accept the fact that the Child-Christ does not spring like Minerva, full-armed from the head of God the Father, but starts as a small thing, humbly laid among the beasts and not even housed in the inn with the humans. The first glimpses of mystical experience

must perforce be very limited because we have not had time to build up through experience a body of images and ideas that shall serve to represent them.   These can only be got together with time, each transcendental experience adding its quota and subsequent rational meditation organising them.

26. Mystics are very apt to make the mistake of thinking that they are following the Star to the place of the Sermon on the Mount, not to the Manger at Bethlehem, the birth-place. It is here that the method of the Tree is so valuable, enabling the transcendent to be expressed in terms of symbolism, and symbolism to be translated into terms of metaphysics ; thus linking the psychic with the spiritual *via* the intellect, and bringing all three aspects of our trinitarian consciousness into focus.

27. It is in Tiphareth that this translation is made, for in Tiphareth are received the mystical experiences of direct consciousness which illuminate the psychic symbols.

II

28. The Central Pillar of the Tree is essentially the Pillar of Consciousness, just as the two side Pillars are the Pillars of the active and passive powers.   When considered microcosmically, that is to say from the point of view of psychology instead of cosmology, Kether, the Divine Spark round which the individualised being builds up, must be regarded as the nucleus of consciousness rather than consciousness itself.   Daath, the invisible Sephirah, is also on the Central Pillar, though, strictly speaking, it always belongs to another plane to that on which the Tree is being considered.   For instance, as we are considering the Tree microcosmically at the moment, Daath would be the point of contact with the macrocosm.   It is not until we come to Tiphareth that we get clear-cut, individualised consciousness.

29. Tiphareth is the functional apex of the Second Triad on the Tree, whose two basal angles consist of Geburah and Gedulah (Chesed).   This Second Triad, emanating from the

First Triad of the Three Supernals, forms the evolving individuality, or spiritual soul.   It is this which endures and
builds up throughout an evolution; it is from this that the
successive personalities, the units of incarnation, are emanated;
it is into this that the active essence of experience is absorbed
at the end of each incarnation when the incarnating unit
dissolves into dust and ether.

30. It is this Second Triad which forms the Oversoul, the
Higher Self, the Holy Guardian Angel, the First Initiator.
It is the voice of this higher self which is so often heard with
the inner ear, and not the voice of discarnate entities, or of
God Himself, as is thought by those who have had no training
in tradition.

31. Overshadowed and directed by the Second Triad, the
Third Triad builds up through the experience of incarnation,
with Malkuth as its physical vehicle.   Brain consciousness is
of Malkuth, and as long as we are imprisoned in Malkuth, that
is all we have.   But the doors of Malkuth are not closely shut
nowadays, and many there are who can peer through the crack
at the phantasmagoria of the astral plane and experience the
psychic consciousness of Yesod.   When this has been achieved
the way opens for the higher psychism, the true seership, which
is characteristic of the consciousness of Tiphareth.

32. Our first experience of the higher psychism, therefore,
is usually in terms of the lower psychism to commence with;
for we have only just risen clear of Malkuth, and are looking
up at the Sun of Tiphareth from the Moon-sphere of Yesod.
Therefore we hear voices with the inner ear and see visions
with the inner eye, but they differ from ordinary psychic consciousness because they are not the direct representations of
astral forms, but symbolic presentations of spiritual things in
terms of astral consciousness.   This is a normal function of
the subconscious mind, and it is very important that it should
be thoroughly understood, for misconceptions on this point
give rise to very serious problems and may even lead to mental
unbalance.

33. Those who are familiar with Qabalistic terminology

know that the first of the greater initiations is said to consist of the power to enjoy the knowledge and conversation of our Holy Guardian Angel; this Holy Guardian Angel, be it remembered, is really our own higher self. It is the prime characteristic of this higher mode of mentation that it consists neither in voices nor visions, but is pure consciousness; it is an intensification of awareness, and from this quickening of the mind comes a peculiar power of insight and penetration which is of the nature of hyper-developed intuition. The higher consciousness is never psychic, but always intuitive, containing no sensory imagery. It is this absence of sensory imagery which tells the experienced initiate that he is on the level of the higher consciousness.

34. The ancients recognised this, and they differentiated between the mantic methods which induced the chthonic, or underworld contacts, and the divine inebriation of the Mysteries. The Mænads rushing in the train of Dionysos were of an entirely different order of initiation to the pythonesses; the pythonesses were psychics and mediums, but the Mænads, the initiates of the Dionysiac Mysteries, enjoyed exaltation of consciousness and a quickening of life that enabled them to perform amazing prodigies of strength.

35. All the dynamic religions have this Dionysiac aspect; even in the Christian religion many saints have left record of the Crucified Christ of their devotion coming to them at last as the Divine Bridegroom; and when they speak of this divine inebriation that comes to them, their language uses the metaphors of human love as its appropriate expression—"How lovely art thou, my sister, my spouse."—"Faint from the kisses of the lips of God . . . " These things tell a great deal to those who have understanding.

36. The Dionysiac aspect of religion represents an essential factor in human psychology, and it is the misunderstanding of this factor which upon the one hand prevents the manifestation of the higher spiritual experiences in our modern civilisation, and upon the other permits of the strange aberrations of religious feeling that from time to time give rise to scandal

and tragedy in the high places of the more dynamic religious movements.

37. There is a certain emotional concentration and exaltation which makes the higher phases of consciousness available, and without which it is impossible to attain them. The images of the astral plane pass over into an intensity of emotion that is like a burning fire, and when all the dross of the nature has gone up in flame the smoke clears, and we are left with the white heat of pure consciousness. By the very nature of the human mind, with the brain as its instrument, this white heat cannot endure for long; but in the brief space of its lasting, changes occur in the temperament, and the mind itself receives new concepts and undergoes an expansion that never wholly retracts. The tremendous exaltation of the experience dies away, but we are left with a permanent expansion of personality, an enhanced capacity for life in general, and a power of realisation of spiritual realities which could never have been ours if we had not been swung forcibly across the great gulf of consciousness by the momentum of ecstasy.

38. Modern spiritual leaders have no knowledge of the technique of the deliberate production of ecstasy and no idea how to direct it when it occurs spontaneously. Revivalists succeed in producing a mild form of it among unsophisticated people by means of personal magnetism, and the worth of a revivalist is judged by his power to inebriate his hearers. But the consequences of this inebriation are apt to be like the consequences of any other inebriation, and life seems exceedingly stale, flat, and unprofitable when the revivalist moves on to other fields of activity. Because the inebriation dies away, the convert thinks he has lost God; no one seems to realise that ecstasy is a magnesium flash in consciousness, and if it were prolonged, would burn up the brain and nervous system. But although it cannot be, and is not meant to be, prolonged, by means of it we swing over the dead centre of consciousness and awake to a higher life.

39. The technique of the Tree gives accurate definition to these spiritual experiences, and those who are trained in that

technique do not mistake the stirring of their own higher consciousness for the voice of God. From the sensory consciousness of Malkuth, through the astral psychism of Yesod, to the formless intuitions and quickened consciousness of Tiphareth they rise and descend smoothly and skilfully; never confusing the planes or suffering them to leak one into another, but bringing them all into focus in a centralised consciousness.

III

40. Tiphareth is called by the Qabalists Shemesh, or the Sphere of the Sun; and it is interesting to note that all sun-gods are healing gods, and all healing gods are sun-gods, a fact which affords us food for thought.

41. The sun is the central point of our existence. Without the sun there would be no solar system. Sunlight plays a very important part in the metabolism, the life-process, of living creatures, and the whole of the nutrition of green plants depends upon it. Its influence is closely allied to that of vitamins, as is proved by the fact that certain vitamins can be used to supplement its activities. We see, therefore, that sunlight is a very important factor in our well-being; we might go even further and say that it is essential to our very existence and that our association with the sun is far more intimate than we realise.

42. The symbol of the sun in the mineral kingdom is gold, pure and precious, which all nations have agreed in calling the metal of the sun and recognising as the most precious metal and the basic unit of exchange. The part played by gold in the polity of nations far exceeds its intrinsic utility as a metal. It is, moreover, the one substance on earth which is incorruptible and untarnishable. It may be dulled by the accumulation of dirt upon its surface, but the metal itself, unlike silver or iron, undergoes no chemical change or decomposition. Neither does water corrode it.

43. The sun is to us truly the Giver of Life and source of all being; it is the only adequate symbol of God the Father, who

may aptly be called the Sun behind the Sun, Tiphareth, in fact, being the immediate reflection of Kether. It is through the mediation of the sun that life comes to the earth, and it is by means of the Tipharetic consciousness that we contact the sources of vitality and draw upon them, both consciously and unconsciously.

44. The sun is, above all things, the symbol of manifesting energy; it is sudden, unaccustomed gushes of solar-spiritual energy that cause the divine inebriation of ecstasy; it is gold, as the basis of money, which is the objective representative of externalised life-force; for verily, money is life and life is money, for without money we can have no fullness of life. Life-force, manifesting on the physical plane as energy and on the mental plane as intelligence and knowledge, can be transmuted by the appropriate alchemy into money, which is a token of the capacity or energy of someone. Money is the symbol of human energy, by means of which we can store up our output of work hour by hour, receiving it back as wages at the end of the week, and spending it on necessities or saving it for future use as we think fit. The gold which backs the notes is a symbol of human energy, and is only earned by an expenditure of that energy; though it may be the energy of a father or a husband, transmitted through an heiress, yet nevertheless it is the symbol of some human being's activity in some sphere, even if it be only the sphere of company-promoting or burglary.

45. The secret, underground movements of gold act in the polity of nations as hormones act in the human body, and there are cosmic laws governing their tidal and epochal movements which economists do not suspect.

46. Kether, Space, the source of all existence, reflects into Tiphareth, which acts as a transformer and distributor of the primal, spiritual energy. We receive this energy directly by means of sunlight, and indirectly by means of the chlorophyll in green plants, which enables them to utilise sunlight, and which we eat at first hand in vegetable foods, and at second hand in the tissues of herbivorous creatures.

47. But the Sun-god is more than the source of life.   He is also the healer when life goes wrong.   For it is life, plus, minus, or misdirected, which is the activity in disease processes; disease has no energy save what it borrows from the life of the organism.   It is therefore by adjustments in the life-force that healing must be brought about, and the sun-gods are the natural gods to invoke in this connection, for life and the sun are so intimately connected.

48. It is by means of their knowledge of the manipulation of the solar influence that the ancient initiate-priests performed their healings, and sun-worship lay at the root of the Æsculapian cult of ancient Greece.

49. We moderns have learnt the value of sunlight and vitamins in our physiological economy, but we have not realised the very important part played by the spiritual aspect of the solar influences in our psychic economy, using that word in its dictionary sense.   There is a Tipharetic factor in the soul of man which, according to ancient tradition, has its physical correspondence in the solar plexus, not in the head or the heart, which is able to pick up the subtle aspect of the solar energy in the same way that the chlorophyll in the leaf of a plant picks up its more tangible aspect.   If we are cut off from this energy and prevented from assimilating it, we become as sickly and feeble in mind and body as plants growing in a cellar cut off from its more tangible aspect.

50. This cutting-off from the spiritual aspect of Nature is due to mental attitudes.   When we refuse to acknowledge our part in Nature, and Nature's part in us, we inhibit this free flow of life-giving magnetism between the part and the whole; and lacking certain elements essential to spiritual function, psychic health is impossible.

51. Psycho-analysts attach great importance to repression as a cause of psychic disease; they learnt to recognise repression because in its extreme form of sex-repression its ill effects are conspicuous.   They did not realise, however, that sex-repression, unless it is caused by circumstances, in which case it does not give rise to dissociation, is but the result of a cause

which lies far deeper than sex, and has its roots in a false spirituality, a spurious refinement and idealism, which has led to the cutting-off of the sympathies, of the recognition, of the gratitude of a living creature from the Giver of Life, the higher aspect of Nature. This is caused by a spiritual vanity which considers the more primitive aspects of nature as beneath its dignity.

52. It is because of our spurious ideals with their false values that we have so much neurotic ill-health in our midst. It is because Priapus and Cloacina are not given their due as deities that we are cursed by the Sun-god and cut off from His benign influence, for an insult to His subsidiary aspects is an insult to Him.

53. When a creature is not in a fit state for reproduction, sexual advances are repellent to it; this is the natural basis of modesty and protects the organism from waste and exhaustion. Because an accumulation of decomposing excreta gives rise to disease, the odour of their excreta is repulsive to living creatures of even the lowliest development, so that they avoid its neighbourhood. Out of these two repulsions, so rational and valuable under natural conditions, under our artificial conditions of civilised life all manner of irrational taboos have grown up. The repulsion is overdone, and no longer serves its biological purpose.

54. Our attitude towards two important sections of natural life implies that they are unnatural, debased, poisonous. Consequently we cut ourselves off from the earth-contacts; then the circuit is broken and the heavenly contacts also fail us. The cosmic current comes down from Kether, through Tiphareth and Yesod, into Malkuth; if the circuit be broken anywhere, it cannot function. True, it is impossible totally to break the circuit during life, for the life-processes are so deeply rooted in nature that we cannot altogether suppress them; but a mental attitude can cause such a kinking of the tube, as it were, can so insulate and inhibit, that only a scanty flow can be sucked through against resistance by the desperate organism.

55. In Tiphareth, the Sun Centre, we have the spiritual manifesting in the natural, and we should give reverence to the Sun-god as representing the naturalisation of spiritual processes ; the spiritualisation of natural processes has had a good deal to answer for in the history of human suffering.

IV

56. The symbols assigned to the Sixth Sephirah become a very illuminating study when we examine them in the light of what we now know about the significance of Tiphareth, for we have here a very clear example of the way in which the symbols assigned to a given Sephirah lace in and out, in and out, in long chains of interrelated associations.

57. The meaning of the Hebrew word Tiphareth is Beauty; and of the many definitions of beauty that have been proposed, the most satisfying is that which finds beauty to lie in a due and just proportion, whatever the beautiful thing may be, whether moral or material. It is interesting, therefore, to find the Sephirah of Beauty as the central point of equilibrium of the whole Tree, and that one of the two Spiritual Experiences assigned to Tiphareth is the Vision of the Harmony of Things.

58. It is curious that two separate and, at first sight, unrelated Spiritual Experiences should be assigned to Tiphareth; it is, in fact, the only Sphere on the Tree where this occurs. It is also unique in having several Magical Images assigned to it; we must therefore ask ourselves why it is that the central Sephirah has these multiple aspects. The answer is to be found in the Yetziratic Text assigned to Tiphareth, which declares that "The Sixth Path is called the Mediating Intelligence." A mediator is essentially a connecting link, an intermediary; consequently Tiphareth, in its central position, must be looked upon as a two-way switch, and we must consider it both as receiving the "influxes of the Emanations" and as "causing that influence to flow into all the reservoirs of the blessings." We may therefore look upon it as the outward manifestation of the five subtler Sephiroth, and also as

the spiritual principle behind the four denser Sephiroth. If looked at from the side of form, it is force; if looked at from the side of force, it is form. It is, in fact, the archetypal Sephirah in which the great principles represented by the five higher Sephiroth are formulated into concepts; "In it are multiplied the influxes of the Emanations," as the *Sepher Yetzirah* declares.

59. The name Zeir Anpin, Lesser Countenance, as distinguished from Arik Anpin, the Vast Countenance, one of the titles of Kether, further bears out this idea. For the formless formulations of Kether take shape in this, the sphere of the higher mind. As previously noted, Kether is reflected into Tiphareth. The Ancient of Days sees Himself reflected as in a glass, and the reflected image of the Vast Countenance is called the Lesser Countenance and the Son.

60. But although a lesser manifestation and a younger generation as viewed from above, Tiphareth is also Adam Kadmon, the Archetypal Man, when viewed from beneath—from the side, that is to say, of Yesod and Malkuth. Tiphareth is Melekh, the King, the husband of Malkah, the Bride, which is one of the titles of Malkuth.

61. It is in Tiphareth that we find the archetypal ideas which form the invisible framework of the whole of manifested creation formulating and expressing the primary principles emanating from the subtler Sephiroth. It is, as it were, a Treasure-house of Images on a higher arc; but whereas the astral plane is peopled by images reflected from forms, the images of the Sphere of Tiphareth are those formulating, and as it were crystallising out, from the spiritual emanations of the higher potencies.

62. Tiphareth mediates between the microcosm and the macrocosm; "As above, so below," is the keynote of the Sphere of Shemesh, wherein the Sun that is behind the sun focusses into manifestation.

63. In the anatomy of the Divine Man is the interpretation of all organisation and evolution; in fact, the material universe is literally the organs and members of this Divine Man; and

it is through an understanding of the soul of Adam Kadmon, which consists of the "influxes of the Emanations," that we can interpret His anatomy in terms of function, which is the only way in which anatomy can be intelligently appreciated. It is because science is content largely to be descriptive, and shrinks from purposive explanations, that it is so barren of all philosophical import.

64. In transcendental psychology, which is the anatomy of the microcosm, the breast is the correspondence assigned to Tiphareth. In the breast are the lungs and the heart, and immediately below these organs, and intimately connected with them and controlling them, is the greatest network of nerves in the body, known as the solar plexus, aptly so named by the ancient anatomists. The lungs maintain a singularly intimate relationship between the microcosm and the macrocosm by determining the ceaseless tidal motion of the atmosphere, in and out, in and out, that never ceases day or night, until the golden bowl is broken and the silver cord is loosed and we cease to breathe. The heart determines the circulation of the blood, and the blood, as Paracelsus truly said, is a "singular fluid." Modern medicine knows well what sunlight means to the blood. It has also discovered that chlorophyll, which is the green substance in the leaves of plants which enables them to utilise the sunlight as their source of energy, has a very potent influence upon the blood-pressure.

65. The three Magical Images of Tiphareth are curious, for at first sight they are so utterly unrelated that each one appears to cancel out the others. But in the light of what we now know concerning Tiphareth, their significance and relationship appears clearly, speaking through the language of symbolism, especially when studied in the light of the life of Jesus Christ the Son.

66. Tiphareth, being the first coagulation of the Supernals, is aptly represented as the new-born Child in the manger at Bethlehem; as the Sacrificed God he becomes the Mediator between God and man; and when He has risen from the dead He is as a king come to his kingdom. Tiphareth is the child

of Kether and the king of Malkuth, and in His own sphere He is sacrificed.

67. We shall not understand Tiphareth aright unless we have some concept of the real meaning of sacrifice, which is very different to the popular one, which conceives of it as the voluntary loss of something dear. Sacrifice is the translation of force from one form to another. There is no such thing as the total destruction of force; however completely it disappears from our ken, it maintains itself in some other form according to the great natural law of the conservation of energy, which is the law that maintains our universe in existence. Energy may be locked up in form, and therefore static; or it may be free from its bondage to form and in circulation. When we make a sacrifice of any sort, we take a static form of energy, and by breaking up the form that imprisons it, put it into free circulation in the cosmos. That which we sacrifice in one form turns up again in due course in another form. Apply this concept to the religious and ethical ideas of sacrifice and some very valuable clues are obtained.

68. The God-name of this sphere is Eloah Va Daath, which associates it intimately with the Invisible Sephirah that comes between it and Kether. This Sephirah, as we have already seen, may best be understood as apprehension, the dawning of consciousness; and we may interpret the phrase "Tetragrammaton Eloah Va Daath" as "God made manifest in the sphere of mind."

69. In the microcosm Tiphareth represents the higher psychism, the mode of consciousness of the individuality, or higher self. It is essentially the sphere of religious mysticism as distinguished from the magic and psychism of Yesod; for be it remembered, the Sephiroth of the Central Pillar of the Tree represent levels of consciousness, and the Sephiroth on the side pillars represent powers and modes of function. Tiphareth is also said to be the Sphere of the Greater Masters; it is the Temple not made with hands, eternal in the heavens and the Great White Lodge. It is here that the initiated adept functions when in the higher consciousness; here that he comes

to meet the Masters, and it is by means of the Name, and by an understanding of the significance of the Name of Aloah Va Daath that he opens up the higher consciousness.

70. For be it noted that it is only in proportion to the significance a word has for us that it becomes a Word of Power. The name of his victim is a word of power to a murderer; and such is its recognised potency that in some countries an instrument to register the changes of blood-pressure is attached to the arm of a suspect while he is being questioned by the police, and the name of the dead man, and other words connected with the crime, are suddenly whispered in his ear, and if these are "words of power" for him, the instrument registers it beyond all question.

71. It is popularly believed that Names of Power exercise direct influence over spirits, angels, demons and such-like, but this is not so.   The Name of Power exercises its influence upon the magician, and by exalting and directing consciousness enables him to get into touch with the chosen type of spiritual influence; if he has had experience of that particular type of influence, the Word of Power will stir potent subconscious memories; if he has not, and approaches the matter in the un-imaginative and incredulous spirit of the scholar, the "bar-barous Names of Evocation" will be just hocus-pocus for him. But be it noted that to the believing Catholic, "hocus-pocus," which is the Protestant's name for deception and superstition and from which is derived the word hoax, means "Hoc est Corpus," which is an altogether different story.   So much lies in the viewpoint in these matters.

72. Therefore it is that a definite spiritual experience is assigned to each Sephirah, and until a person has had that experience he is not an initiate of that Sephirah, and cannot make use of its Names of Power even if he knows them.   As tradition has it, it is not enough to know a Name of Power, one must also know how to vibrate it.   It is generally believed that the vibration of a Name of Power is the right note on which to chant it;   but magical vibration is something much more than that.   When one is deeply moved, and at the same

time devotionally exalted, the voice drops several tones below its normal pitch and becomes resonant and vibrant; it is this tremor of emotion combined with the resonance of devotion which constitutes the vibration of a Name, and this cannot be learnt or taught; it can only be spontaneous. It is like the wind, it bloweth where it listeth. When it comes, it shakes one from head to heel with a wave of fiery heat, and all who hear it involuntarily come to attention. It is an extraordinary experience to hear a Word of Power vibrated. It is an even more extraordinary experience to vibrate it.

73. The archangel of Tiphareth is Raphael, the "spirit that standeth in the sun," who is also the angel of healing.

74. When the initiate is "working on the Tree," that is to say is building up in his imagination a diagram of the Tree of Life in his aura, he formulates Tiphareth in his solar plexus between the abdomen and the breast; if he intends to work in the sphere of the Sixth Sephirah, and concentrates the power in this centre, he will find that he himself has suddenly become a spirit standing in the sun, with the blazing photosphere all round him. It is one thing to formulate a Sephirah in one's aura; but it is quite another to find oneself right inside the Sephirah. Although one can receive the influence of a Sephirah by means of the former operation, and it is a good routine method for daily meditation, it is not until one has everted—as it were, turned clean inside out, so that the position is reversed, and instead of the Sphere being inside one, one is inside the Sphere—that one can work with the power of a Sephirah. It is this experience which is the culmination of the initiation of a Sephirah.

75. The Order of Angels of Tiphareth are the Malachim, or Kings. These are the spiritual principles of natural forces— and no one can control, or even safely make contact with elemental principles unless he holds the initiation of Tiphareth, which is that of a minor adept. For he must have been accepted by the Elemental Kings, that is to say he must have realised the ultimate spiritual nature of natural forces before he can handle them in their elemental form. In their sub-

jective elemental form they appear in the microcosm as powerful instincts of combat, of reproduction, of self-abasement, of self-aggrandisement, and all those emotional factors known to the psychologist. It is obvious, therefore, that if we stir and stimulate these emotions in our natures it must be in order that we may use them as servants of the higher self, directed by reason and spiritual principle. It is necessary, therefore, that when we operate the elemental forces we do so through the Kings, under the presidency of the Archangel and by the invocation of the Holy Name of God appropriate to the sphere. Microcosmically, this means that the powerful elemental driving-forces of our nature are correlated with the higher self, instead of being dissociated into the Qliphothic underworld of the Freudian unconscious.

76. Elemental operations are not, of course, performed in the Sphere of Tiphareth, but it is essential that they should be controlled from the Sphere of Tiphareth if they are to remain White Magic. If there is no such higher control, they will soon slide off into Black Magic. It is said that at the Fall the four lower Sephiroth became detached from Tiphareth and assimilated to the Qliphoth. When the elemental forces become detached from their spiritual principles in our concepts so that they become ends in themselves, even if no evil but merely experimentation is intended, a Fall takes place and degeneration soon follows. But when we clearly realise the spiritual principle behind all natural things, they are then in a state of innocence, to use a theological term with a definite connotation; they are unfallen, and we can safely work with them and advantageously develop them in our own natures; thus bringing about the unrepression and equilibrium so necessary to mental health. This correlation of the natural with the spiritual, thus maintaining it unfallen and in a state of innocency, is a very important point in all practical workings in any form of magic.

V

77. As has already been seen, two spiritual experiences go to make up the initiation of Tiphareth, the Vision of the Harmony

of Things and the Vision of the Mysteries of the Crucifixion. We have already seen in another connection that there are two aspects to Tiphareth, and therefore must be two spiritual experiences in its initiation.

78. In the Vision of the Harmony of Things we see deep into the spiritual side of Nature; in other words, we meet the Angelic Kings, the Melachim. Through this experience we understand that the natural is but the dense aspect of the spiritual, the "Outer Robe of Concealment" covering the "Inner Robe of Glory." It is this understanding of the spiritual significance of the natural which is so lamentably lacking in our religious life to-day, and which is responsible for so much neurotic ill-health and so much married un-happiness.

79. It is through this Vision of the Harmony of Things that we are made one with Nature, not by means of elemental contacts. Human beings who are in anywise raised by culture above the primitive cannot become one with Nature upon the elemental level, for to do so is degeneration, and they become beastly in both senses of the word. The nature contacts are made through the Angelic Kings of the Elements in the Sphere of Tiphareth—in other words, through the realisation of the spiritual principles behind natural things—and the initiate then comes to the elemental beings in the name of their presiding King. He descends into the elemental king-doms from above, as it were, bringing with him his manhood; thus he is an initiator to the elementals; but if he meets them on their own level, he abrogates his manhood and returns to an earlier phase of evolution. Elemental force, not limited and kept in check by the limitations of an animal brain, is bound to be unbalanced force when it flows through the wide channels of a human intellect, and the result is chaos, which is one of the Kingdoms of the Qliphoth.

80. The Mysteries of the Crucifixion are both macrocosmic and microcosmic. In their macrocosmic aspect we find them in the myths of the Great Redeemers of mankind, who are always born of God and a Virgin mother, thus again emphasis-

ing the dual nature of Tiphareth, wherein form and force meet together. But let us not forget their microcosmic aspect, as an experience of mystical consciousness. It is by means of an understanding of the Mysteries of the Crucifixion, which concern the magical power of sacrifice, that we are able to transcend the limitations of brain consciousness, limited to sensation and habituated to form, and enter into the wider consciousness of the higher psychism. We thus become able to transcend form and thereby release the latent force, changing it from static to kinetic and rendering it available for the Great Work, which is regeneration.

81. The characteristic virtue of the Sphere of Tiphareth is Devotion to this Great Work. Devotion is a very important factor in the Way of Initiation that leads to the higher consciousness, and we must therefore examine it carefully and analyse it into the factors of which it consists. Devotion might be defined as love for something higher than ourselves; something that evokes our idealism; which, while we despair of becoming equal to it, yet makes us aspire to become like it; "Beholding as in a glass the glory of the Lord, are changed into the same image from glory to glory." When a stronger emotional content is infused into devotion and it becomes adoration, it carries us across the great gulf fixed between the tangible and the intangible, and enables us to apprehend things that eye hath not seen, nor ear heard. It is this Devotion, rising to Adoration, in the Great Work, which initiates us into the Mysteries of the Crucifixion.

82. The Vice assigned to Tiphareth is Pride, and in this attribution we have some very true psychology. Pride has its roots in egoism, and as long as we are self-centred we cannot be made one with all things. In the true selflessness of the Path the soul overflows its boundaries and enters into all things through limitless sympathy and perfect love; but in pride the soul tries to extend its boundaries till it possesses all things, and it is a very different matter to possess a thing to being made one with it, wherein it equally possesses us in perfect reciprocity. It is this one-sided arrangement which

is the vice of the adept.   He must give as well as receive, and
he must give himself unreservedly if he would participate in
mystical union, which is the fruit of the sacrifice of crucifixion.
"Let him who would be the greatest among you be the servant
of all," said Our Lord.

83. The symbols associated with Tiphareth are the lamen;
the Rose Cross; the Calvary Cross; the truncated pyramid;
and the cube.

84. The lamen is the symbol upon the breast of the adept
and indicates the force he represents.   An adept performing
work in the Sphere of Shemesh, for instance, would wear upon
his breast an image of the sun in splendour.   A lamen is the
magical weapon of Tiphareth; and it therefore becomes
necessary to say something concerning the nature of magical
weapons in general in order that the function of a lamen can
be understood.

85. A magical weapon is some object which is found to be
suitable as a vehicle for force of a particular type.   For
instance, the magical weapon of the Element of Water is a cup
or chalice; the magical weapon of the Element of Fire is a
lighted lamp.   These objects are chosen because their nature
is congenial to that of the force to be invoked; or in modern
language, because their form suggests the force to the imagination by association of ideas.

86. Tiphareth is traditionally associated with the breast,
both by virtue of the network of nerves which is called the
solar plexus, and by its position when the Tree is built up in the
aura.   Consequently the breast jewel of the adept is held to be
the focus of the Tipharetic force, whatever operation may be
performed.   The actual force, operating in its own sphere, is
represented by the magical weapon assigned to it.   For
instance, an adept performing an operation of the Element of
Water would have as his magical weapon the Cup, and with the
Cup would make all signs, and upon the Cup would concentrate the force called down by invocation.   But upon his
breast would be the sigil of the Element of Water, and this
would be recognised as representing the spiritual factor in

the operation, and as referring to the archangel over that particular kingdom. Unless the adept understands the significance of his lamen, as distinguished from his magical weapon, he is no adept, but a wizard.

87. The Rose Cross and the Calvary Cross are both given as symbols of the Sphere of Tiphareth. In order to understand their significance, it is necessary to say something concerning crosses in general, and how they are used in systems of symbolism. Although the cross with which we are most generally familiar is the Calvary Cross, owing to its association with Christianity, there are many other forms of cross, and each has its own significance. The Equal-armed Cross, such as the Red Cross of the army medical service, is called by initiates the Cross of Nature, and represents power in equilibrium. It is to be found at the top of some Keltic crosses, often enclosed in a circle, so that a Keltic cross actually consists of a tapering shaft ending in a nature cross, and has no relationship whatever to the Calvary Cross, which is the Cross of Christianity. The tapering shaft of the Keltic cross is, in actual fact, a truncated pyramid, and examples of this type of Keltic cross exist which leave no doubt upon this point whatsoever. Some archaic forms suggest the imposition of the cross and circle upon the conical phallic stone which is so universal an object in primitive worship.

88. The Swastika is also a nature cross, and is sometimes called the Cross of Thor, or the Hammer of Thor, its form being supposed to indicate the whirling action of his thunderbolts.

89. The Calvary Cross is the Cross of Sacrifice, and should properly be coloured black. Its shaft should be three times the length of its arms, and the length of each arm three times its width. Meditation on this cross brings initiation through suffering, sacrifice, and self-abnegation. The Crucifix is, of course, an elaboration of the Calvary Cross.

90. The circle upon the cross is an initiatory symbol, especially when the cross is raised upon three steps, as it should be in this form. The circle indicates eternal life; also wisdom;

and we see a form of it in the emblem of the Theosophical
Society, which has for its badge the "serpent that holdeth his
tail in his mouth." A Calvary Cross with the circle superimposed means initiation by the Way of the Cross, and the
three steps are the three degrees of illumination. It is this
which is the so-called Rose Cross. The fanciful object with
brambles growing over it is not an initiatory symbol at all.
The Rose associated with the Cross in Western symbolism is
the Rosa Mundi, and is a key to the interpretation of the nature
forces. On its petals are marked the thirty-two signs of the
natural forces; these correspond to the twenty-two letters of the
Hebrew alphabet and the Ten Holy Sephiroth; these in their
turn are assigned to the Thirty-two Paths of the Tree of Life,
and this is the key to the understanding of the Rosa Mundi.
The curious scribbles that are called the sigils of the elementary spirits are made by drawing lines from one to another of
the letters of their names on the Rose.

91. In the light of this explanation we are at no loss to
understand the value of the claims of those organisations
which sport a floral emblem as their symbol. They are on a
par with those of the gentleman who demanded of his haber-
dasher a Public School tie with a bit of red in it.

92. The cube is usually said to be assigned to Tiphareth
because it is a six-sided figure, and six is the number of Tiphareth. But there is more than this in the symbolism of the
cube. The cube is the simplest form of solid, and as such is
the appropriate symbol of Tiphareth, in whose sphere is
found the first foreshadowing of form. The symbol of
Malkuth is the double cube, which symbolises "As above,
so below."

93. The pyramid symbolises the perfected man, broad-
based on earth and tapering to unity in the heavens; in other
words, the Ipsissimus. The truncated pyramid symbolises the
initiated adept, or Adeptus Minor, who has passed within the
Veil but has not yet completed his grades. This pyramid, to
whose six sides correspond the six central Sephiroth which
constitute Adam Kadmon, or the Archetypal Man, is com-

pleted by the addition of the Three Supernals which terminate in the unity of Kether.

94. The Sixes of the Tarot suits are also assigned to Tiphareth, and in them the harmonious and balanced nature of this Sephirah shows clearly.   The Six of Wands is the Lord of Victory.   The Six of Cups, the Lord of Joy.   Even the maleficent suit of Swords is tuned to harmony in this sphere, and the Six of Swords is known as the Lord of Earned Success —that is to say, success achieved after struggle.   The Six of Pentacles is Material Success;   in other words, power in equilibrium.

PART III

CHAPTER XXI

THE FOUR LOWER SEPHIROTH

1. The Ten Holy Sephiroth, when arranged upon the Tree of Life in their traditional pattern, fall into three main horizontal divisions, as well as the three vertical divisions of the Pillars. The highest of these horizontal divisions consists of the Three Supernals, which for all practical purposes are beyond the sphere of our comprehension. We posit them as fundamental principles which must exist if subsequent manifestations are to be explained. They represent Pure Being and the opposing principles of Activity and Passivity, and they are well described by calling them the Supernal Triangle.

2. The next functional triangle upon the Tree consists of Chesed, Geburah, and Tiphareth. These represent the active principles of Anabolism, Katabolism, and Equilibrium, and might best be described by calling them the Abstract Triangle.

3. All these six higher Sephiroth we have considered in detail, and we have seen how the three Supernal principles form the basis of manifestation, and the three Abstract principles give expression to manifestation. The three higher are latent, and the three lower are potent. If we understand these things, we find we have a system for explaining the infinite diversity of manifestation of the planes of form by reducing them to their primary principles, which renders the relations between them and the mode of their interaction and development clearly comprehensible; which it never has been, and never can be when the attempt is made to reduce all things to terms of form, instead of resolving them into terms of force.

4. The lowest functional unit on the Tree of Life consists,

not of a triangle, but of a quaternary, and this quaternary is said by the Qabalists to have been affected by the Fall, the head of Leviathan rising out of the Abyss to a point between Yesod and Tiphareth. Beyond this it was not permitted to go, and the six higher Sephiroth retained their innocency. In other words, the four lower Sephiroth belong to the planes of form, wherein force is no longer free-moving, but "cabined, cribbed, confined"; only to be freed by works of destruction.

5. Tiphareth, as has already been seen, is the centre of equilibrium of the Tree. Equilibrium gives rise to stability, and stability to cohesion. From now onwards in the descent of life upon the Path of Involution we find the principle of cohesion playing an increasingly predominant part, until in Malkuth it reaches its apogee.

6. We may well conceive that the active principles of the Abstract Triangle underwent subdivision and specialisation in the course of the descent of life through Netzach, and in Yesod attained to a considerable degree of stereotyping by means of which the forms of Malkuth were determined. Once Malkuth, which is the plane of pure form, attained development, the evolutionary stream began to turn back towards spirit, freeing itself from the bondage of form while retaining the capacities acquired by experience of the discipline of form.

7. We may conceive, then, of numerous abstract principles of life-function becoming clothed upon with form owing to the influence of the experience of their outward manifestations in the Kingdom of Form. Or, in the language of the Qabalists, the influence of the Fall is felt by them, and they have lost their innocency.

8. These considerations give us an insight into the nature of the Quaternary of the Planes of Form, and enable us to tread the Middle Way between credulity and scepticism in this Sphere of Illusion, as it has somewhat unkindly been called.

9. The great tide of evolving life, which issued as an emanation from Tiphareth, is broken up in the Sephirah Netzach as by a prism into many-rayed manifestation; whence comes the

Yetziratic description of this Sephirah as "the refulgent splendour." In Hod these multifarious forces are clothed upon with form; and in Yesod they act as etheric moulds for the final emanations in Malkuth.

10. Manifestation in Malkuth completes the outgoing arc of involution, and life turns back upon itself to pursue a parallel course on the returning arc of evolution. Human intelligence develops, and begins to meditate upon causation and discerns the gods. Be it noted that primitive man has never achieved monotheism in a single stride; he has always conceived of causation as multiform, and it has required many generations of culture to reduce the many to the One.

11. This brings us to the great question, which might almost be called the Dweller on the Threshold of occult science, the horror which confronts every adventurer into the Unseen; which unites in itself the functions of the Sphinx, and asks a question of the soul upon the answer to which hangs his fate. Shall he be condemned to wander in the realms of illusion? Shall he be turned back on to the planes of form, or shall he be permitted to pass on into the Light? This question is, Do you believe in the gods? If he answers Yes, he will be a wanderer in the planes of illusion, for the gods are not real persons as we understand personality. If he answers No, he will be turned back at the gate, for the gods are not illusions. What then shall he answer?

12. The intuition of a poet has given us the answer.

"For no thought of man made Gods to love and honour
    Ere the song within the silent soul began,
    Nor might earth in dream or deed take heaven upon her
    Till the word was clothed with speech by lips of man."

13. Therein we have the clue to the riddle. The gods are the creations of the created. They are made by the adoration of their worshippers. It is not the gods that do the work of creation. This is done by the great natural forces working each according to its nature; the gods come in their procession after the Swan of the Empyrean has laid the egg of manifestation in the darkness of the cosmic night.

14. The gods are emanations of the group-minds of races; they are not emanations of Eheieh, the One and Eternal. Nevertheless, they are immensely powerful, because by means of their influence over the imaginations of their worshippers they link the microcosm with the macrocosm; for by meditation on the ideal beauty of Apollo the soul of man is opened to beauty in general.

15. As man has analysed life and discerned factor by factor its prime motives, he has apotheosised them. Because man in all parts of the globe has found that the same needs and motives actuate him, he has evolved comparable pantheons. Because temperaments differ, he has evolved as different pantheons as the blood-thirsty fiends of Mexico and the radiant beings of Hellas.

16. We may ask ourselves, then, whether the gods are wholly subjective; whether they live solely in the imaginations of their worshippers, or whether they have an independent life of their own? The answer to this question is to be found in a fact of occult experience which cannot be explained by what we know of natural science, but which has to be taken for granted by every practical occultist before he can obtain results. In fact, one might say that the results he obtains are in proportion to his faith, for it becomes true for him as soon as he believes in it. This fact is, that only a very small proportion of the existing mind-stuff of the universe, whatever that may be, is organised into the brains and nervous systems of sentient creatures. The vast mass of what, for want of a better name, we call mind-stuff, because that is its nearest analogy among known things, is free-moving upon what occultists call the astral plane, organised into forms within itself, but not necessarily attached to matter. Different occultists refer to this free mind-stuff by different names. Mme Blavatsky calls it Akasha; Eliphas Lévi calls it the reflecting ether. Netzach represents the force aspect, and Hod the form aspect of this Akasha.

17. Out of this mind-stuff are formed the moulds of all forms; and within these moulds are built up the framework of

etheric stresses that function in the sphere of Yesod, and within which are held the molecules of matter which form the body of manifestation on the physical plane.

18. Normally these forms are built by the cosmic consciousness expressed as natural forces, functioning each according to its nature; but as consciousness began to develop in the creatures of the Creator, it exercised its function in varying degrees upon the astral mind-stuff which, by its nature, was amenable to the influences of consciousness; consequently, "the thought of man made Gods to love and honour." These forms, once built, became channels of the specialised forces they were designed to represent, concentrating them upon their worshippers. In this enlightened sense initiates not only believe in, but adore the gods.

CHAPTER XXII

NETZACH

TITLE: Netzach, Victory. (Hebrew spelling: נצח: Nun, Tzaddi, Cheth.)

MAGICAL IMAGE: A beautiful naked woman.

SITUATION ON THE TREE: At the foot of the Pillar of Mercy.

YETZIRATIC TEXT: The Seventh Path is called the Occult Intelligence because it is the refulgent splendour of the intellectual virtues which are perceived by the eyes of the intellect and the contemplations of faith.

TITLE GIVEN TO NETZACH: Firmness.

GOD-NAME: Jehovah, Tseva'oth, the Lord of Hosts.

ARCHANGEL: Haniel, Grace of God.

ORDER OF ANGELS: Elohim, Gods.

MUNDANE CHAKRA: Nogah, Venus.

SPIRITUAL EXPERIENCE: Vision of beauty triumphant.

VIRTUE: Unselfishness.

VICE: Unchastity. Lust.

CORRESPONDENCE IN THE MICROCOSM: Loins, hips, and legs.

SYMBOLS: Lamp and girdle. The rose.

TAROT CARDS: The four Sevens.

> SEVEN OF WANDS: Valour.
> SEVEN OF CUPS: Illusory success.
> SEVEN OF SWORDS: Unstable effort.
> SEVEN OF PENTACLES: Success unfulfilled.

COLOUR IN ATZILUTH: Amber.

„ „ BRIAH: Emerald.

„ „ YETZIRAH: Bright yellowish green.

„ „ ASSIAH: Olive, flecked with gold.

I

1. Netzach, the Sphere of Venus, is best understood by contrasting it with Hod, the Sphere of Mercury, these two representing force and form on a lower arc, as has already been seen. Netzach represents the instincts and the emotions they give

rise to, and Hod represents the concrete mind.   In the macrocosm they represent two levels of the process of the concretion of force into form.   In Netzach force is still relatively
free-moving, being bound only into exceedingly fluidic and
ever-shifting shapes, and in Hod taking on for the first time
definite and permanent form, though of an exceedingly
tenuous nature.   In Netzach a particular form of force
represents itself as a type of beings, flowing backwards and
forwards over the boundaries of manifestation in an exceedingly elusive manner.   Such beings have no individualised
personalities, but are like the armies with banners that can be
seen in the sunset clouds.   In Hod, however, individualisa-
tion into units has taken place, and there is continuity of
existence.   All mind is group-mind in Netzach, but in Hod
the human mind has its beginnings.

2. Let us now consider Netzach itself, both in its microcosmic and macrocosmic aspects, bearing constantly in mind
that we are now in the sphere of illusion, and that what is about
to be described in terms of form are appearances as represented
by the intellect to itself and projected back into the astral light
as thought-forms.   This is a very important point, and should
be thoroughly understood in order to avoid falling into
superstition.   Everything that is perceived by the "eyes of
the intellect and the contemplations of faith," as the Yetziratic
Text so graphically puts it, has its metaphysical basis in
Chokmah, the Supernal Sephirah at the head of the Pillar of
Mercy.   But with Netzach a great change comes over our
mode of apprehending the different types of existence assigned
to each sphere.   Hitherto we have perceived by means of
intuition; our apprehensions have been formless, or at least
represented by highly abstract symbols; there are no more of
these after Tiphareth, but we come to such concrete symbols
as the rose, assigned to Venus, for Netzach, and the caduceus,
assigned to Mercury, for Hod.

3. As has been seen, we conceive of the higher Sephiroth
under the aspect of factors of manifestation and functions.
We saw in our study of Tiphareth how the Mediating In-

telligence, as the *Sepher Yetzirah* calls it, broke up the White Light of the One Life as in a prism so that it becomes the Refulgent Splendour of many-rayed hues in Netzach. Here we have not force, but forces; not life, but lives. Appropriately, therefore, the Order of Angels assigned to Netzach are the Elohim, or gods. The One has been reduced to the Many for the purposes of manifestation in form.

4. These rays are not represented as the pure white light by which we see everything in its true colours, but as many-hued, each one of which brings out and intensifies some specialised aspect of manifestation, just as a ray of blue light will only show up those colours that are sympathetic to it, and will make its complementary colours look black. Every life or form of force manifesting in Netzach is a partial but specialised manifestation; therefore no being that has for its sphere of evolution the sphere of Netzach can ever have an all-round development, but must always be a creature of one idea, one single, simple, stereotyped function.

5. It is the Netzach factor in ourselves that is the basis of our instincts, each of which, in their unintellectualised essence, gives rises to appropriate reflexes, just as an infant's lips will suck anything that is inserted between them.

6. The beings of Netzach, the Elohim, are not so much intelligences as the embodiments of ideas.

7. These Elohim, to give them their Hebrew name, are the formative influences whereby the creative force expresses itself in Nature. Their true character is to be discerned in Chesed, where they are described by the *Sepher Yetzirah* as the "Holy Powers." In Netzach, however, which represents the upper stratum of the reflecting ether, they undergo a change, the image-making mind of man has begun to work upon them, moulding the astral light into forms that shall represent them to his consciousness.

8. It is very important that we should realise that these lower Sephiroth of the Plane of Illusion are densely populated by thought-forms; that everything which the human imagination has been able to conceive, however dimly, has a form built

about it out of the astral light, and that the more the human imagination has dwelt upon it to idealise it, the more definite that form becomes. Consequently, subsequent generations of seers, when they seek to discern the spiritual nature and innermost essence of any form of life, are met by these images, the "creations of the created," and will be deceived thereby, mistaking them for the abstract essence itself, which is not to be found upon any plane that yields images to psychic vision, but only upon those that are discerned by pure intuition.

9. When his mentality was still primitive man worshipped these images, by means of which he represented to himself the great natural forces so all-important to his material well-being, thus establishing a link with them, by means of which a channel was developed whereby the forces they represented were poured into his soul, thus stimulating the corresponding factor in his own nature and thereby developing it. The operations of this worship, especially when it became highly organised and intellectualised, as in Greece and Egypt, built up exceedingly definite and potent images, and it is these that are generally understood as the gods. Generations of worship and adoration build a very strong image in the astral light, and when sacrifice is added to worship, the image is brought a step farther down the planes into manifestation and acquires a form in the dense ethers of Yesod, and is a very potent magical object, capable of independent action when ensouled by the concrete ideas generated in Hod.

10. We see, then, that every celestial being conceived by the mind of man has as its basis a natural force, but that upon the basis of this natural force is built up a symbolic image representative thereof, which is ensouled and rendered active by the force it represents. The image, then, is but a mode of representation indulged in by the human mind for its own convenience, but the force that the image represents, and which ensouls it, is a very real thing indeed, and under certain circumstances can be exceedingly powerful. In other words, although the form under which the god is represented is pure

imagination, the force associated with it is both real and active.

11. This fact is the key, not only to talismanic magic in its broadest sense, which includes all consecrated objects used in ceremonial and for meditation, but to many things in life that we cannot fail to observe but for which we have no explanation. It explains a great many things in organised religion that are very real to the believer but very baffling to the unbeliever, who can neither explain them nor explain them away.

12. In Netzach, however, we have the most tenuous form of these things, and they are perceived far more by the "contemplations of faith" than by the "eyes of the intellect." In the Sphere of Hod are performed all manner of magical operations in which the intellect itself is brought to bear upon these tenuous and fleeting images to give them form and permanency; but in the Sphere of Netzach such operations do not take place to any great degree; all god-forms in Netzach are worshipped by means of the arts, not conceived by means of philosophies. Nevertheless, for all practical purposes it is impossible to separate the activities of Hod and Netzach, which are a functional pair, just as Geburah and Chesed make up the two aspects of metabolism, the katabolic and the anabolic. The functions of Netzach are implicit in Hod because Netzach emanates Hod, and the powers developed by evolution in the Sphere of Netzach are the basis of the capacities of Hod. Consequently all magical operations of the Sphere of Hod work upon a basis of the tenuous life-forms of Netzach; and because the human intellect works up from Sphere to Sphere, a good deal of the powers of Hod have been carried over into Netzach by initiated souls going on ahead of evolution. The two Spheres, therefore, are not clear-cut in their division and classification, but in each one a certain type of function very definitely predominates.

13. The contacts of Netzach are not made by means of conceiving its life philosophically, nor by means of ordinary image-making psychism, but by "feeling with," as Algernon Blackwood has so graphically expressed it in his novels, into

which so much of the Sphere of Netzach enters. It is by means of dance and sound and colour that the Netzach angels are contacted and evoked. The worshipper of a god in the Sphere of Netzach enters into communion with the object of his adoration by means of the arts; and in proportion as he is an artist in some medium or other, and can therein represent his deity symbolically, will he be able to make the contact and draw the life into himself. All rites which have rhythm and movement and colour in them are aworking in the Sphere of Netzach. And as Hod, the Sphere of magical workings, draws its force from Netzach, it follows that any magical operation of the Sphere of Hod must have a Netzach element in it if it is to be ensouled effectually; and in order to provide a basis of manifestation, etheric substance has to be provided by some form of sacrifice, even if it be only the burning of incense. This question will be dealt with fully in studying the Sphere of Yesod, to which it belongs. It is necessary to refer to it here, because the significance of the rites of Netzach cannot be understood without a realisation of the means whereby manifestation is effected, and the god brought near to his worshippers.

II

14. Let us now consider Netzach from the point of view of the microcosmic Tree of Life—that is to say, the subjective Tree within the soul, wherein the Sephiroth are factors in consciousness.

15. The Three Supernals, and the first pair of manifesting Sephiroth, Chesed and Geburah, represent the Higher Self, with Tiphareth as the point of contact with the Lower Self. The four lower Sephiroth, Netzach, Hod, Yesod, and Malkuth, represent the Lower Self, or personality, the unit of incarnation, with Tiphareth as the point of contact with the Higher Selt, which is sometimes called the Holy Guardian Angel.

16. From the point of view of the personality, Tiphareth represents the higher consciousness, aware of spiritual things; Netzach represents the instincts, and Hod the intellect. Yesod

represents the fifth element, Æther, and Malkuth the four elements which are the subtle aspect of matter. All that the average human intellect can realise is the nature of dense matter, Malkuth, and of the intellect, Hod, both concrete aspects of existence. It has no appreciation of the forces which build the forms, as represented by Netzach, the Sphere of the instincts, and Yesod, the etheric double or subtle body. Consequently we must make a careful study of Netzach because its nature and importance are so little understood.

17. We shall comprehend the nature of Netzach in the microcosm best if we remember that it is the Sphere of Venus, with all that that implies. Translated from the symbolic language of the Qabalah into plain English, it means that we are concerned here with the function of polarity, which is a very great deal more than mere sex as popularly conceived.

18. It is important to note in this respect that Venus, or in her Greek form, Aphrodite, is not a fertility goddess at all, such as are Ceres and Persephone; she is the goddess of love. Now in the Greek concept of life, Love embraced much more than the relationship between the sexes, it included the comradeship of fighting men and the relationship of teacher and pupil. The Greek hetaira, or woman whose profession is love, was something very different to our modern prostitute. The Greek kept the simple physical relation of the sexes for his lawful wife, who was secluded in the gynæceum, or harem, and was kept simply for breeding purposes in order that he might have lawful heirs; and she was a woman without education though of good blood, and was not encouraged to render herself attractive or ply the arts of love. Still less was she encouraged to worship the goddess Aphrodite, who presides over the higher aspects of love; the deities of her adoration were expected to be the gods of hearth and home; Ceres the earth-mother was the ruler of the Mysteries of the Greek women.

19. The Aphrodite cult was something very much more than the simple performance of an animal function. It was concerned with the subtle interaction of the life-force between

two factors; the curious flow and return, the stimulus and the reaction, which plays so important a part in the relations of the sexes, but extends far beyond the sphere of sex.

20. The Greek hetaira was expected to be a woman of culture; there were, of course, all grades among them, from the lower, who approximated to the Japanese geisha, to the higher, who held salons after the manner of the famous French blue-stockings, and were women of clean physical virtue to whom no man would dare to make sensual advances; but because of the reverence in which the function of sex was held among the Greeks, it is probable that at no grade of society did the hetaira approximate to the degradation of the modern professional prostitute.

21. The function of the hetaira was to minister to the intellect of her clients as well as their appetites; she was a hostess as well as a mistress, and to her resorted the philosophers and poets to receive inspiration and sharpen their wits; for it was well realised that there is no greater inspiration to an intellectual man than the society of a vital and cultured woman.

22. In the temples of Aphrodite the art of love was sedulously cultivated, and the priestesses were trained from childhood in its skill.   But this art was not simply that of provoking passion, but of adequately satisfying it on all levels of consciousness; not simply by the gratification of the physical sensations of the body, but by the subtle etheric exchange of magnetism and intellectual and spiritual polarisation.   This lifted the cult of Aphrodite out of the sphere of simple sensuality, and explains why the priestesses of the cult commanded respect and were by no means looked upon as common prostitutes, although they received all comers.   They were engaged in ministering to certain of the subtler needs of the human soul by means of their skilled arts.   We have brought to a higher pitch of development than was ever known to the Greeks the art of stimulating desire with film and revue and syncopation, but we have no knowledge of the far more important art of meeting the needs of the human soul for etheric and mental interchange of magnetism, and it is for this

reason that our sex life, both physiologically and socially, is so unstable and unsatisfactory.

23. We cannot understand sex aright unless we realise that it is one aspect of what the esotericist calls polarity, and that this is a principle that runs through the whole of creation, and is, in fact, the basis of manifestation. It is represented on the Tree by the two Pillars of Severity and Mercy. The whole of the activity of force is comprised in the principle of polarity, just as the whole of the function of form is comprised in the principle of metabolism.

24. Polarity really means the flowing of force from a sphere of high pressure to a sphere of low pressure; high and low being always relative terms. Every sphere of energy needs to receive the stimulus of an influx of energy at higher pressure, and to have an output into a sphere of lower pressure. The source of all energy is in the Great Unmanifest, and it makes its way down the levels, changing its form from one to the other, till it is finally "earthed" in Malkuth. In every individual life, in every form of activity, in every organised social group for whatever purpose, whether army, church, or limited company, we see the exemplification of this flowing of energy in circuit. The great point we need to realise is that in the microcosmic Tree there is a flow down and up the positive and negative aspects of our own subjective levels of consciousness, whereby the spirit inspires mind, and mind directs the emotions, and the emotions form the etheric double, and the etheric double moulds the physical vehicle, which is the "earth" of the circuit. This is a fact that is generally realised, and its implications are easily seen as soon as attention is drawn to them.

25. But a point we do not so readily realise is that there is a flow and return between each "body" or level of consciousness and its corresponding aspect in the macrocosm. Just as there is an intake and output on the level of Malkuth whereby food and water are received into the body as nutriment and rejected as excreta, which is the food of the vegetable kingdom under the polite name of manure—so is there an intake and output between the etheric double and the astral light, and

between the astral body and the mind side of nature, and so on up the planes, with the subtler factors represented by the six higher Sephiroth. The essence of the Magical Qabalah, which is the practical application of the Tree of Life, is to develop these magnetic circuits of the different levels, and so strengthen and reinforce the soul. Just as the physical body is nourished by eating and drinking, and kept healthy by adequate excretion, which might be called the operations of the Sphere of Malkuth, so is the soul of man energised by the operations of the Sphere of Tiphareth, which is also called the Sphere of the Redeemer, who brings health to the soul. We know how initiation develops the powers of the higher psychism and enables the human understanding to apprehend spiritual truths; what we do not realise is that for the full gamut of human development we need also to develop our power to contact natural energy in its essential form as represented by the Sphere of Netzach. We are accustomed to take the line that the spiritual and the natural are mutually antagonistic and that we must rob Peter to pay Paul, and to conclude that if the spiritual is the highest good, the natural must necessarily be the lowest evil; we do not realise that matter is crystallised spirit, and spirit is volatilised matter, and that there is no difference of substance between them, any more than there is between water and ice, but both are different states of the One Thing, as the alchemists call it; this is the great secret of alchemy which forms the philosophic basis of the secret doctrine of transmutation.

26. But the transmutation of metals is of little save academic importance compared to the transmutation of energy within the soul. It is this that the initiates deal with by means of the technique of the Tree of Life; and as consciousness transmutes up and down the Central Pillar of Mildness, or Equilibrium, so does energy transmute up and down the Pillar of Mercy, of which Netzach is the base, and form transmute up and down the Pillar of Severity, of which Hod, the intellect, is the base.

27. In Chokmah, then, we get the tremendous drive of life, which is the great male potency of the universe; in Chesed we get the organisation of forces into interacting wholes; and in

Netzach we get a sphere wherein evolution, ascending from Malkuth as organised force ensouling vivified form, is able to contact essential force once more. Netzach, the Sphere of Nogah, which is the Hebrew name for Venus-Aphrodite, is therefore an exceedingly important Sphere from the point of view of the practical work of occultism. It is because most people who go in for occultism work up the Central Pillar only, which is the Pillar of Consciousness, and pay no attention to the side pillars, which are the Pillars of Function, that such negligible results are obtained from initiation. The blind are leading the blind, and the average would-be initiator in modern occult fraternities, who is usually more of a mystic than an occultist, does not realise that he has got to initiate subconsciousness as well as consciousness, and illuminate the instincts as well as the reason.

III

28. We have considered Netzach from the objective and the subjective points of view; it now remains to study the symbolism assigned to this Sephirah in the light of the knowledge we have already obtained.

29. We shall observe at once that the symbolism contains two distinct ideas—the idea of power and the idea of beauty; and we are reminded of the love that existed between Venus and Mars according to the old myth. Now these myths are not fabulous, save in the historical sense, but represent truths of the spirit; and when we find the same idea recurring in different pantheons, when we find Hebrew Qabalist and Greek poet, whose mentalities were as far removed from each other as the poles, presenting the same concept in different forms, we must conclude that it is not accidental, but will repay careful scrutiny.

30. Let us depart from our usual method of analysing the symbols in the given order, and classify them according to the two types into which they fall.

31. The Hebrew title of the Seventh Sephirah is Netzach, meaning Victory. Its additional title is Firmness, which

carries out the same idea of masterful and victorious energy. The God-name is Jehovah Tseva'oth, meaning the Lord of Hosts, or God of Armies. The Order of Angels assigned to Netzach are the Elohim, or gods, the rulers of Nature.

32. The four Tarot cards assigned to this Sephirah all contain the idea of battle, even if in a negative form. It is curious to note, however, that it is only the Seven of Wands which has a good, or positive, significance, the other three Sevens are all cards of ill fortune. The reason for this becomes clear, however, when we understand the symbolism as a whole, so we will put it aside for the moment, and reconsider it later.

33. Let us now turn to the consideration of the other set of symbolic images. The Mundane Chakra of Netzach is the planet Venus, and the magical image is, appropriately enough, "a beautiful naked woman." The spiritual experience assigned to this sphere is the Vision of Beauty Triumphant. The virtue is Unselfishness—that is to say, the capacity to polarise from the negative pole. The vices are the obvious ones of love abused—unchastity and lust.

34. The correspondence in the microcosm is with the loins, hips, and legs. These, it will be noted, form the setting of the generative organs, but not the generative organs themselves, and bear out the idea previously shadowed forth, that the goddess of Love and the fertility goddess are not one and the same thing.

35. The symbols assigned to Netzach are the Lamp, the Girdle, and the Rose. The Girdle and Rose are self-explanatory, for they are traditionally associated with Venus. The Lamp, however, requires more explanation, for the classical associations afford us no clue on this point. We must turn to alchemy.

36. The four Elements are associated with the four lower Sephiroth, and of these the Element of Fire is associated with Netzach. The Lamp is the magical weapon used in operations of the Element of Fire. Hence the association with Netzach. The Element of Fire is associated with the fiery energy at the

heart of Nature, and connects up with the Mars aspect of the Venus Sephirah.

37. We see, then, from a study of the foregoing symbolism, that the Mars, or Victory, symbolism is associated with the Macrocosm, and the Venus, or Love, symbolism with the Microcosmic or subjective aspect. This gives us the key to a very important psychological truth, well understood by the ancients, but which had to await the work of Freud for its interpretation in modern language. This may best be expressed by saying that elemental energy, or the fundamental dynamism of an individual, is very closely connected with the sex life of that individual.

38. This is a very important fact in our psychic life, well understood by psychologists though but little appreciated by mystics and psychics, who generally incline to an idealism which seeks to escape from matter and its problems. But to escape like this is to leave unconquered fortresses in our rear; and the wiser way, the only way that can produce wholeness of life and a balanced temperament, is to give due place to Netzach, which balances the intellectuality of Hod and the materiality of Malkuth, remembering always that the Tree consists of the two Pillars of Polarity and the Path of Equilibrium between them.

39. The true secret of natural goodness lies in the recognition of the contending rights of the Pairs of Opposites; there is no such antinomy as between Good and Evil, but only the balance between two extremes, each of which is evil when carried to excess, both of which give rise to evil if insufficient for equipoise. Unbridled licence leads to degradation; but unbalanced idealism leads to psychopathology.

40. There are three types of persons who pass within the Veil—the mystic, the psychic, and the occultist. The mystic aspires to union with God, and achieves his end by putting aside all that is not of God in his life. The psychic is a receiver of subtle vibrations, but not a transmitter. The occultist must needs be to some extent at least a receiver, but his primary aim is to be able to control and direct in the

invisible kingdoms in the same way that the man of science has learnt to control and direct in the kingdom of Nature.

41. In order to achieve this end he must work in harmony with the invisible forces in the same way that the scientist masters Nature by understanding her. Of these invisible forces some are spiritual, descending from Kether, and some are elemental, working up from Malkuth. The Kether forces of the Macrocosm are picked up by the Tiphareth-centre in the Microcosm, to use the Qabalistic terminology; the elemental forces are picked up by the Yesod-centre, but—and this is the important point—they are directed and controlled by the manner in which the equilibrium is maintained between Netzach and Hod.

42. Netzach, in the Microcosm, represents the instinctive, emotional side of our nature, and Hod represents the intellect; Netzach is the artist in us, and Hod is the scientist. According as our moods shift between restraint and dynamism will be the polarity of Hod and Netzach in the Microcosm which is the soul. If there is no Netzach influence to introduce a dynamic element, the over-preponderance of Hod will lead to all theory and no practice in occult matters. No one can handle magic in whom the Sphere of Netzach is not in function, for the scepticism of Hod will kill all magical images before their birth. Like all things in nature, Hod, unfertilised by its opposing polarity, is sterile. There must be something of the artist in every occultist who wants to do practical work. The intellect alone, however powerful, does not confer powers. It is through the Netzach in our own nature that the elemental forces obtain access to consciousness; without Netzach, they remain in the subconscious Sphere of Yesod, working blindly. It is taught in the Mysteries that each level of manifestation has its own ethic, or standard of right and wrong, and that we must not confuse the planes by expecting from one the standard of another, which is not applicable thereon. In the realm of mind, the ethic is Truth; on the astral plane, which is the sphere of the emotions and instincts, the ethic is Beauty. We must learn to understand the righteousness of Beauty, as well

as the beauty of righteousness, if we want to bring all the provinces of the inner kingdom into obedience to the central power of unified consciousness.

43. In entering upon the region of the four lower Sephiroth we are coming into the sphere of the human mind. Subjectively considered, they constitute the personality and its powers. It is the aim of occult initiation to develop these powers and, if taken from the higher standpoint, as it always should be if it is not to degenerate into black magic, to unite them with Tiphareth, which is the focussing-point of the higher self, or Individuality. In discussing Netzach, therefore, we have definitely passed within the portal of the Mysteries, and are treading upon the sacred ground reserved for initiates.

44. I am no advocate of a secrecy which is simply priest-craft, but there are certain practical secrets of the Mysteries which it is inadvisable to cry aloud lest they be abused. There is also the inveterate tendency of human nature to apply its own definitions to familiar terms, and to refuse to recognise them apart from their familiar associations. If I lift a corner of the Veil of the Temple and reveal the fact that sex is simply a special instance of the universal principle of polarity, the immediate assumption is that polarity and sex are synonymous terms. If I say that although sex is a part of polarity, there is a great deal of polarity that has nothing to do with sex, my explanation is ignored. Perhaps I shall be understood better if I substitute the terminology of physics for that of the more appropriate psychology, and say that life will only flow in circuit; insulate it, and it becomes inert. Let us take the human personality as an electrical machine; it must be connected up with the power-house, which is God, the Source of all Life, or there will be no motive power; but equally it must be "earthed," or the power will not flow. Every human being must be "earthed" to the earth, both literally and metaphorically. The idealist tries to induce a complete insulation of all earth-contacts in order that the inflowing power may not be wasted; he fails to realise that the earth is one great magnet.

45. Tradition declares from of old that the key to the

Mysteries was written upon the Emerald Tablet of Hermes, whereon were inscribed the words, "As above, so below." Apply the principles of physics to psychology, and the riddle will be read. He that hath ears to hear, let him hear.

46. Finally we come to the consideration of the significance of the Tarot cards associated with Netzach. These are the four Sevens of the Tarot pack.

47. As we are now coming within the sphere of influence of the earth-plane, it may be as well to explain what these lesser cards of the Tarot pack represent in divination. They symbolise the different modes of function of the different Sephirothic forces in the four worlds of the Qabalists. The suit of Wands corresponds to the spiritual level; Cups to the mental level; Swords to the astral plane; and Pentacles to the physical plane. Consequently, if the Seven of Pentacles turns up in a divination, it means that the influence of Netzach is playing a part on the physical level. There is an old proverb, "Lucky in love, unlucky at cards," which is but another way of saying that the person who is attractive to the opposite sex is usually in perpetual hot water. Venus is a disturbing influence in worldly affairs. She distracts from the serious business of life. As soon as her influence comes through to Malkuth, she must hand over the sceptre to Ceres and leave well alone. It is children, not love, that keep the home together. The Qabalistic name of the Seven of Pentacles is "Success Unfulfilled," and we have only to look at the lives of Cleopatra, Guinevere, Iseult, Héloïse to realise that Venus upon the physical plane has for her motto, "All for love, and the world well lost."

48. The suit of Swords is assigned to the astral plane. The secret title of the Seven of Swords is "Unstable Effort." How well does this express the action of Venus in the sphere of the emotions, with its short-lived intensity.

49. The secret title of the Seven of Cups is "Illusory Success." This card represents the working of Venus in the sphere of mind, where her influence is by no means conducive to clear-sightedness. We believe what we want to believe when we

are under the influence of Venus.   Upon this plane her motto might well be "Love is blind."

50. Only in the sphere of the spirit does Venus come into her own.   Here her card, the Seven of Wands, is called "Valour," which well describes the dynamic and vitalising influence she exerts when her spiritual significance is understood and employed.

51. Very interestingly do the four Tarot cards assigned to Netzach reveal the nature of the Venusian influence as it comes down the planes.   They teach us a very important lesson, for they show how essentially unstable this force is unless it is rooted in spiritual principle.   The lower forms of love are of the emotions, and essentially unreliable; but the higher love is dynamic and energising.

CHAPTER XXIII

HOD

TITLE: Hod, Glory. (Hebrew spelling; הוד:Hé, Vav, Daleth.)

MAGICAL IMAGE: An hermaphrodite.

SITUATION ON THE TREE: At the foot of the Pillar of Severity.

YETZIRATIC TEXT: The Eighth Path is called the Absolute or Perfect Intelligence because it is the mean of the Primordial, which has no root by which it can cleave or rest, save in the hidden places of Gedulah, from which emanates its proper essence.

GOD-NAME: Elohim Tseva'oth, the God of Hosts.

ARCHANGEL: Michael, Like unto God.

ORDER OF ANGELS: Bene Elohim, the Sons of the Gods.

MUNDANE CHAKRA: Kokhav, Mercury.

SPIRITUAL EXPERIENCE: Vision of Splendour.

VIRTUE: Truthfulness.

VICE: Falsehood. Dishonesty.

CORRESPONDENCE IN THE MICROCOSM: Loins and legs.

SYMBOLS: Names and Versicles and Apron.

TAROT CARDS: The four Eights.

        EIGHT OF WANDS: Swiftness.

        EIGHT OF CUPS: Abandoned success.

        EIGHT OF SWORDS: Shortened force.

        EIGHT OF PENTACLES: Prudence.

COLOUR IN ATZILUTH: Violet-purple.

    ,,   ,,   BRIAH: Orange.

    ,,   ,,   YETZIRAH: Russet-red.

    ,,   ,,   ASSIAH: Yellowish black, flecked with white.

I

1. The two root-powers of the universe are represented on the Tree of Life by Chokmah and Binah, Positive and Negative Force. It is held by the Qabalists that although each Sephirah emanates its next in numerical order, that these two Supernals,

the Tree being once established, are reflected down it diagonally in a particular way. This is clearly indicated in the Yetziratic Text of this Sephirah, wherein it says that Hod "has no root by which it can cleave or rest, save in the hidden places of Gedulah, from whence emanates its proper essence." Gedulah, be it remembered, is another name for Chesed.

2. Binah is the Giver of Form. Chesed is cosmic anabolism, the organisation of the units formulated by Binah into complex, interacting structures; Hod, the reflection of Chesed, is in its turn a Sephirah of Form, and represents this coagulating principle in another sphere.

3. Chokmah, on the other hand, is the dynamic principle; it reflects into Geburah, which is the Cosmic Katabolist, representing the breaking-down of the complex into the simple, thus releasing latent energy; and this reflects again into Netzach, the life-force of Nature.

4. It is important for the understanding of the five lower Sephiroth to note that the present stage of evolution has brought some degree of development of human consciousness in their Spheres. Tiphareth represents the higher consciousness wherein the individuality unites with the personality: Netzach and Hod represent the force and form aspects of astral consciousness respectively. Because human consciousness has made a degree of development in these spheres, their purely cosmic nature is considerably overlaid by its influences; and as human consciousness, being developed in Malkuth, is a consciousness of forms derived from the experience of physical sensations, the conditions of Malkuth are reflected back, though in a rarefied form, into Hod and Netzach, and in a lesser degree into Tiphareth; Yesod is even more markedly conditioned by the rising influence of Malkuth.

5. This is due to the fact that the mind of any being of a sufficient degree of development to have achieved an independent will works objectively on its environment, thereby modifying it. Let us make this clear by an illustration. Creatures of a lowly development, such as the simple forms of life that have no motile power, like sea-anemones, can exercise

very little influence over their environment; but a higher and more intelligent type of creature can exercise a great deal, forcing its environment, by its energy and intelligence, to conform to its will, as when a beaver builds a dam. Human beings, the highest of all the creatures of matter, have learnt to exercise a profound influence on their environment, so that the material globe is gradually being brought into subjection to man, whole spheres, in fact, being thus harnessed.

6. The conditions with regard to each level of consciousness are precisely analogous. The mind builds up out of mind-stuff and the spiritual nature out of the spiritual forces of the Cosmos in exactly the same way that the sea-anemone builds up its substance out of the nutriment brought to it by the water. The higher types of personality, however, are analogous to the higher types of animals in that they can in an increasing degree, according to their energy and capacity, influence their subtle environment; the mind, built up out of mind-stuff, making its influence felt in the plane of mind.

7. We observe in dealing with the astral plane, which is essentially the level of function of the denser aspects of the human mind, that the forces and factors of this plane present to consciousness as ethereal forms of a distinctly human type; and if we approach the subject philosophically, and not credulously, we are at a loss to explain how this can be. The initiate, however, has his explanation. He declares that it is the human mind itself which has created these forms by representing these intelligent natural forces to itself as having forms of a human type; reasoning by analogy that, because they are individualised, their individuality must have the same kind of vehicle for its manifestation as his own individuality.

8. This, of course, does not necessarily follow. In fact, these forms of life, left to their own devices, achieve incarnation in natural phenomena, their vehicles being co-ordinations of natural forces such as a river, a range of mountains, or a storm. Wherever man comes in touch with the astral, whether as psychic or magician, he always anthropomorphises, and creates forms in his own likeness to represent to himself the

elusive subtle forces that he is endeavouring to contact, understand, and harness to his will. He is a true child of the Great Mother, Binah, and carries his natural propensities for organising and form-making to whatever plane he is able to exalt consciousness.

9. The forms perceived on the astral plane by those who can see there, are the forms that have been made by the imagination of men to represent these subtle natural forces of other forms of evolution than the human. The intelligences of other forms of evolution than ours, if they come into touch with human life, can sometimes be persuaded to make use of these forms, just as a man puts on a diving-dress and descends into another element. A certain, and fundamental, type of magic deals with the making of these forms and the inducing of entities to ensoul them.

10. Let us consider what is done when such a process is afoot. Primitive man, who is much more psychic than civilised man, his mind not being so elaborately organised by education, is intuitively aware that there is a subtle something behind any highly organised unit of natural force that differentiates it from every other unit. Humans are subconsciously aware of this to a greater degree than they will admit; it is not for nothing that a ship is "she," and that we speak of "Father Thames." A savage, then, feeling this life behind phenomena, tries to get into touch with it in order that he may come to terms with it. As he obviously cannot hope to conquer it, he must make terms with it, just as he would with other alien lives ensouled in the bodies of another tribe. In order to come to terms there must be a parley. One cannot make terms with persons who will not parley. The savage thinks, reasoning by his own primitive method of analogy, that the beings behind the phenomena dwell in a kingdom similar to that in which his own dream-life goes on; as daydreams are close akin to the dreams of sleep, and have the advantage of being inducible at will, he tries to approach these beings of another sphere by entering their kingdom; that is to say, he fabricates in day-dream or phantasy the closest approach

he can to the visions of the night, and if he can achieve a high degree of concentration, he is able to close down his waking consciousness and enter voluntarily into the dream-state in a dream of his own determining.

11. In order to achieve this end, he builds up in his imagination a mental picture intended to represent the being that is the presiding genius of the natural phenomenon he wishes to come to terms with; he builds it up repeatedly; he adores it; he prays to it; he invokes it. If his invocation be sufficiently fervent, the being he is seeking will hear him telepathically and may become interested in what he is doing; if his adoration and sacrifices are agreeable to it, its co-operation may be obtained. Gradually it may become tamed and domesticated; and finally, it may be persuaded to ensoul from time to time the form that has been built up out of mind-stuff for its vehicle. Success in this operation depends, of course, on the degree to which the worshipper can appreciate through sympathy the nature of the being he is bent upon invoking, and he can only do this in proportion as his own temperament partakes of its nature.

12. If this process is successful, then we have the domestication of a portion of the life of Nature, and its incarnation in a form built for it by its worshippers. As long as the astral form is kept alive by the appropriate kind of worship, carried out by worshippers who have the necessary capacity to enter into sympathetic communion with that kind of life, there is an incarnated god, available for contacting, brought down within the range of human perception. Should the worship cease, the god withdraws to his own place in the bosom of Nature. Should other worshippers come along, however, who possess the knowledge necessary to build a form in accordance with the nature of the life that is to be invoked, and the imaginative sympathy necessary to invoke it, it is a comparatively simple matter to attract into the form once more the life that was accustomed to ensoul it; no more difficult, at least, than to catch with a basket of oats a horse that has run wild on the ranges.

13. Now, it may be said, all this is the wildest speculation and sheer dogmatism. How do I know that that is the way

in which primitive man went to work? Because that is the way of going to work that has come down in the secret Mystery Tradition from very ancient times, and because when it is used by anyone who has acquired the necessary degree of skill in concentration and knows the symbols that are used for building the different forms, the method works, and back come the Old Gods to the altar fires re-kindled. Definite results are obtained in the consciousness of the worshippers; and if they borrow the technique of the spiritualist, and a materialising medium is available, phenomena of a very definite kind are produced.

14. It is the method that is used in working the Mass by those priests who have knowledge. There are two types of priest in the Roman Church: the beneficed parish clergy and the men who belong to monastic Orders and undertake parish, and especially home mission, work as part of their service. These monks frequently bring to the working of the Mass a very high degree of magical power, as any psychic can testify. It is the ensouling of an astral form with spiritual force which is the real act of Transubstantiation. It is in the knowledge of these things, and in the possession of organised bodies of men and women trained in their use in the encloistered Orders, that the strength of the One Catholic and Apostolic Church lies; it is the lack of any such inner knowledge which is the weakness of the schismatic communions, a lack that makes the Anglican rituals, even when worked with full ceremonial, as water unto wine when compared with the Roman rituals; for the men who work them have no knowledge of the secret workings which are traditional in the Roman communion, and are not trained in the technique of visualising. I am not a Catholic, and never shall be, because I would not submit to their discipline, nor do I believe that there is only One Name under heaven whereby men may be saved, much as I revere that Name, but I know power when I see it, and I respect it.

15. But the power of the Roman Church does not lie in charter, but in function. It is powerful, not because Peter received the Keys (which he probably didn't), but because it

knows its job.   There is no reason why priests of the Anglican communion should not work with power if they apply the principles I have explained in these pages.

II

16. For the full understanding of the philosophy of magic we must remember that single Sephiroth are never functional; for function one must have the Pair of Opposites in balanced equilibrium, resulting in an equilibrated Third which is functional.   The Pair of Opposites, by themselves, are not functional because they are mutually neutralising; it is only when they unite in balanced force to flow forth as a Third, after the symbolism of Father, Mother, and Child, that they achieve dynamic activity, as distinguished from the latent force which is for ever locked up in them, awaiting to be called forth.

17. The functioning triangle of the Lower Triad consists of Hod, Netzach, and Yesod.   Hod and Netzach, as we have noted before, are respectively Form and Force on the astral plane.   Yesod is the basis of etheric substance, Akasha, or the Astral Light, as it is variously called.   Hod is especially the Sphere of Magic, because it is the sphere of the formulation of forms, and is therefore the sphere in which the magician actually works, for it is his mind that formulates the forms, and his will that makes the link with the natural forces of the Sphere of Netzach that ensoul them.   Be it noted, however, that without the contacts of Netzach, the force aspect of the astral, there could be no ensouling; and with Netzach, being the Sphere of emotions, the contacts are made through sym-

pathy and "feeling with." The power of the will projects
the magician out of Hod, but only the power of sympathy can
take him into Netzach. A cold-blooded person of dominating
will can no more be an adept working with power than can a
fluidically sympathetic person of pure emotion. The power of
the concentrated will is necessary to enable the magician to
gather himself together for his work, but the power of imaginative sympathy is essential to enable him to make his contacts.
For it is only through our power to enter imaginatively into
the life of types of existence different to our own that we can
pick up our contacts with the forces of Nature. To attempt
to dominate them by pure will, cursing them by the Mighty
Names of God if they resist, is sheer sorcery.

18. As we have already noted, it is through the corresponding factors in our own temperaments that we come into touch
with the forces of Nature. It is the Venus within that puts us
in touch with the influences symbolised by Netzach. It is the
magical capacity of our own mind that puts us in touch with
the forces of the Sphere of Hod-Mercury-Thoth. If there is no
Venus in our own nature, no capacity to respond to the call of
love, the gates of the Sphere of Netzach will never open to us
and we shall never receive its initiation. Equally, if we have
no magical capacity, which is the work of the intellectual
imagination, the Sphere of Hod will be a closed book to us.
We can only operate in a Sphere after we have received the
initiation of that Sphere, which, in the language of the Mysteries, confers its powers. In the technical working of the
Mysteries these initiations are conferred on the physical plane
by means of ceremonial, which may be effectual, or may not.
The gist of the matter lies in the fact that one cannot waken
into activity what is not already latent. Life is the real
initiator; the experiences of life stimulate into function the
capacities of our temperaments in such degree as we possess
them. The ceremony of initiation, and the teachings that
should be given in the various grades, are simply designed to
make conscious what was previously subconscious, and to
bring under the control of the will, directed by the higher

intelligence, those developed reaction-capacities which have hitherto only responded blindly to their appropriate stimuli.

19. Be it well noted that it is only in proportion as our capacities for reaction are lifted out of the sphere of emotional reflexes and brought under rational control that we can make of them magical powers. It is only when the aspirant, having the capacity to respond on all planes to the call of Venus, can easily and without effort refrain at will from responding, that he can be made an initiate of the Sphere of Netzach. This is why it is said of the adept that he has the use of all things, but is dependent upon nothing.

20. These concepts are shadowed forth for those who have eyes to see in the symbolism of Hod. The Yetziratic Text declares that Hod is the Perfect Intelligence because it is the mean of the Primordial. In other words, it is power in equilibrium, for the word "mean" implies a position half-way between two extremes.

21. The concept of inhibited reaction and satisfaction foregone is expressed in the title of the Eight of Cups of the Tarot pack, whose secret name is "Abandoned Success." The suit of Cups, in the Tarot symbolism, is under the influence of Venus and represents the different aspects and influences of love. "Abandoned Success," the inhibition of the instinctive reaction which would give satisfaction—in other words, sublimation—is the key to the powers of Hod. But remember that sublimation is not the same thing as either repression or eradication, and it applies to the instinct of self-preservation as well as to the instinct of reproduction, with which it is exclusively associated in the popular mind.

22. The same concept reappears in the secret title of the Eight of Swords, which is "The Lord of Shortened Force." We get a clear image in these words of the checking, or braking of dynamic power in order that it may be brought under control.

23. In the Eight of Pentacles, which represents the nature of Hod manifesting on the material plane, we have the Lord of Prudence—again a checking and inhibiting influence. But all

these three negative, inhibiting cards are summed up under the presidency of the Eight of Wands, which represents the action of the Sphere of Hod on the spiritual plane, and this card is called the Lord of Swiftness.

24. We see, then, that it is through inhibitions and refrainings on the lower planes that the dynamic energy of the highest plane is rendered available. It is in the Sphere of Hod that the rational mind imposes these inhibitions on the dynamic animal nature of the soul; condensing them; formulating them; directing them by limiting them and preventing diffusion. This is the operation of the magic that works with symbols. By its means the free-moving natural forces are constrained and directed to ends that are willed and designed. This power of direction and control is only obtained by the sacrifice of fluidity, and Hod is therefore aptly said to be the reflection of Binah through Chesed.

25. Having considered the general principles of the Sphere of Hod, we are now in a position to consider its symbolism in detail.

26. The meaning of the Hebrew word Hod is Glory, and this suggests at once to the mind that in this, the first Sphere in which forms are definitely organised, the radiance of the Primordial is shown forth to human consciousness. Physicists tell us that light is only rendered visible as blue sky owing to its reflection from the particles of dust in the atmosphere. Absolutely dustless atmosphere is absolutely dark atmosphere. And so it is in the metaphysics of the Tree. The glory of God can only shine forth in manifestation when there are forms to manifest it.

27. The Magical Image of Hod affords a very interesting subject for meditation. Those who have grasped the significance of the preceding pages will see how well the form-and-force nature of magical working is summed up in this symbol of the being in whom are combined the male and female elements.

28. Hod is essentially the sphere of forms ensouled by the forces of Nature; and conversely, it is the sphere in which the forces of Nature take on sensible form.

29. The Yetziratic Text has already been discussed at length, and to that discussion the reader can refer for its elucidation.

30. The God-name of Hod, Elohim Tseva'oth, God of Hosts, contains the hermaphroditic symbol in a very interesting way, for the word Elohim is a feminine noun with a masculine plural, thus indicating in the manner of the Qabalists that it represents a dual type of activity, or force functioning through an organisation. All three Sephiroth in the Negative Pillar of the Tree have the word Elohim as part of the God-name. Tetragrammaton Elohim in Binah; Elohim Gibbor in Geburah; and Elohim Tseva'oth in Hod.

31. The word Tseva'oth means a host or army, and so we get the idea of the Divine Life manifesting in Hod by means of a host of forms ensouled with force, in contradistinction to the fluidic activity of Netzach.

32. The assignation of the mighty Archangel Michael to Hod again gives us food for thought. He is always represented as trampling upon a serpent and piercing it with a sword, and frequently holds in his hand a pair of balances, symbolic of equilibrium and expressive of the same idea as the Yetziratic words, "Mean of the Primordial."

33. The serpent upon which the great Archangel treads is primitive force, the phallic serpent of the Freudians; and this glyph teaches us that it is the restrictive "prudence" of Hod which "shortens" primitive force and prevents it from overflowing its boundaries. The Fall, be it remembered, is represented on the Tree by the Great Serpent with seven heads which overpasses the bounds set for it and raises its crowned heads even unto Daath. It is very interesting to observe the manner in which the symbols weave in and out of each other, and reinforce and interpret each other's significance and yield their fruits to Qabalistic contemplation.

34. The Order of Angels functioning in Hod are the Bene Elohim, the Sons of the Gods. Again we have the concept of the "God of Hosts" or armies. One of the most important concepts of arcane science concerns the working of the Creator through intermediaries. The uninitiated and profane con-

ceive of God as working as the labourer works, who adds brick to brick with his hands, fashioning the edifice; but the initiated conceive of God as working as the Great Architect of the Universe, designing His plans on the plane of archetypes; to Whom come the overseers, the archangels, for their instructions, these last directing the armies of humble toilers who add stone to stone according to the archetypal plan of the Most High. Whenever did the architect designing the edifice work upon it with his two unaided hands? Never, not even when the universe was abuilding.

35. The Mundane Chakra, as we have already noted, is Mercury, and its symbolism as Hermes-Thoth we have already considered.

36. The Spiritual Experience assigned to this Sephirah is the Vision of Splendour, which is the realisation of the glory of God manifesting in the created world. The initiate of Hod sees behind the appearance of created things and discerns their Creator, and in the realisation of the splendour of Nature as the garment of the Ineffable he receives his illumination and becomes a co-worker with the Great Artificer. It is this realisation of the spiritual forces manipulating all manifestations and appearances which is the key to the powers of Hod as wielded in the Magic of Light. It is by making himself a channel for these forces that the Master of White Magic brings order into the disorder of the Spheres of Unbalanced Force, not by deflecting the invisible powers to his personal will. He is the equilibrator of the unbalanced, not the arbitrary manipulator of Nature.

37. In this Sphere, which is the Sphere of Mercury-Hermes, god of science and books, how clearly can we see that the supreme virtue is truthfulness, and that the obverse aspect of this Sephirah is that which reveals Mercury in his aspect as the god of thieves and cunning rogues. In esoteric ethics it is realised that each plane has its own standard of right and wrong. The standard of the physical plane is strength; the standard of the astral plane is beauty; the standard of the mental plane is truth; and the standard of the spiritual plane is that of right

and wrong as we understand the terms; therefore there is no ethic except in terms of spiritual value; all else is at best expediency. In the Sphere which is essentially the Sphere of the concrete mind how right it is that the Qabalah should give the supreme virtue as truthfulness.

38. The Correspondence in the Microcosm is given as the loins and legs, in accordance with the astrological ruling of the planet Mercury.

39. The symbols associated with Hod are given as the names and versicles and the apron. The names are the Words of Power wherein the magus sums up and evokes into conscious-ness the multiform potencies of the Beni Elohim. These names are by no manner of means arbitrary and barbaric vocables, without etymology or meaning. They are philo-sophical formulæ. In some cases their interpretation is etymo-logical, as in the case of the Egyptian deities, whose names are built up out of the names of potencies and symbols when used to indicate composite forces. In all systems of magic, however, which have their root in the Qabalah, the magical names are built up out of the numerical value of the consonants of whatever sacred alphabet is used; there is a Greek, an Arabic, and a Coptic Qabalah, as well as the better-known Hebrew one. These consonants, when replaced by the appropriate numerals, yield a number, which can be dealt with mathe-matically in many ways. Some of these ways are according to the methods of pure mathematics, the results being then translated back into letters again, and showing very interesting correspondences with the names of similar or related potencies. This is a very curious aspect of Qabalistic lore, and in the hands of competent exponents yields interesting results; it is, how-ever, full of pitfalls for the unwary, for there is no limit to what it can be made to yield, and only a sound knowledge of first principles can tell us when the analogies are legitimate or otherwise, and prevent us from falling into credulity and superstition.

40. The versicles are mantric phrases, a mantra being a sonorous phrase which, when repeated over and over after the

manner of a rosary, works upon the mind as a special form of auto-suggestion, the psychology of which is too complex to be entered upon now.

41. The apron has immediate associations for the initiates of Solomon the Wise; it is the characteristic garment of the initiate in the Lesser Mysteries, who is always deemed figuratively to be a craftsman, that is a maker of forms, and as the Sephirah Hod is the Sphere of the operations of the makers of magical forms, it will be seen that this symbolism is again apposite. The apron covers and conceals the Moon-centre, Yesod, concerning which we shall speak in its appropriate place. As has already been noted, Yesod is the functional aspect of the Pair of Opposites of the astral plane.

42. Concerning the four Eights of the Tarot pack, assigned to this Sephirah, we have already spoken on a previous page.

43. To sum up, then, in Hod we have the Sphere of formal magic as distinguished from simple mind power. The forms that are formulated thereon by the magician initiating the forces of nature are the Beni Elohim, or Sons of the Gods.

CHAPTER XXIV

YESOD

TITLE: Yesod, the Foundation. (Hebrew spelling: יסוד: Yod, Samech, Vav, Daleth.)

MAGICAL IMAGE: A beautiful naked man, very strong.

SITUATION ON THE TREE: Towards the base of the Pillar of Equilibrium.

YETZIRATIC TEXT: The Ninth Path is called the Pure Intelligence because it purifies the Emanations. It proves and corrects the designing of their representations, and disposes the unity with which they are designed without diminution or division.

GOD-NAME: Shaddai El Chai, the Almighty Living God.

ARCHANGEL: Gabriel, Strong man, or Hero, of God.

ORDER OF ANGELS: Keruvim, the Strong.

MUNDANE CHAKRA: Levanah, the Moon.

SPIRITUAL EXPERIENCE: Vision of the Machinery of the Universe.

VIRTUE: Independence.

VICE: Idleness.

CORRESPONDENCE IN THE MICROCOSM: Reproductive organs.

SYMBOLS: The Perfumes and sandals.

TAROT CARDS: The four Nines.

> NINE OF WANDS: Great strength.
> NINE OF CUPS: Material happiness.
> NINE OF SWORDS: Despair and cruelty.
> NINE OF PENTACLES: Material gain.

COLOUR IN ATZILUTH: Indigo.

„ „ BRIAH: Violet.

„ „ YETZIRAH: Very dark purple.

„ „ ASSIAH: Citrine, flecked with azure.

I

1. The study of the symbolism of Yesod reveals two apparently incongruous sets of symbols. Upon the one hand

we have the conception of Yesod as the foundation of the universe, established in strength; this is indicated by the recurrence of the idea of strength, as in the Magical Image of a beautiful naked man, very strong, the God-name of Shaddai, Almighty, the Keruvim, the strong angels, and the Nine of Wands, whose secret name is the Lord of Great Strength. But upon the other hand we have the Moon symbolism, which is very fluidic, in a continual state of flux and reflux, under the presidency of Gabriel, the archangel of the element of Water.

2. How are we to reconcile these conflicting concepts? The answer is to be found in the words of the Yetziratic Text, which says of the Ninth Path that it "purifies the Emanations. It proves and corrects the designing of their representations, and disposes of the unity with which they are designed without diminution or division." This concept is further illuminated by the nature of the Spiritual Experience assigned to Yesod, which is described as "the Vision of the Machinery of the Universe."

3. We get the concept, then, of the fluidic waters of chaos being finally gathered up and organised by means of the "representations" that were "designed" in Hod; this final "proving, correcting, and disposing of the unity" of these "representations" or formative images resulting in the organisation of the "Machinery of the Universe," the·vision of which constitutes the spiritual experience of this Sephirah. In fact, Yesod might aptly be described as the Sphere of the Machinery of the Universe. If we liken the kingdom of earth to a great ship, then Yesod would be the engine-room.

4. Yesod is the sphere of that peculiar substance, partaking of the nature of both mind and matter, which is called the Æther of the Wise, the Akasha, or the Astral Light, according to the terminology that is being used. It is not the same as the ether of the physicists, which is the fire element of the Sphere of Malkuth; but is to that ether what that ether is to dense matter; it is, in fact, the basis of the phenomena which the physicist attributes to his empirical ether. The Æther of the Wise might, in fact, be called the root of the ether of physics.

5. The material universe is an insoluble riddle to the materialist because he insists on trying to explain it in terms of its own plane. This is a thing that can never be done in any sphere of thought. Nothing can ever be explained in terms of itself, but only by being resumed in a greater whole. The four elements of the ancients find their explanation in a fifth, the Æther, as initiates have always maintained. For it is a doctrine of esoteric philosophy that any four visible states always have their root in a fifth, an invisible state. For instance, the Four Worlds of the Qabalists have their root behind the Veils of the Unmanifest. It is only by positing this unmanifest fifth, and assigning to it certain attributes deduced from the manifest four as being essential in the prime cause, that we are able to arrive at any understanding of the nature of the four. So do we find in Yesod the unmanifest fifth of the four elements of Malkuth, the fire of the ancients answering to the ether of the moderns, and earth, water, and air to the solid, liquid, and gaseous states of matter.

6. Yesod, then, must be conceived of as the receptacle of the emanations of all the other Sephiroth, as is taught by the Qabalists, and as the immediate and only transmitter of these emanations to Malkuth, the physical plane. As the Yetziratic Text says, it is the function of Yesod to purify the emanations, and to prove and correct them; consequently it is in the Sphere of Yesod that all operations are carried out which are designed for the correcting of the Sphere of dense matter, or in any way to dispose of its unity of design. Yesod, then, is the all-important Sphere for any magic which is designed to take effect in the physical world.

7. Now be it well noted that all Spheres operate according to their nature, and that that nature cannot in any way be altered by any magical or miraculous influence, however powerful; we can only "correct" the "designing" of the representations. The things represented remain constant. The conditions of the material world cannot therefore be arbitrarily disposed of, even by the highest spiritual force, as is believed by those who pray to God to intervene on their

behalf, healing their diseases or giving rain upon earth; neither can they any more be influenced by the most powerful wizard with his spells. The only approach to Malkuth is through Yesod, and the approach to Yesod is through Hod, where the "representations" are "designed." Let us once and for all disabuse our minds of the idea that spirit can work directly upon matter; it never does so. Spirit works through mind, and mind works through the Æther; and the Æther, which is the framework of matter and the vehicle of the life-forces, can be manipulated within the limits of its nature, which are by no means inconsiderable. All miraculous and supernatural happenings, therefore, are brought about by the manipulation of the natural qualities of the Æther, and if we understood the nature of the Æther, we should understand the rationale of their production. We should no more attribute them to the direct intervention of God, or to the activities of the spirits of the departed, than we attribute nowadays the phenomena of combustion to the activities of phlogiston, which a previous generation believed to be the active principle of fire, whose presence or absence determined whether a given substance would burn or not. There are men living to-day who learnt about phlogiston in their school-days, and have seen the change of thought come about; equally, the day will come when men will look upon psychic phenomena and "spiritual" healing as we look upon phlogiston.

8. At the present state of our knowledge it is not possible to give a very full account of the nature of the Yesodic Æther. We can, however, state certain things about it that have been learnt by experience. Much has been learnt by experiments with ectoplasm, which is very close akin to it in nature; in fact, one might describe it as organic Æther, in contradistinction to the ether of physics, which is inorganic Æther. We know that ectoplasm takes on forms, and holds them and relinquishes them with equal readiness, showing that it is not the form which confines the life, but the life that determines the form. We likewise know that ectoplasm can be emanated and absorbed, though we do not know the conditions that

govern this phenomenon. Ectoplasm is, in fact, a kind of ethereal protoplasm; and we might conceive of the Æther or Astral Light as bearing the same relationship to ectoplasm as ectoplasm bears to protoplasm.

9. But although we no more know the ultimate nature of the astral Æther than we understand the ultimate nature of electricity, nevertheless we know by observation that it possesses certain properties. We do not merely deduce these properties; we know they exist by experience, because they enable us to manipulate this subtle substance in certain definite ways, within, as has already been explained, the limits of its own nature. Two of these properties are all-important to the work of the practical occultist, forming, in fact, the basis of his whole system.

10. The first of these properties is the capacity of the astral Æther to be moulded into forms by the mind; the second is the capacity of the astral Æther to hold the molecules of dense matter in its mesh-like lines of tension as in a rack of pigeon-holes. It may be asked, how do we know that the Æther possesses these qualities, so vital to our magical hypothesis? We answer that the existence of these properties is the only explanation of the properties of living matter and conscious mind. We cannot explain either mind or matter in terms of themselves alone; we cannot explain mind without employing terms of sensation, and we cannot explain living matter without employing terms of consciousness. Sensation must always be an affair of both mind and matter, inexplicable in isolation. To explain neural sensation we must posit a substance that is intermediate between mind and matter; to understand purposive movement we equally require the existence of such a substance—that is, which possesses the power to receive and hold the impress of thought and to in-fluence the position in space of the atomic units of matter. These are the properties we assign to our hypothetical astral Æther, advancing the same arguments in justification of this proceeding as have been accepted on behalf of a similar pro-ceeding in the case of the ether of physics. We plead prece-

dent for our hypothesis; and if the arguments in favour of the ether of physics are acceptable, it is difficult to see why an Æther should not be permitted to psychology. It is an old maxim that hypotheses should not be unnecessarily multiplied, but when an hypothesis such as that of ether has proved so fruitful, we are surely amply justified in experimenting with a similar one in the sister science of psychology. One thing is quite certain, psychology never made any real progress while it limited itself to the materialistic viewpoint and regarded consciousness as an epiphenomenon, that is to say as an irrelevant and purposeless by-product of physiological activity —if anything in Nature can be called irrelevant and purposeless. Let us learn a lesson from coal-tar, the irrelevant and purposeless by-product of the production of gas—to be practically given away to anyone who wanted to tar a fence, subsequently found to be the source of most valuable chemicals, dye-stuffs, and drugs.

II

11. From the point of view of magic, Yesod is the all-important Sephirah, just as Tiphareth is the functional sphere of mysticism, with its transcendent contacts with the Supernal. If the Tree of Life be considered as a whole, it will be seen clearly that it works in triads. The Three Supernals having their correlatives on a lower arc in Chesed, Geburah, and Tiphareth. Anyone who has had experience of practical Qabalism knows that for all practical purposes Tiphareth is Kether for us while we tabernacle in this house of flesh, for no man may look upon the face of God and live. We can only see the Father reflected in the Son, and Tiphareth "shows us the Father."

12. Netzach, Hod, and Yesod form the Lower Triad, overshadowed by Tiphareth as the Lower Self is overshadowed by the Higher Self. One might, in fact, say that the four lower Sephiroth form the Personality, or unit of incarnation, of the Tree; the Higher Triad of Chesed, Geburah, and

Tiphareth form the Individuality, or Higher Self, and the Three Supernals correspond to the Divine Spark.

13. It will be observed that although each Sephirah is considered to emanate its successor, the Triads are always represented, when once emanated and in equilibrium, as a Pair of Opposites manifesting in a Functional Third. In this, the Lower Triad, then, we find Netzach and Hod equilibrated in Yesod, which is conceived as receiving their emanations. But it also received the emanations of Tiphareth, and through Tiphareth, of Kether, because there is always a line of force working down a Pillar; consequently, as it received also from Netzach and Hod the influences that they in their turn have received from their respective Pillars, it may aptly be called, in the words of Qabalists, the "receptacle of the emanations"; and it is from Yesod that Malkuth receives the influx of the Divine forces.

14. Yesod also is of supreme importance to the practical occultist, because it is the first Sphere with which he makes acquaintance when he commences to "rise on the planes," and lifts consciousness above Malkuth. Having trodden the terrible Thirty-second Path of the Tav or Cross of Suffering, and of Saturn, he enters Yesod, the Treasure House of Images, the sphere of Maya, Illusion. Yesod, considered by itself, is unquestionably the Sphere of Illusion, because the Treasure House of Images is none other than the Reflecting Æther of the Earth-sphere, and corresponds in the microcosm to the Unconscious of the psychologists, filled with ancient and forgotten things, repressed since the childhood of the race. The keys that unlock the doors of the Treasure House of Images and enable us to command its denizens are to be found in Hod, the Sphere of Magic. It is truly said in the Mysteries that no degree becomes functional until one has taken the next. Anyone who tries to function as a magician in Yesod soon learns his error, for although he can perceive the Images in the Treasure House, he has no word of power with which to command them. Therefore in initiation upon the Western Path, at any rate (I cannot answer for the Eastern, not knowing

it), the grades of the Lesser Mysteries go straight up the Central Pillar to Tiphareth, and do not follow the line of the Lightning Flash. In Tiphareth the initiate takes the first grade of adepthood, and from there returns, if he so desires, to learn the technique of the magician relative to the Personality of the Tree, that is to say the macrocosmic unit of incarnation. If he does not desire this, but wishes to become free from the wheel of Birth and Death, he proceeds up the Central Pillar, which is also called by the Qabalists the Path of the Arrow, and passes over the Abyss into Kether. He who enters this Light cometh not forth again.

15. Yesod is also the Sphere of the Moon; therefore to understand its significance we must know something about the way in which the Moon is regarded in occultism. It is held by initiates that the Moon separated from the Earth at a period when evolution was on the cusp between the etheric phase of its development and the phase of dense matter. Those who are familiar with the terminology of astrology will know that the cusp is that phase between two signs wherein the influence of both is intermingled. The Moon, then, has something of the material in its composition, hence the luminous globe we see in the sky; but the really important part of its composition is etheric, because it was during the phase of evolution when life was developing the etheric form that the Moon had its heyday, and for this reason this phase is called by some occultists the Luna Phase of evolution. Those who want to know more of this subject will find it dealt with in *The Rosicrucian Cosmo-conception*, by Max Heindel, and *The Secret Doctrine*, by Mme Blavatsky. As the Qabalists use a different system of classification to the Vedantists, we cannot open up the vast subject of the "Rays and the Rounds" in these pages. It must suffice to give dogmatically certain facts known to occultists and indicate where the reader can find further information if he desires it.

16. The Moon and the Earth, according to the occult theory, share one etheric double, though their two physical bodies are separate, and the Moon is the senior partner; that

is to say, in etheric matters the Moon is the positive pole of
the battery, and the Earth the negative one. Yesod, as we
have already seen, reflects the Sun of Tiphareth, which in its
turn is Kether on a lower arc. Astronomers have long told
us that the Moon shines by borrowed light, reflected from the
Sun, and they are now beginning to hint that the Sun may
receive its fiery energy from outer space. Translated into
Qabalistic terminology, outer space would be the Great
Unmanifest, and the Qabalists have taught this doctrine since
the days when Enoch walked with God and was not, for God
had taken him—in other words, he had received the initiation
of Kether.

17. It will be seen from the above that Yesod-Luna is ever
in a state of flux and reflux, because the amount of sunlight
received and reflected waxes and wanes in a twenty-eight day
cycle. Malkuth-Earth is also in a state of flux and reflux in
a twenty-four hour cycle, and for the same reason. Likewise
Malkuth-Earth has a three hundred and sixty-five day cycle, of
which the phases are marked by the Equinoxes and the Solstices.
It is the interacting set of these tides which is all-important to
the practical occultist, because so much of his work depends
upon them. The charts of these tides have always been kept
secret, and some of them are exceedingly complex. As these
concern the secret workings, the genuine and legitimate occult
secrets, which are only given after initiation, they cannot be
dealt with in these pages. Enough has been said, however,
to indicate that certain tides in the lunar Æther exist and are
important, and that students of the occult are probably wasting
their time if they try to operate without the necessary charts.

18. These lunar tides play a very important part in the
physiological processes of both plants and animals, and
especially in the germination and growth of plants and the
reproduction of animals, as witness the twenty-eight day lunar
sexual cycle of the human female. The male has a sexual cycle
based on the solar year, but in the artificially lit and heated
houses of civilisation this cycle is not so marked, though the
poet drew our attention to the fact that "In the spring a young

man's fancy lightly turns to thoughts of love," and the reference has been found so apt that it is almost too hackneyed for quotation.

19. It is the light of the Moon which is the stimulative factor in these etheric activities, and as Earth and Moon share one etheric double, all etheric activities are at their most active when the Moon is at its full. Likewise, during the dark of the Moon, etheric energy is at its lowest, and unorganised forces have a tendency to rise up and give trouble. The Dragon of the Qliphoth raises his multiple heads. In consequence, practical occult work is best let alone during the dark by all but experienced workers. The life-giving forces are relatively weak and the unbalanced forces relatively strong; the result, in inexperienced hands, is chaos.

20. All psychics and sensitives are conscious of the set of these cosmic tides, and even those who are not avowedly sensitive are affected by them far more than is generally realised, especially in illness when the physical energies are low.

21. Not a great deal can be said concerning Yesod, because in her are hidden the keys of the magical workings. We must therefore content ourselves with elucidating the symbolism in a somewhat cryptic form, though he that hath ears to hear is at liberty to use them.

22. We have already noted the curious two-sided nature of Netzach and Hod, the magical image of Hod being a hermaphrodite, and Venus-Aphrodite sometimes being represented among the ancients as bearded. In Yesod again we meet with this dual symbolism, and yet again, as we shall see presently, in Malkuth. This indicates clearly that in these Sephiroth belonging to the lower levels of the Tree we must very definitely recognise a form and force side in each one. This comes out very clearly in both Yesod and Malkuth, to which both gods and goddesses have to be assigned.

23. Yesod is essentially the Sphere of the Moon, and as such comes under the presidency of Diana, the moon-goddess of the Greeks. Now Diana was primarily a chaste goddess, ever-virgin, and when the over-presumptive Actæon annoyed

her, he was torn to pieces by his own hunting-hounds. Diana, however, was represented at Ephesus as the Many-breasted, and regarded as a fertility goddess. Moreover, Isis is also a lunar goddess, as indicated by the lunar crescent upon her brow, which in Hathor becomes the cow-horns, the cow being among all peoples the especial symbol of maternity. In the Qabalistic symbolism, the generative organs are assigned to Yesod.

24. All this is very puzzling at first sight, for the symbols appear to be mutually exclusive. Carried a step further, however, we begin to find connecting links between the ideas.

25. The Moon has three goddesses assigned to her, Diana, Selene or Luna, and Hecate, the latter being the goddess of witchcraft and enchantments, and also presiding over childbirth.

26. There is also a very important moon-god, none other than Thoth himself, Lord of Magic. So then, when we find Hecate in Greece and Thoth in Egypt both assigned to the Moon, we cannot fail to recognise the importance of the Moon in matters magical. What then is the key to the magical Moon, who is sometimes a virgin goddess and sometimes a fertility goddess?

27. The answer is not very far to seek. It is to be found in the rhythmical nature of the Moon, and, in fact, in the rhythmical nature of sex-life in the female. There are times when Diana is many-breasted; there are times when her hounds tear the intruder to pieces.

28. In dealing with the rhythms of Luna we are dealing with etheric, not physical, conditions. The magnetism of living creatures waxes and wanes with a definite tide. It is a thing that is not difficult to observe when one knows what to look for. It shows itself most clearly in relations between persons in whom magnetism is fairly evenly balanced. Sometimes one will be in the ascendant, and sometimes the other.

29. Now, it may be asked, if the Sphere of Yesod is etheric, why are the generative organs assigned to this sphere, for

surely their function is physical, if anything is? The answer
to that question is to be found in the knowledge of the subtler
aspects of sex which appears to be entirely lost to the Western
world. It cannot be entered upon in detail in these pages, and
it must suffice to point out that all the more important aspects
of sex are etheric and magnetic. We might liken it to an ice-
berg, five-sixths of whose bulk is below the surface. The
actual physical reactions of sex form a very small proportion,
and by no means the most vital portion of its functioning. It
is owing to our ignorance of this that so many marriages fail
to fulfil the purpose of the welding of two halves into a
perfect whole.

30. We take no account of the magical side of marriage,
despite the fact that the Church classes it as a sacrament. Now
a sacrament is defined as an outward and visible sign of an
inward and spiritual grace, and it is that inward and spiritual
grace which is so seldom found in the marriage act of the
Anglo-Saxon races, with their relatively frigid temperament
and contempt for the body. That inward and spiritual grace
which makes of marriage a true sacrament after its kind is
not the grace of sublimation, or renunciation, or a purity of
denial and abstention; it is the grace of the blessing of Pan in
the joy in natural things so beautifully expressed by Walt
Whitman in his poem-series, "Children of Adam."

31. The assignation to Yesod of the perfumes and sandals
is very significant. These two things play a very important
part in magical operations. The sandals, or soft heelless
slippers that give free play to the foot, are always used in
ceremonial work to tread the magical circle. They are as
important a part of the equipment of the practical occultist as
his rod of power. God said unto Moses, "Put off thy shoes
from off thy feet, for the place whereon thou standest is
holy ground." The adept makes holy ground for himself by
placing upon his feet the consecrated sandals. The floor-cloth,
of the appropriate colour and marked with the appropriate
symbols, is also an important piece of lodge furniture. It is
designed to concentrate the earth magnetism used in the

operation in the same way that the altar is the focus of the spiritual forces. Through our feet we pick up the earth magnetism; and when that magnetism is of a special kind, we use special slippers that shall not inhibit it.

32. The perfumes, too, are very important in ceremonial operations, for they represent the etheric side of the affair. Their psychological influence is well known, but the fine art of using them psychologically has been but little studied outside occult lodges. The use of perfumes is the most effectual way of playing on the emotions, and consequently of changing the focus of consciousness. How quickly do our thoughts turn away from earthly things when the drifting smoke of incense comes to us from the high altar; how quickly do they return to them again when we get a whiff of patchouli from the next pew!

33. And in the four Tarot cards assigned to this Sephirah how clearly do we see the workings of the etheric magnetism appearing. There is Great Strength when we are on the earth-contacts and blessed of Pan; there is also Material Happiness; in fact, without the blessing of Pan there can be no material happiness because there is no peace of the nerves. On its negative side, however, are to be found the depths of Despair and Cruelty; but with the earth-contacts firm under our feet there comes Material Gain because we are adequate to deal with the material plane.

CHAPTER XXV

MALKUTH

TITLE: Malkuth, the Kingdom. (Hebrew spelling: מלכות:
Mem, Lamed, Kaph, Vav, Tav.)

MAGICAL IMAGE: A young woman, crowned and throned.

SITUATION ON THE TREE: At the base of the Pillar of
Equilibrium.

YETZIRATIC TEXT: The Tenth Path is called the Resplendent
Intelligence because it is exalted above every head and
sits upon the Throne of Binah. It illuminates the
splendours of all the Lights, and causes an influence to
emanate from the Prince of Countenances, the Angel of
Kether.

TITLES GIVEN TO MALKUTH: The Gate. The Gate of Death.
The Gate of the Shadow of Death. The Gate of Tears.
The Gate of Justice. The Gate of Prayer. The Gate
of the Daughter of the Mighty Ones. The Gate of the
Garden of Eden. The Inferior Mother. Malkah, the
Queen. Kallah, the Bride. The Virgin.

GOD-NAME: Adonai Melekh or Adon ha-Arets.

ARCHANGEL: Sandalphon.

CHOIR OF ANGELS: Ishim, Souls of Fire.

MUNDANE CHAKRA: Olam ha-Yesodoth, Sphere of the
Elements.

SPIRITUAL EXPERIENCE: Vision of the Holy Guardian Angel.

VIRTUE: Discrimination.

VICE: Avarice. Inertia.

CORRESPONDENCE IN THE MICROCOSM: The feet. The anus.

SYMBOLS: Altar of the double cube. The Equal-armed cross.
The magic circle. The triangle of art.

TAROT CARDS: The four Tens.
       TEN OF WANDS: Oppression.
       TEN OF CUPS: Perfected Success.
       TEN OF SWORDS: Ruin.
       TEN OF PENTACLES: Wealth.

Colour in Atziluth: Yellow.
    ,,   ,,   Briah: Citrine, olive, russet, and black.
    ,,   ,,   Yetzirah: Citrine, olive, russet, and black, flecked with gold.
    ,,   ,,   Assiah: Black, rayed with yellow.

I

1. It will be observed that the conformation of the Tree falls naturally into three functional triangles, but that Malkuth participates in no such triangle, but stands apart, and it is said by the Qabalists that it receives the influences or emanations of all the other Sephiroth. But although Malkuth is the only Sephirah that does not participate in a triangle, it is also the only Sephirah that is represented as parti-coloured instead of a unit, for it is divided into four quarters, which are assigned to the four elements of Earth, Air, Fire, and Water. And although it is not functional in any triangle, it represents the end-results of all the activities of the Tree. It is the nadir of evolution, the outermost point on the outgoing arc, through which all life must pass before returning whence it came.

2. Malkuth is said to be the Sphere of Earth; but we must not make the mistake of thinking that the Qabalists meant by Malkuth only the terrestrial sphere. They meant also the Earth-soul—that is to say, the subtle, psychic aspect of matter; the underlying noumenon of the physical plane which gives rise to all physical phenomena. Likewise with the four elements. These are not earth, air, fire, and water as known to the physicists, but are the four conditions in which energy can exist. The esotericist distinguishes these from their mundane counterparts by referring to them as the Air of the Wise, or the Earth of the Wise, as the case may be. That is to say, the Element of Air or of Earth as it is known to the initiate.

3. The physicist recognises the existence of matter in three states. Firstly, as solid, wherein the particles of which it is composed adhere firmly to each other; secondly, liquid, in which the particles move freely over each other; thirdly, gaseous, in which the particles all try to get as far away from

each other as possible, or in other words to diffuse. These three modes of matter correspond to the three elements of Earth, Water, and Air, and electrical phenomena corresponds to the element of Fire. Esoteric Science classifies all phenomena manifesting upon the physical plane under these four headings, as giving the best clue to the real understanding of their nature ; and it recognises that any given force can pass from one stage to another under certain conditions, just as water can exist in a state of ice and steam as well as its normal fluidity.

4. The esotericist sees in Malkuth the end-result of all operations; not until the Pairs of Opposites have achieved the settled equilibrium which gives the state of Earth, or coherence, can they be said to have completed any given cycle of experience. When this is achieved, they build a permanent vehicle of manifestation and stereotype its reactions; the machinery of expression thus evolved becomes self-regulating, and will continue to function with the minimum of attention, just as the human heart opens and shuts its valves with perfect regularity in response to a stereotyped cycle of nervous impulses and the pressure of the blood.

5. The great point to remember in connection with Malkuth is that herein is achieved stability. It is in the inertia of Malkuth that its virtue lies. All the other Sephiroth are in varying degrees mobile; even the Central Pillar only achieving equilibrium in function, just as a tight-rope walker achieves it.

6. Like all the other Sephiroth, Malkuth can only be understood when considered in relation to its neighbours. But in this case there is only one neighbour—Yesod. No understanding of Malkuth can be arrived at save through an understanding of Yesod.

7. For while Malkuth is essentially the sphere of form, all coherence of parts, save simple mechanical stresses and electromagnetic attractions and repulsions, depend upon the functions of Yesod. And Yesod, though it is essentially a form-giving Sephirah, depends for the manifestation of its activities upon the substance provided by Malkuth. The forms of Yesod are " such stuff as dreams are made on " till they have picked up

the material particles of Malkuth to body forth their forms. They are systems of stresses into whose framework the physical particles are built.

8. And equally with Malkuth, it is inanimate matter until the powers of Yesod ensoul it.

9. We should conceive of the material plane as the outward and visible sign of invisible etheric activity. Malkuth, in its prime essence, is only known to the instruments of the physicist. It goes without saying that where there is life, there is Yesod, because Yesod is the vehicle of life; but it should also be realised that where there is any kind of electrical activity or conductivity, whether of crystals, metals, or chemicals, there is Yesodic force in function. It is this fact which makes certain substances suitable for use as talismans, because they will take a charge of astral force.

10. It is not possible in these pages to go into a detailed study of esoteric physics; enough must be said, however, to give the student an understanding of the principles underlying this concept of the material world, which sees it as visible drapery upon an invisible framework.

11. The exact nature of the relationship between Yesod and Malkuth must be clearly understood, because it is all-important for practical occult work. Yesod is, of course, the form-giving principle, and whatever form is built up in its Sphere will be bodied forth in the Sphere of Malkuth unless it contains incompatibles, for it will tend to draw to itself the conditions of material expression. Material particles, however, are extremely resistant and unresponsive in their nature, and it is only by working upon the most tenuous aspect of matter, to which initiates give the name of the Element of Fire, that Yesodic forces can produce any effects. Once a response can be obtained from this Elemental Fire, the other Elements can in their turn be influenced.

12. Elemental Fire, however, is a kind of over-state of matter with which only the most advanced physics has any acquaintance. It might best be called a state of relationships rather than a thing in itself. Elemental Air might be de-

scribed as a capacity to achieve these relationships, and as such, is the vital principle of physical life; for it is only in so far as matter has a capacity for organisation that organic substance is possible. Elemental Water, the Water of the Wise, is just plain protoplasm; and Elemental Earth is inorganic matter.

13. Now each of these types of organised force and reaction-capacity has its own very definite nature, from which it will depart no hair's-breadth for any force in the manifested cosmos. But as there are definite interrelations of influence and expression between these four elemental states, it is possible, by using their influence one over the other, to achieve results which for want of understanding are called magical. It is, of course, the method of magic to manipulate these tenuous elemental forms; but it is also the method of life to do the same thing, and if magic is to be anything more than auto-suggestion, it must use the methods of life—that is to say, it must work through the intermediation of protoplasm, for protoplasm, in its curious web-like structure, carries the subtle magnetic force of the Fire of the Wise, transmitted through elemental air. In other words, the operator has to use his own body as a self-starter; for it is the magnetism of his own protoplasm that supplies the basis of manifestation of any force that is being brought through into the Sphere of Malkuth. Carried to its logical conclusion, this is the principle of generation, whether of protozoa or spermatozoa.

14. The modern concept of matter approximates very closely to that which has been held by esoteric science from time immemorial. What our senses perceive are the phenomena attributable to activities of different types of force, usually in organisation and combination. Only through an understanding of the nature of these forces is the nature of matter to be understood. Exoteric science is dealing with the problem by refining its concept of matter till there is no substance left in it. What the physicist now knows as matter is very far removed from the obvious.

15. The esotericist, approaching the problem from the opposite direction, points out that matter and mind are two

sides of the same coin, but that there comes a point in one's investigation when it is profitable to change over one's terminology, and talk of forces and forms in terms of psychology, as if they were conscious and purposive.   This, he says, enables us to deal with the phenomena we encounter much better than we can do if we limit ourselves to terms only applicable to inanimate matter and blind, undirected force. We must always, by the nature of our intellect, use analogy as a help to understanding; if the analogies we use on this level of the investigation are the analogies of inanimate matter, we shall find them so inadequate as to be very limiting and misleading, and darkeners of counsel in general.

16. If, however, we use the terminologies of life and intelligence and purposive will, duly diluted to the requirements of the very rudimentary state of development of that with which we have to deal, we shall find we have an analogy which is illuminating instead of limiting, and which will lead on to advancement in understanding.

17. It is for this reason that the esotericist personifies the subtler forces and calls them Intelligences.   He then proceeds to deal with them as if they were intelligent, and he finds that there is a subtle side of his own nature and consciousness which responds to them, and to which, he fondly believes, they respond.   At any rate, whether the response is mutual or not, his powers of dealing with them are, by this means, greatly extended beyond those which he possesses when he regards them as "a fortuitous concourse of uncorrelated incidents."

II

18. Malkuth is the nadir of evolution, but it should be looked upon, not as the ultimate depth of unspirituality, but as the marking-buoy in a yacht race.   Any yacht that puts about on to the homeward course before it has rounded the marking-buoy is disqualified.   And so it is with the soul.   If we try to escape from the discipline of matter before we have mastered the lessons of matter, we are not advancing heaven-

wards, but suffering from arrested development. It is these spiritual defectives who flock from one to another of the innumerable wildcat uplift organisations that come to us from the Far East and the Far West. They find in cheap idealism an escape from the rigorous demands of life. But this is not a way of advancement, but a way of retreat. Sooner or later they have to face the fence and clear it. Life brings them up to it again and again, and presently begins to use the whip and spur of psychological sickness; for those who will not face life, dissociate; and dissociation is the prime cause of most of the ills that mind is heir to.

19. If we study the lessons of history we shall get much light on moral and spiritual problems from an unexpected angle. We see that all civilisation and inspiration arose in the East; a point to which those who are of Eastern race or follow an Eastern tradition point proudly, saying that the West must sit at the feet of the East if it is to learn the secrets of life.

20. Now it cannot be denied that there are many things, especially the more recondite aspects of psychology, concerning which the East knows a great deal more than the West, and which we should be wise to learn; but it also cannot be denied that, having originated in the East, the growing-point of evolution is now to be found in the West, and that for every advance in the art of living on this terrestrial planet, the East must look to the West unless it is content to go back to the spinning-wheel standard of life. But let it not be forgotten that with the primitive standard of life goes also the primitive standard of death. A primitive culture can only support a sparse population. A great many people have got to die, mostly the old and the young. When we return to Nature, she deals with us after her own manner with her red tooth and claw. The unsoftened impact of Nature is not a pleasant thing. When human beings get too thick on the ground, she wipes them out with disease and starvation. With the white man's civilisation goes the white man's sanitation. By refraining from all action one may achieve release from the bondage of the body more quickly and effectually than one

bargains for, if among the actions refrained from·are those connected with communal cleanliness in a densely populated land.

21. The Greeks understood the principle of Malkuth better than did anybody else, and they were the founders of the European culture. They taught us to see beauty in perfect proportion and function, and nowhere else. The frieze of figures upon the Grecian urn turned the mind of Keats to the contemplation of ideal Truth and Beauty. There can be no higher ideal than this for the finite mind to contemplate, for in it the Law and the prophets are lifted far above the grim forbiddings of the Mosaic code into the inspiration of an ideal to be pursued.

22. It is in the Sphere of Malkuth that civilisation has wrought for the last thousand years. It does not need any astrologer to tell us that the Great War marked the end of an epoch, and that we are now in the dawn of a new phase. According to Qabalistic doctrine, the Lightning Flash, having come down the Tree till it ends in Malkuth, is now replaced by the symbolism of the Serpent of Wisdom, whose coils loop upwards on the Paths till its head rests beside Kether. The Lightning Flash represents the unconscious descent of force, building the planes of manifestation, passing from active to passive and back again in order that equilibrium may be maintained. The Serpent coiling upon the Paths represents the dawn of objective consciousness and is the symbol of initiation; by the Path whereon the initiates have gone, ahead of their time, evolution is beginning to go, taking with it the race as a whole. It is now becoming normal for the average man to do what only the initiates used to do.

23. We see the growing-point of evolution, then, beginning to rise out of Malkuth and reach out towards Yesod. This means that science, both pure and applied, is passing beyond the study of inanimate matter and is beginning to take account of the etheric and psychic side of things. This changing phase is visible all around us for those who can read the signs of the times. We see it in medicine, in international relationships, in

industrial organisation. Last, and most reluctantly, we see it making itself felt in the sciences of physiology and psychology, which cling tenaciously to a materialistic explanation of all things, and especially the life-processes, even after physics, which avowedly deals with inanimate matter, has abandoned the materialistic position and talks in terms of mathematics.

24. The occult division of Malkuth into the Four Elements gives us a very valuable key. We should regard matter as we know it as Earth of Malkuth. The different types of physical activity, whether in molecules or masses, can be classified under the two headings of anabolism and katabolism, that is to say the building-up and the breaking-down processes; these can be classified in esoteric terminology as the Water or Air of Malkuth, and whatever is said by esoteric philosophy or pagan mythology in relation to these elements will be applicable to these two metabolic processes and functions. The Fire of Malkuth is that subtle electro-magnetic aspect of matter which is the link with the processes of consciousness and life, and to it all life-myths apply.

25. When this principle of classification is understood, the terminology of the alchemists becomes less recondite and absurd, for it is seen that the classification into Four Elements really refers to four modes of manifestation on the physical plane. This method of classification is of very great value, because it enables the relationship and correspondence between the physical plane and the life-processes behind it to be readily seen. It is especially important in the study of physiology and pathology, and in its practical application it is a most important key to therapeutics. The more advanced physicians are beginning to feel their way towards this position, and the classifications of Paracelsus are being quoted to-day by more than one leader of medical thought. The concept of diathesis or constitutional predisposition is receiving attention. Psycho-therapy, again, is beginning to see that the old classification into the four temperaments affords a useful guide to treatment, and that it does not do to handle everyone in the same way; nor yet that similar results always spring from similar causes

in the realms of mind, because temperament intervenes and falsifies the results. For instance, apathy in the phlegmatic type may simply mean boredom; whereas the same degree of apathy in the sanguine type may mean a complete breakdown of the whole personality. The analogies between material and mental things can be very misleading; whereas the analogies between mental and material things can be very enlightening.

26. The four elements correspond to the four temperaments as described by Hippocrates, the four Tarot suits, the twelve signs of the Zodiac, and the seven planets. If the implications of these statements are worked out, it will be seen that herein are contained some very important keys.

27. The Element of Earth corresponds to the Phlegmatic Temperament; the suit of Pentacles; the signs of Taurus, Virgo, and Capricorn; and the planets Venus and Luna.

28. The Element of Water corresponds to the Bilious Temperament; the suit of Cups; the signs of Cancer, Scorpio, and Pisces; and the planet Mars.

29. The Element of Air corresponds to the Choleric Temperament; the suit of Swords; the signs of Libra, Gemini, and Aquarius; and the planets Saturn and Mercury.

30. The Element of Fire corresponds to the Sanguine Temperament; the suit of Wands; the signs of Aries, Sagittarius and Leo; and the planets Sol and Jupiter.

31. It will be seen, then, that if we classify mundane affairs and phenomena in terms of the Four Elements, we shall immediately see their relationship to astrology and the Tarot. Now classification is the stage that immediately follows observation in scientific method. A very great deal of scientific work simply consists in these two processes; in fact, for the rank and file of science these represent the total range of their activities. If science is limited to these two activities, as it would be if we listened to our more pedestrian scientists, it would be no more than a compiling of lists of natural phenomena, as if the brokers were in on the universe. But the imaginative scientist, who alone is worthy of the name of research worker, uses classification not so much as a means of

putting things away tidily, but to enable him to recognise relationships.

32. From the imaginative scientist who perceives to the philosophic scientist who interprets is but a step; and from the philosophical scientist who interprets in terms of causation to the esoteric scientist who interprets in terms of purpose, and so links science to ethics, is but another step. It is the tragedy of Esoteric Science that its exponents have nearly always been inadequately equipped upon the plane of Malkuth, and consequently unable to co-ordinate their results with those obtained by workers in other fields. As long as we rest content with this state of affairs we shall continue to have muddle-headed thinking and credulous assumptions as our inalienable lot. Esoteric Science needs to observe the rule of the yacht race, and make each magical operation round the marking-buoy of Malkuth before it is reckoned to have achieved completion.

33. Let us now interpret this simile from the point of view of technical occultism. Every magical operation is designed to bring power down the planes into the reach of the operator, who then applies it to whatever ends he may design. Many operators are content if they can obtain purely subjective results—that is to say, a sense of exaltation; others aim at the production of psychic phenomena. It should be recognised, however, that no operation is completed until the process has been expressed in terms of Malkuth, or, in other words, has issued forth in action on the physical plane. If this is not done, the force that has been generated is not properly " earthed," and it is this loose force left lying around that causes the trouble in magical experiments. It may not cause trouble in a single experiment, as few operators generate enough power to cause anything, let alone trouble; but in a series of experiments the effect may be cumulative, and result in the general psychic upheaval and run of bad luck and queer happenings so often reported by experimenters. It is these sort of things that give experimental magic a bad name, and lead to its being regarded as dangerous and compared to drug addiction. The

true analogy, however, would be with the dangers of X-ray research in its early days. It is faulty technique that gives rise to trouble, as it always must when active potencies are being handled. Perfect your technique and you get rid of your troubles and have a very potent force available for use.

III

34. The only means of transition from Yesod to Malkuth is through the mediumship of living substances. Now there are various degrees of livingness. The esotericist recognises life wherever there is organised form, for he says that life alone is the organiser of form, though in what are popularly called inorganic substances the proportion of life is very small, and in some cases infinitesimal. In some forms of inorganic matter, however, there is a by no means negligible proportion of life, just as in plants there is a by no means negligible proportion of intelligence. It is only recent advances in experimental work, notably those of Sir Jagindranath Bhose, that have demonstrated this fact, but it has long been known empirically to the practical occultist. He has always made use of crystalline and metallic substances as storage batteries of subtle forces. He has always regarded silk as an insulator. He has, in fact, availed himself of the properties of the same substances that the electrician employs to-day. The best talismans are considered to be disks of pure metal engraven with suitable devices and kept wrapped in silk of a colour appropriate to the force with which the talisman is charged. A precious stone, which is of course a coloured crystal, is a very important part of certain operations, because it is held to act as a focus for the force. It is also a very important part of certain types of wireless receivers. The influence of colours on mental states is now well recognised. No worker is allowed to work for a lengthy period in the red light rooms of the manufacturers of photographic supplies, because it is recognised that such workers are liable to emotional disturbance and even temporary mental unbalance. All these things

we are rediscovering by means of modern scientific method and its instruments, but they were well known to the ancients, and their practical applications were worked out to an extent that is not dreamed of to-day, save among the few who are popularly known as "cranky."

35. Plants also we find credited with a varying degree of "psychic activity." This is especially attributed to aromatic plants. The ancients had an elaborate system of attribution of plants to the different forms of subtle force. Some of these, of course, are fantastic, but there are certain broad principles which give guidance. Wherever we find a plant traditionally associated with any deity we may be fairly certain that that plant has been proven to have affinities with the type of force that that deity represents. It may be that the association appears to our modern eyes to be superficial and irrational, such associations as Freud has shown us that the dreaming mind employs; but the worshippers of the deity, if the association is hallowed by tradition, will have built up the psychic connection between the plant and the force, and as in all such traditional associations, once established, the link is easily recoverable by those who know how to make use of the constructive imagination. Whether there is any intrinsic relationship between the nature of the plant and the nature of the force to which it is assigned, as in the case of the rose to Venus and the lily to the Virgin Mary, such a relationship is speedily established by the worshippers of a cult and equally speedily recoverable by those who follow in their footsteps, even after a lapse of centuries. Therefore for all practical purposes there is such a relationship, not only in relation to the plants assigned to a particular deity, but in relation to animals as well.

36. An attribution which has especial practical importance is that of perfumes and colours. The colour attributions have already been given in the tables at the head of each chapter. Concerning the perfumes, it is less easy to lay down hard and fast rules, as the available perfumes are almost countless, and the forces in practical working often tend to run one into the

other. For instance, it is difficult, and in fact undesirable, to keep the forces of Netzach separated from those of Tiphareth, or those of Hod from Yesod, or Yesod from Malkuth; and anyone who tries working Geburah without Gedulah would burn his fingers.

37. Perfumes are used not only to enable the deity to manifest, but to tune the imagination of the operator. To this latter end they are most efficacious, as anyone will discover for themselves if they try to work a ceremony without the appropriate perfume. With inexperienced operators it is advisable to dispense with the use of perfumes in case the psychic effect is too drastic for comfort or convenience.

38. Broadly speaking, we can divide perfumes into those which exalt consciousness and those which stir the subconscious to activity. Of those which exalt consciousness the aromatic gums stand by themselves, and these are employed exclusively in the manufacture of ecclesiastical incense. In addition to these, certain essential oils possess similar properties, especially those which are aromatic and astringent rather than sweet and spicy. These substances are of value in all operations in which the aim is increased intellectual clarity or exaltation of the mystical type.

39. The perfumes that awaken the subconscious mind are of two types, the Dionysiac and the Venusian. The Dionysiac odours are of the aromatic, spicy type, such as smouldering cedar- or sandal-wood or pine-cones. The Venusian odours are of a sweet, cloying nature, such as vanilla. In actual practice these two types of odours shade one into the other, and characteristic flower odours are to be found in both divisions. In the practical work of compounding the perfumes a blend of ingredients is almost always employed, as they enhance each other. Many perfumes which by themselves are crude and acrid, or cloying and sickly, become admirable when blended.

40. It has been said that synthetic perfumes are useless for magical work. In my experience this is not the case, provided the essence is of good quality. Good synthetic essences

are indistinguishable from the natural products save by chemical tests. As the value of perfumes is psychological, their action being upon the operator, not upon the power invoked, the chemical nature of the substance is immaterial provided one gets the appropriate effect.

41. The same applies to precious stones, rank heresy though it be to say so. All one needs is a crystal of the appropriate colour, and whether it is a Burmese ruby or a Burma one makes no difference to anything except one's bank balance. That the ancients knew this is witnessed by the fact that in the lists of precious stones sacred to various deities alternative gems are always given. For instance, Crowley, in "777," gives pearls, moon-stones, crystal, and quartz as all being sacred to the moon-forces, and the ruby or any red stone as sacred to Mars.

42. It is believed by the occultist that the mental concentration of a current of will, backed by the imagination, has an effect upon certain crystals, metals, and oils. He makes a use of this property in order to conserve in them forces of a particular type so that these forces can be readily re-awakened at will, or even exercise their influence all the time by means of a steady emanation. Most ceremonial depends in some degree at least upon the principle of the consecrated magical weapons. It is noteworthy that all the more important equipment of a church is always consecrated before it is taken into use. Whether this consecration is effective is not a matter of opinion. Any good psychic will readily distinguish between consecrated and unconsecrated objects, provided, of course, that the consecration has been effectual. It is a matter of experience with any practical occultist that a very definite change takes place in him when he takes his accustomed magical instruments in hand or puts on his accustomed robes. He can do with these what he cannot do without them. He also knows that it takes time to "break in" a new magical instrument. It is interesting to note in this respect that I am quite unable to write anything about the "Mystical Qabalah" without my ancient and battered "Tree

of Life" beside me.   It is also interesting to note that when
this Tree of Life, which was originally prepared for me by
someone else, became so dingy as to be almost indecipher-
able, I repainted it myself, and found thereafter that it
immediately took on a marked increase in magnetism: thus
bearing out the old tradition that one should always prepare
one's magical weapons as far as possible with one's own
hands.

43. The great problem in the practical working is to bring
things through to the Sphere of Malkuth.   Many methods are
described by the ancients—with how much truth one has no
means of knowing.   How far were actual materialisations
obtained by the method of blood-sacrifice described by Virgil,
and how far did the exalted imagination of the participants in
these awe-inspiring rites supply the basis of manifestation?

44. But whatever may be the facts, the holocausts of
the ancients are not a practicable method for the modern
experimenter to follow.   The basis of the idea, however, lies
in the fact that freshly shed blood gives off ectoplasm.   There
are, of course, materialising mediums who also give off ectoplasm without the shedding of blood.   But those who give
off an appreciable quantity are few and far between.   When
a number of psychically developed people are gathered
together in a circle for the purpose of evocation they may,
between them, give off sufficient ectoplasm to form the
necessary basis for physical phenomena.   Such a method
is not without its difficulties, not to say risks, and the
esotericist, who is a philosopher rather than an experimenter, seldom makes use of it.   It is sufficient for him if
he gets manifestations in the Sphere of Yesod and perceives
them with the inner vision.

45. The only satisfactory channel of evocation is the
operator himself.   In the Egyptian method of evocation,
known as the assumption of the god-forms, the operator
identifies himself with the god and offers himself as the channel
of manifestation.   It is his own magnetism that bridges the
gulf between Malkuth and Yesod.   There is no other method

so satisfactory, for the amount of magnetism in a living being is far greater than in any metal or crystal, however precious.

46. This ancient method is also known to us under another name; it is called by moderns, mediumship. When the spirit speaks through the entranced medium, precisely the same thing is happening as happened in ancient Egypt when the priest with the mask of Horus spake with the voice of Horus.

47. When we consider the microcosmic Tree, the physical body is Malkuth; the etheric double is Yesod; the astromental body is Hod and Netzach; and the higher mind is Tiphareth. Whatever the higher mind can conceive can readily be brought through into manifestation in the subjective Malkuth. We do better to rely upon this method of evocation rather than the extraneous devices of extruded ectoplasm or the outpouring of vital fluids, even if this latter device were practicable in our modern civilisation.

48. The best magical weapon is the magus himself, and all other contrivances are but a means to an end, the end being that exaltation and concentration of consciousness which makes a magus of an ordinary man. "Know ye not that ye are the temple of the living God?" said a Great One. If we know how to use the symbolic furniture of this living temple, we have the keys of heaven in our hands.

49. The key to this use is given in the microcosmic attributions of the Tree. Interpreting these in terms of function, and function in terms of spiritual principles, we can unlock the door of the Storehouse of Force. The best and most complete manifestation of the power of God is through the energised enthusiasm of the trained and dedicated man. We would be wiser if we looked for the end-result of a magical operation to come about through natural channels rather than to expect an interference with the course of Nature—an expectation that in the very nature of things is doomed to disappointment.

50. Let us make this clear by illustration. Supposing we desire to heal sickness, we should, working by the method of the Tree, employ a rite or meditation of Tiphareth. But

are we, for this reason, to limit our operations to the Sphere of Tiphareth and require the healing to be a purely spiritual healing, as do the Christian Scientists? Or shall we modify our method sufficiently to allow of the laying on of hands and the anointing with oil, which are operations of the Sphere of Yesod, designed to conduct magnetic force? Or shall we, which appears to me the wiser method, make use of an operation of Malkuth also, thus bringing the power steadily down the planes into manifestation without break or gap in the transmutation and conduction?

51. And what is an operation of the Sphere of Malkuth? It is simply action on the physical plane. In an invocation of healing, therefore, I think we do better to invoke the Great Physician to manifest His power to us through the human physician, for that is the natural channel, than to rely upon a spiritual force for which the only channel of evocation is the spiritual nature of the patient, who may or may not be able to rise to the occasion.

52. That great spiritual forces can be brought to bear effectually upon the healing of our diseases is beyond question, but they must have a channel of manifestation; and why be at great pains to build a psychic one when there is a natural one ready to hand? God moves in a mysterious way His wonders to perform when natural law is a sealed book to us; but when we understand the ways of Nature's working, we see that God moves in a perfectly natural way, through the regularly established channels; the difference between the supernatural and the natural does not lie in the channels of manifestation that are used, but in the amount of power that comes through them. Not in quality but in quantity does the flow of power alter when spiritual forces are successfully invoked.

53. The whole problem of Malkuth is a problem of channels and connecting links. The rest of the work is done by the mind on the subtler planes; the real difficulty lies in the transition from the subtle to the dense, for the subtle is so ill-equipped to work on the dense. This transition is effected by means of the magnetism of living things, whether or-

ganic or inorganic.   *Ce n'est que le dernier pas qui coûte* in magical
operations.

IV

54. Three ideas issue from a contemplation of the Yetziratic
Text related to Malkuth—the concept of the Resplendent In
telligence which illuminates the splendour of all the Lights;
the relationship between Malkuth and Binah; and the function
of Malkuth in causing an influence to emanate from the Angel
of Kether.

55. It may seem a curious idea that Malkuth, which is the
material world, should be the illuminator of the Lights; we
can understand this, however, if we refer to the analogy of
physics, which tells us that the sky only appears blue and
luminous owing to the reflection of light from the innumerable
dust particles floating in the atmosphere; absolutely dustless
air is unilluminated, and our sky would have the darkness of
interstellar space if it were not for these dust particles. We
also learn from the study of physics that we see objects solely
by means of the rays of light they reflect from their surfaces.
When there is little or no reflection, as with black cloth, it is
almost invisible in a dim light, a property made much use of
by conjurers and illusionists.

56. It is the formative, concreting function of Malkuth
which finally renders tangible and definite what was, upon the
higher planes, intangible and indefinite, and this is its great
service to manifestation and its characteristic power. All the
Lights, that is to say the emanations of all the other Sephiroth,
become illuminated, visible, when reflected from the concrete
aspects of Malkuth.

57. Every magical operation must come through to Malkuth before it can be reckoned to have attained completion,
for only in Malkuth is the force finally locked home into form.
Therefore all magical work is better carried out in the form of
a ritual performed on the physical plane, even if the operator
is working alone, than simply as a form of meditation operating upon the astral plane only. There must be something

upon the physical plane, even if it be no more than lines drawn on a talisman, or the writing of signs upon the air,· which brings the action through to the plane of Malkuth. Experience proves that an operation so terminated is a very different matter to an operation which begins and ends on the astral.

58. The relationship between Malkuth and Binah is very clearly indicated in the titles assigned to both these Sephiroth. Binah is the Superior Mother and Malkuth the Inferior Mother. As we have already seen, Binah is the primordial Giver of Form. Malkuth being the Sphere of Form, the relationship is obvious. That which had its inception in Binah has its culmination in Malkuth. This point gives us an important clue by means of which to guide our researches among the ramifications of the polytheistic pantheons. The Qabalistic system is explicit concerning the doctrine of Emanations, whereby the One unfolds into the Many, and the Many are reabsorbed into the One. No other system is specific upon this point, though in all of them it is hinted under the guise of genealogies. The begettings and matings of the gods and goddesses, by no means always in holy wedlock, give definite indication of the implicit doctrines of emanation and polarity, and are not merely ribald phantasies of primitive man, creating the gods in his own image and likeness.

59. A careful comparison of the information that has come down to us concerning the rites by which the ancients worshipped their many gods soon reveals that the clear-cut myths so delightfully retold for children have little bearing on the actual religion of the folk who used them as the means of expression for spiritual teachings. The gods and goddesses melt one into the other in the most perplexing fashion, so that we get the Bearded Venus, and Hercules, of all persons, arrayed in female clothes.

60. It is clear from a study of ancient art that the persons and characteristics of the various gods and goddesses were used as a form of picture-writing to indicate definite abstract ideas, of which the convention was well understood by the

priesthood. Having to deal with an illiterate population for the most part, for learning was limited to a very few in those days, they wisely said, Look on this symbol and think about this story; you may not know what it means, but you are looking in the right direction, the direction whence light arises; and in proportion as you are able to receive it, light will flow into your soul if you contemplate these ideas.   It is probable to the point of certainty that the illumination given in the Mysteries included the elucidation of the metaphysics of these myths.

61. Persephone, Diana, Aphrodite, Hera, all exchange their symbols, functions, characteristics, and even subordinate titles in a bewildering manner in Greek myths and art.   Likewise do Priapos, Pan, Apollo, and Zeus. The best we can say of them is that all the goddesses are Great Mothers and all the gods are Givers of Life; the difference between them lying not in function, but in the level upon which they function. A distinction is drawn between the Celestial Venus and the goddess of earthly love of the same name; the discerning can see an equal distinction, and an equal underlying identity, between Zeus the All-Father, and Priapos, equally addicted to fatherhood, but after another manner, the one being earthly where the other is celestial.   Nevertheless, they are not two gods, but one god: just as Binah and Malkuth are not two distinct types of force, but the same force functioning on different levels.   This is the key to the understanding of the significance of phallic worship, which plays so important a part in all ancient and primitive faiths, a part so little under- stood by their scholastic interpreters.   Its real meaning is the bringing down of the godhead into manhood in the hope of taking manhood up into godhead.   A process which is also the basis of the Freudian therapy.

62. The statement that Malkuth causes an influence to emanate from the Angel of Kether further bears out this idea. We see that the Great Mother, which is Malkuth, polarises with the All-Father, which is Kether.

63. This classification, however, is too simple to serve us adequately, whether we are reducing a pagan pantheon to

its simplest terms or dealing with the chances and changes of personal life. But in the four quarters, or elements, into which Malkuth is divided we find the key that we need.

64. These four elements are said to be the Earth, Air, Fire, and Water of the Wise—that is to say, four types of activity. They are represented in the notation of esoteric science by four different types of triangle. Fire is represented by a triangle point upwards; Air by a similar triangle with a bar across it, thus indicating that Air may be esteemed as akin in nature to Fire, but denser. In fact, we should not go far wrong if we called Air, Negative Fire, or Fire, Positive Air. Water is represented by a triangle point downwards, and Earth by the same triangle with a bar across it; and to these two symbols the same principles apply as to their predecessors.

65. Supposing, then, we consider the Fire triangle as representing unconditioned force and the Air triangle as representing conditioned force, the Earth triangle as representing totally inert form and the Water triangle as representing an active type of form, we have another mode of classification available. In the most ancient myths, the air, or space-god, is the parent of the sun, celestial fire, and water is the matrix of earth. This comes out clearly on the Central Pillar of the Tree of Life, where Kether, space, overshadows Tiphareth, the sun-centre, and the watery Yesod, the moon-centre, overshadows the earthy Malkuth.

66. Or supposing we arrange the symbols composing the glyph after another manner, which it is the glory of the Tree that it enables us to do, and place them as the four Elements, citrine, olive, russet, and black, in the sphere of Malkuth, and consider the life-force descending from Kether as operating after the manner of an alternating current of electricity, which the doctrine of alternating polarity teaches us to do, we find that force will sometimes be flowing from Malkuth to Kether, and sometimes from Kether to Malkuth.

67. Now this is an all-important point when applied to the microcosm, for it teaches us that we need to be in circuit with the Earth-soul just as much as with the God of Heaven; there

is an inspiration that rises up from the unconscious quite as much as there is an inspiration that flows down from the superconscious.

68. This comes out clearly in the Greek myths, wherein we find such positive earth-forces as Pan, who, by virtue of his goat-symbolism, cannot be assigned otherwise than to the Sphere of Earth, for Capricorn is the most earthy of the earthy triplicity. Pan represents the positive magnetism of the earth uprushing in its return to the All-Father. Ceres, on the other hand, or many-breasted Diana, who are both very earthly Venuses and far from virgin, represent the final earth-ing of the heavenly force in dense matter. Hera, who has been called the Celestial Venus or heavenly Aphrodite, repre-sents the return of the uprushing earth-force to heaven, and is earth-positive on a celestial level.

69. These are things difficult to elucidate to those who have not seen the sun at midnight. They yield much to meditation, but little to disputation.

V

70. In the Sphere of Malkuth are worked all divinations. Now the object of any method of divination is to find a set of things on the physical plane which correspond accurately and comprehensively to the invisible forces in the same way that the movements of the hands of a clock correspond to the passage of time.

71. For revealing general trends and conditions it is agreed by universal experience of those who have studied such matters that astrology is the best system of correspondences. But for obtaining an answer to a single question it is not sufficiently specific, for too many factors may come in to modify the result. The initiated diviner, therefore, makes use of the more specific systems, such as divination by the Tarot or geomancy, when he wants to obtain an answer to a specific question.

72. But it is of little use to go into a shop and buy a pack of Tarot cards unless there is the knowledge necessary to build

up the astral correspondences to each card.   This takes time,
as there are seventy-two cards to work with.   Once it is done,
however, the operator can take the cards into his hands with a
considerable degree of confidence that his subconscious mind,
whatever that may be, will all unwittingly deal the cards that
refer to the matter in question.   Exactly how the shuffle and
deal is affected we do not know, but one thing is certain, when
the Great Angel of the Tarot has been contacted, the cards are
remarkably revealing.

73. Having considered the general principles of the Sphere
of Malkuth, we are now in a position to study its special
symbolism with profit.

74. It is called the Kingdom—in other words, the sphere
ruled by the King—and the King is the title of Microprosopos,
who consists of the six central Sephiroth, excluding the Three
Supernals.   We may regard Malkuth, or the material Sphere,
as the sphere of manifestation of these six central Sephiroth,
which themselves are emanated by the Three Supernals.
Everything, then, ends in Malkuth, even as everything begins
in Kether.

75. The Magical Image of Malkuth is a young woman,
crowned and veiled; this is the Isis of Nature, her face veiled
to show that the spiritual forces are hidden within the outer
form.   This idea is also present in the symbolism of Binah,
which is summed up in the concept of "the outer robe of
concealment."   Malkuth, as is clearly set forth in the Yetziratic Text, is Binah upon a lower arc.

76. Now Binah is called the Dark Sterile Mother, and
Malkuth is called the Bride of Microprosopos, or the Bright
Fertile Mother, and these correspond to the dual aspects of
the Egyptian moon-goddess as Isis and Hathor, Isis being
the positive aspect of the goddess, and Hathor the negative
aspect.   In Greek symbolism these would correspond to
Aphrodite and Ceres.   Now Aphrodite is the positive aspect
of the female potency, for be it remembered that under the law
of alternating polarity that which is negative on the outer
planes is positive on the inner, and *vice versa*.   Aphrodite, the

Celestial Venus, is the giver of magnetic stimulus to the spiritually negative male; it is because her function is not understood in modern life that so much is wrong with modern life. Binah, the higher aspect of Isis, is, however, barren, because the positive pole is always the giver of the stimulus, but never the producer of the result. The Malkuth aspect of Isis is the Bright Fertile Mother, the goddess of fecundity, thus indicating the end-result of the operation of Isis on the physical plane.

77. The situation of Malkuth at the foot of the Pillar of Equilibrium places it in the direct line of the descent of power from Kether, transmuted in Daath, the Invisible Sephirah, and passing on to the planes of form *via* Tiphareth. This is the Path of Consciousness, whereas the two Side Pillars are Paths of Function; but the two Side Pillars also converge on Malkuth *via* the Thirty-first and Twenty-ninth Paths. Consequently everything ends in Malkuth.

78. We who are incarnated in physical bodies are standing in Malkuth, and when we set out upon the Way of Initiation our route lies up the Thirty-second Path to Yesod. This Path, straight up the Central Pillar, is called the Path of the Arrow, which is shot from Qesheth, the Bow of Promise; it is by this route that the mystic rises upon the planes; the initiate, however, adds to his experience the powers of the Side Pillars as well as the realisations of the Middle Pillar.

79. This aspect of the Central Pillar is expressed in the Yetziratic Text wherein it states that Malkuth causes an influence to emanate from the Prince of Countenances, the Angel of Kether.

80. The additional titles assigned to Malkuth bring out its attributes clearly. It is regarded as the Gate and the Mate. These two ideas are in essence one idea, for the womb of the Mother is the Gate of Life. It is also the Gate of Death, for birth into the plane of form is death to higher things.

81. Malkuth is also said to be Kallah, the Bride of Microprosopos, and Malkah, the Queen of Melekh, the King. This clearly indicates the function in polarity that prevails between

the planes of form and the planes of force; the planes of form being the female aspect, polarised and made fertile by the influences of the planes of force.

82. The God-name in Malkuth is Adonai Melekh, or Adon ha-Arets, which titles mean, the Lord who is King, and the Lord of Earth. Herein we clearly see the assertion of the supremacy of the One God in the Kingdoms of Earth, and every magical operation, wherein the operator takes power into his own hands, should commence with the invocation of Adonai to indwell his temple of earth and rule therein, that no force may break from its allegiance to the One.

83. Those who call upon the Name of Adonai call upon God made manifest in Nature, which is the aspect of God adored by initiates of the Nature Mysteries, whether Dionysian or Isiac—which concern the different ways of opening super-consciousness *via* subconsciousness.

84. The archangel is the great angel Sandalphon, who is sometimes called by Qabalists the Dark Angel; whereas Metatron, the Angel of the Countenance, is the Bright Angel. These two angels are held to stand behind the right and left shoulders of the soul in its hours of crisis. They might be taken to represent good and bad karma. It is in reference to the function of Sandalphon as the Dark Angel presiding over the Karmic Debt that Malkuth is called the Gate of Justice and the Gate of Tears. It has been said by a wit, with more truth than he knew, that this planet was actually some other planet's hell. It is in very fact the sphere in which karma is normally worked out. Where there is sufficient knowledge, however, karma can be worked out deliberately on the subtler planes, and this method is one of the forms of spiritual healing.

85. The Order of Angels assigned to Malkuth are the Ishim, the Souls of Fire, or Fiery Particles, of which Mme Blavatsky says some very interesting things. A Soul of Fire is in actual fact the consciousness of an atom; the Ashim therefore represent the natural consciousness of dense matter; it is these which bestow on it its characteristics. It is these

Fiery Lives, these infinitesimal electrical charges, which are for
ever weaving backwards and forwards with tremendous
activity in the background of matter and form its basis.
Everything that we know as matter builds up on this groundwork. It is with the help of these Fiery Lives that certain
types of magic are worked. There are but few who can work
such magic, for the denser the plane to be manipulated, the
greater must be the power of the Magus who commands it.

86. The Mundane Chakra of Malkuth is the Sphere of the
Elements. These we have already considered in such detail
as is possible in these pages.

87. The Spiritual Experience of Malkuth is the Vision of
the Holy Guardian Angel. Now this angel, which according
to the Qabalists is assigned to each soul at birth and com-
panions him till death, when it takes him into its keeping and
presents him before the face of God for judgment, is in
actuality the Higher Self of each one of us, which builds up
around the Divine Spark that is the nucleus of the soul and
endures for an evolution, sending down a process into
matter at each incarnation to form the basis of the new
personality.

88. When the Higher Self and the Lower Self become united
through the complete absorption of the lower by the higher,
true adepthood is gained; this is the Great Initiation, the Lesser
Divine Union. It is the supreme experience of the incarnate
soul, and when this takes place, it is freed from any compulsion
to rebirth into the prison-house of flesh. Thenceforth it is
free to go on up the planes and enter into its rest, or, if it so
elects, to remain within the earth-sphere and function as a
Master.

89. This, then, is the spiritual experience which is assigned
to Malkuth—the bringing down of the Godhead into manhood, just as the spiritual experience of Tiphareth is the taking
up of manhood into the Godhead.

90. The especial virtue of Malkuth is said to be Discrimination. This idea is further carried out in the curious symbolism of the ancients which declared the correspondence in the

microcosm to be with the anus.   Whatever in life is effete has
to be excreted, and the macrocosmic excretion is into the
Qliphothic spheres which depend below Malkuth, whence
the cosmic excreta cannot return to the planes of organised
form until they find balance in equilibrium.   There is, therefore, in the Qliphothic world, a sphere which is not Hell, but
Purgatory; it is a reservoir of disorganised force emanated
from broken-up forms, cast out from evolution; it is Chaos
upon a lower arc.   It is from this reservoir of force that
is accustomed to form, and therefore organises readily, that
the Shells, or imperfect entities, build up their vehicles.
It is also said to be drawn upon for the lower types of
magic of an evil kind.   The tendency of such forces as are
available in the Qliphothic sphere must always be to assume
once more such forms as they were accustomed to before they
were disintegrated and reduced to their primal state; as these
forms were at least out of date, if not actively evil, it naturally
follows that this matter of chaos is not a desirable substance
to work in; and had best be left there till its purification is
complete and it has filtered back through the Sphere of Earth
by the natural channels, and been drawn once again into the
stream of evolution.   It is for this reason that all the underworld cults and the evocation of the departed are undesirable,
for the forms the manifesting entities assume must be built in
part at least of this substance of Chaos.

91. It is the especial virtue of Malkuth, then, to act as a
kind of cosmic filter, casting out the effete and preserving that
which still retains its usefulness.

92. The characteristic vices of the functioning of Malkuth
are said to be avarice and inertia.   It is easy to see how the
stability of Malkuth can be overdone, and so give rise to
sluggishness and inertia.   The concept of avarice, though
not so obvious upon the surface, soon yields its significance to
investigation; for the over-retentiveness of avarice is a kind
of spiritual costiveness, the exact opposite of the discrimination which rejects the excreta of life through the cosmic anus
into the cosmic cesspool of the Qliphoth.   It is interesting to

note that Freud declares that the miser is invariably con-
stipated, and associates the dream of money with fæces.

93. One of the most important things we have to do before
we can rise out of the limitations of life in Malkuth and
breathe a wider air, is to learn how to let go; how to sacrifice
the lesser to the greater and so buy the pearl of great price.   It
is discrimination which enables us to know which is the lesser
value that has to be given up in order to obtain the greater, for
there is no gain without sacrifice.   What we do not realise is
that every sacrifice should yield a substantial profit in treasure
laid up in heaven where neither moth nor rust do corrupt;
otherwise it is mere useless waste.

94. We have already noted one of the correspondences
assigned to Malkuth in the microcosm.   It is also said, however, that Malkuth corresponds to the feet of the Divine Man.
Here again we have an important concept; for unless the feet
are firmly planted on Mother Earth, no stability is possible.
There are altogether too many top-heavy mystics who like to
think that the Divine Man ends at the neck like a cherub, and
give no place to the generative organs of Yesod, or the anus
of Malkuth.   They need to learn the lesson that the heavenly
dream taught to St Peter, that nothing which God made is
unclean unless we allow it to become so.   We should recognise the Divine Life in all its functions, and so bring the manhood up into Godhead and sanctify it.   Cleanliness is next to
godliness, especially internal cleanliness.   If we evade and
avoid a thing, how are we to keep it clean and wholesome?
The taboos of a primitive people have been altogether overdone in our civilised life, with disastrous consequences to the
health and wholesomeness of humanity.

95. The symbols of Malkuth are the altar of the double
cube and the equal-armed cross, or cross of the elements.

96. The altar of the double cube is symbolic of the Hermetic
maxim, "As above, so below," and teaches that what is visible
is the reflection of what is invisible, and corresponds with it
exactly.   This cubical altar is the altar of the Mysteries, in
contradistinction to the table-altar, which is the altar of the

Church.   For the table-altar stands in the east, but the cubical altar stands in the centre.   It is said to be in proper proportion when it is the height of the navel of a six-foot man, and its breadth and depth are half its height.

97. The equal-armed cross, or cross of the elements, represents the four elements in balanced equilibrium, which is the perfection of Malkuth.   It is represented on the Tree by the division of Malkuth into four quarters, coloured citrine, olive, russet, and black, with the citrine towards Yesod and the black towards the Qliphoth; the olive towards Netzach and the russet towards Hod.   These are the reflections of the Three Pillars and the Qliphothic sphere, dulled and tempered by the veil of earth.

98. Thus are all things summed up in Malkuth, though seen in a glass darkly, by reflection, and not face to face.

99. The four Tarot cards yield curious results when subjected to meditation in the light of what we know about Malkuth.   The Ten of Wands is called the Lord of Oppression; the Ten of Cups, the Lord of Perfected Success; the Ten of Swords, the Lord of Ruin; and the Ten of Pentacles, the Lord of Wealth.

100. As we have already seen, it is in Malkuth that spiritual forces come to their fulfilment on the plane of form, and by taking these completed forms, and "sacrificing" them, we can translate them back into spiritual potencies.

101. These four Tarot cards, it will be observed, are alternately good and bad in their significance; in fact, the Ten of Swords is said to be the worst card in the pack to turn up in a divination.   There is a curious alchemical doctrine which has a bearing on this point.   It is taught that the signs of the planets are compounded out of three symbols—the solar disk, the lunar crescent, and the cross of corrosion or sacrifice; and these symbols, rightly interpreted, give the key to the alchemical nature of the planet and its practical use in the Great Work of transmutation.   For instance, Mars, in whose symbol the cross surmounts the circle, is said to be outwardly corrosive, but inwardly solar ; Venus, in which the circle

surmounts the cross, is said to be outwardly solar, but inwardly corrosive, or in the words of Scripture, sweet in the
mouth, but in the belly bitter.

102. In these four Tarot tens the same principle is seen to
prevail.   Each card represents the working of a certain type
of spiritual force on the plane of dense matter.   The most
spiritual of these cards, the ten of the suit whose ace is said
to be the Root of the Powers of Fire, is called the Lord of
Oppression.   This teaches us that the higher spiritual forces
are apt to be outwardly corrosive when operating upon the
plane of matter.   The powers of Fire, at their highest potency
in the ten of Wands, are a refining fire.   "As gold is tried in
the furnace, so the heart must be tried by pain."

103. On the other hand, all the symbolism of the suit of
Cups, or Chalices, shows the Venusian influence very clearly;
it is in this suit we find the Lords of Pleasure, Material Happiness, and Abundance.   But we also find the Lords of Illusory
Success, Abandoned Success, and Loss in Pleasure, which
shows clearly that this suit, though outwardly solar, is inwardly
corrosive.

104. Swords, again, are under the Martian influence, and
the Lord of Ruin shows the total sacrifice of all material
things.

105. But in Pentacles, earth of earth, the position is again
reversed, and we find that the ten of Pentacles is the Lord of
Wealth.

106. It will be seen, therefore, that those cards which are
of suits primarily spiritual in nature are outwardly corrosive on
the physical plane ; and those cards of suits that are primarily
material in nature are outwardly solar, or beneficent on the
material plane.   This teaches a very useful lesson, and gives
a very important key when used in those systems of divination which are designed to give discernment of the spiritual
influences operating in a case.

107. All mundane affairs rise and fall like the waves of
the sea, crest following trough, and trough following crest
in rhythmical progression; therefore, when any mundane

condition is at either its zenith or nadir we know that a change of tide is to be expected in the near future. This knowledge is embodied in many popular sayings, such as "It's a long lane that has no turning," and "The darkest hour is before the dawn." Harriman, the great American millionaire, said that he made his fortune by always buying on a falling market and selling on a rising one—which is the exact opposite to what everyone else tries to do. Nevertheless, it is a far-sighted proceeding, for a boom always topples over into a depression, and a depression issues forth into a boom. This has happened so often even within living memory that one would have thought speculators would have learnt the lessons of history, but they never do. It was a knowledge of this fact that enabled the Society of the Inner Light to be piloted steadily amidst the post-war difficulties, and come through without having to curtail any of its activities. There are times when it is necessary to be modest in order to be solvent; but there are times when one can launch out boldly, despite all outward seeming, because one knows that the tide is rising under one.

108. These four cards, then, give a very true insight into the nature of the operation of forces in Malkuth, and when they turn up in a divination, one always prepares for the outward gold to turn to corrosion, and the outward corrosion to turn to gold sooner or later, and one takes in or spreads one's sails accordingly.

109. This is the true use of divination—to enable one to discern the spiritual forces concerned in any happening, and act accordingly. Of what use, then, is the divination performed by one who has not spiritual discernment? And can one expect to find spiritual discernment in the hack occultist who gives so much for half-a-crown, and so much more for ten shillings? Spiritual things are not done in this way. Among the ancients, divination was a religious rite, and so it should be among us, if it is not to bring a trail of bad luck in its wake.

CHAPTER XXVI

THE QLIPHOTH

1. In a previous chapter we have referred to the Qliphoth, the evil and averse Sephiroth; the time has now come to study them in detail, even though "these are awful forms, dangerous even to think upon."

2. It may be asked why, since these forms are reputed to be so dangerous even to think about, it is necessary to study them. Were it not better to turn the mind away from them and prevent the images of such evil forces from formulating in consciousness? In answer to this question we may cite the precepts of Abramelin the Mage, whose system of magic is the most potent and complete that we possess. According to his system, the operator, after a prolonged period of purification and preparation, evokes not only the angelic forces, but also the demoniac ones.

3. A good many people have burnt their fingers with the system of Abramelin, and the reason is not far to seek; for if we examine their records we find that they have never followed the system in its entirety, but picked out a ceremony here and an invocation there for performance as the mood took them. Consequently Abramelin's system has got a bad name as being a singularly dangerous formula; whereas, performed in its entirety, it is a singularly safe one, because it deals with all the reactions of the invoked forces under what might be termed laboratory conditions and neutralises them.

4. Whoever attempts to work with the positive aspect of a Sephirah must remember that it also has a negative aspect, and unless he can maintain the necessary equilibrium of forces, that negative aspect is liable to come uppermost and swamp the

20

operation.   There is a point in every magical operation when
the negative aspect of the force comes up to be dealt with, and
unless dealt with will lure the experimenter into the pit which
he has digged.   It is a sound magical maxim not to invoke
any force unless you are equipped to deal with its averse
aspect.

5. Dare you invoke the fiery energy of Mars (Geburah) into
your nature unless you have sufficiently purified and disciplined yourself to be sure that you can prevent the Martian
force from going to extremes and leading to cruelty and
destructiveness?   If you have any insight into human nature
at all, you must be aware that everyone has the faults of his
qualities—that is to say, if he is vigorous and energetic he is
liable to fall into cruelty and oppression; if he is calm and
magnanimous he is liable to the temptations of *laissez-faire*
and inertia.

6. The Qliphoth are aptly termed the evil and averse
Sephiroth, for they are not independent principles or factors in
the cosmic scheme, but the unbalanced and destructive aspect
of the Holy Stations themselves.   There are, in fact, not two
Trees, but one Tree, a Qliphah being the reverse of a coin
of which the obverse is a Sephirah.   Whoever uses the
Tree as a magical system must perforce know the Spheres
of the Qliphoth, because he has no option but to deal
with them.

7. It is only upon the plane of Atziluth that there is but
one Name of Power associated with a Sephirah, and that
is the Deity Name.   To the archangel corresponds the devil,
and to the choir of angels the cohort of demons, and the
Sephirothic Spheres have their correspondence in the Infernal
Habitations.

8. The student must carefully distinguish between what the
occultist calls positive and negative evil.   This is a very
important point in esoteric philosophy, and a failure to realise
its significance leads into far-reaching practical errors and
cripples the whole life and work of the initiate, or, for the
matter of that, of any human being who is endeavouring to

develop a modicum of free-will and self-governance. It is a point which is but little understood, but it is a singularly important point in practice, because it influences so immediately our outlook, judgment, and conduct.

9. Positive evil is a force which is moving against the current of evolution; negative evil is simply the opposition of an inertia which has not yet been overcome, or of a momentum which has not yet been neutralised. Let us make these definitions clear by an example. The natural conservatism of a mature mind is regarded as evil by the would-be reformer; the natural iconoclasm of youth is regarded as evil by the administrator who has established his system. Nevertheless, we cannot dispense with either of these opposing factors if society is to be maintained in a healthy state; between them we achieve a steady progress that neither disorganises society nor permits it to sink into inertia and decay. Both these factors are indispensable to social welfare, yet either of them, unchecked, would lead to harm.

10. We cannot consider either of them, then, as a social evil unless it is overdone. We should therefore, in the terminology of esoteric philosophy, classify conservatism as negative evil when considered from the standpoint of the reformer, and iconoclasm as negative evil when considered from the standpoint of the conservative.

11. Positive evil is a different matter. It may be of the nature of an iconoclasm carried too far that descends into sheer anarchy; or of conservation carried too far, and becoming class privilege and vested interest militating against the general welfare. Or it may take the form of actual political corruption, which destroys the efficiency of the administrative machine; or of social corruption, such as organised prostitution or child-labour, which undermines the health of the body politic.

12. The conservative impulse and the radical impulse will both draw to themselves those who are in sympathy with their viewpoints, and their supporters will soon organise themselves into political parties; these parties are not evil save in the

prejudiced eyes of their political opponents; the main body of the nation opposes and supports them impartially and turn about, recognising that they represent compensating factors. Equally, the corrupt and criminal elements in society will tend to organise a Tammany Hall of their own. Now the Conservative and Radical parties might be likened to Chesed and Geburah respectively; Tammany Hall might be compared to the Qliphah corresponding to Geburah, the Burning and Contending Forces; and the organised Diehards to the Qliphah of Chesed, the Permitters of Destruction.

13. Negative evil is the practical corollary of the principle of Equilibrium. Equilibrium is the result of the balance of contending forces; consequently they must pull one against the other. We must not make the mistake of classing one of a pair of contending forces as good and the other as evil; to do so is to fall into the fundamental heresy of dualism.

14. The instructed and enlightened expositors of all religions regard dualism as a heresy; it is only ignorant adherents of a faith who believe in the conflict between light and darkness, spirit and matter, which shall eventually result in the triumph of the good and the total abolition and elimination of all opposing influences. Protestant Christianity forgets that Lucifer is the Light-bearer, Satan a fallen angel, and that Our Lord did not limit His ministrations to humanity, but descended into Hell and preached to the spirits in prison. We cannot deal with evil by cutting it off and destroying it, but only by absorbing and harmonising it.

15. In all our calculations and conceptions we must carefully distinguish between the resistance of the compensating Sephirah and the influence of the corresponding Qliphah. The two Trees, Divine and Infernal, Sephirothic and Qliphothic, are usually represented as they would appear if the obverse Tree were a reflection of the Celestial Tree in a mirror at its base, reaching downwards in proportion as the other reaches upwards. We should get a better concept if we conceived of the two glyphs as inscribed upon either side of a sphere, so that if a pendulum swinging between Geburah

and Gedulah (Mars and Jupiter) overreached itself in either direction it would commence to circle round to the reverse side of the globe and come into the sphere of influence of the corresponding averse Sephirah. If it swung too far towards Geburah (Severity) it would come into the Sphere of the Burning and Destroying Forces and of Hatred; if it swung too far in the direction of Mercy it would come into the Sphere of the Permitters of Destruction, and there is much significance in that name.

16. The mystic tells us that it is his aim to work in the sphere of pure spirit without any alloy of earth, and therefore he calls upon the Name of God alone; but the occultist replies : As long as you are in a body of earth you are a child of earth, and spirit for you cannot be without alloy. When you call upon the love of God it cannot come to you save through a Redeemer. The Sphere of the Redeemer is Tiphareth and its archangel is Raphael, the healer, for do we not recognise the influence of the Redeemer through its healing influence upon body and soul? But the reverse of the Redeemer who harmonises are the Zourmiel, the Disputers, "the great black giants ever working against each other." Do we not see their influence in the harsher doctrines of Christianity, in the idea of everlasting punishment under the dominion of the Devil as contrasted with everlasting reward under the dominion of the vengeful and venal Jehovah? If these are not Dual Contending Forces, what are they? Modern religious thought makes a great error in not realising that one can have too much of a good thing.

17. The only time when there is perfect equilibrium of force is during a Pralaya, a Night of the Gods. Force in equilibrium is static, potential, never dynamic, because force in equilibrium implies two opposing forces which have perfectly neutralised each other and thus rendered each other inert, inoperative. Upset the equilibrium, and the forces are freed for action, change can take place; growth, evolution, organisation can occur. There is no possibility of progress in perfect equilibrium; it is a state of rest. At the end of a

Cosmic Night it is said that equilibrium is overset, and in consequence an outflowing of power takes place once more and evolution begins again.

18. The equilibrium of the universe may best be likened to the swing of a pendulum rather than the grip of a clamp. It is not *held* immobile, and there is all the difference in the world between those two concepts. For in poise there is always a slight vibration, a push-pull between the opposing forces that holds it steady; it is a stability, not of inertia, but of strain.

19. This is represented on the Tree by the two Pillars of Mercy and Severity which pull against each other. Geburah (Severity) pulls against Gedulah (Mercy). Binah (Form) pulls against Chokmah (Force). If this counter-pull ceased, the universe would collapse, as a man who is pulling on a rope collapses if the rope breaks. We must clearly realise that this tension, this resistance against which we have to strain in whatever we may be doing, is not evil; it is the necessary counterpoise of whatever force we are employing.

20. As was pointed out in a previous chapter, each Qliphah arose primarily as an emanation of unbalanced force in the course of the evolution of the corresponding Sephirah. There was a period when the forces of Kether were overflowing to form Chokmah, and the Second Path was in process of becoming, but not yet fully established; therefore Kether must have been out of equilibrium—overflowing but not yet compensated. We see this phenomenon of the pathological transition stage clearly exhibited in the case of the adolescent who has ceased to be a child under control, and has not yet become an adult and self-controlled.

21. It was this inevitable period of unbalanced force, the pathology of transition, that gave rise to each Qliphah in turn. It follows then that the solution of the problem of evil and its eradication from the world is not to be achieved through its suppression, cutting off, or destruction, but through its compensation and consequent absorption back into the Sphere whence it came. The unbalanced force of Kether, which gave rise to the Dual Contending Forces, must be neutralised

by a corresponding increase in the activity of Chokmah, Wisdom.

22. The unbalanced force of each Sephirah then, which arose unchecked during the temporary phases of disequilibrium that occur periodically in the course of evolution, forms the nucleus around which were organised all the thought-forms of evil arising in the consciousness of sentient beings or through the operation of blind forces that happen to be out of equilibrium, each kind of inharmony seeking its own place. It will follow, then, that what was at first a mere overplus of a force, both pure and good in its intrinsic nature, may, if not compensated, become in the course of ages a highly organised and developed centre of positive and dynamic evil.

23. An example will once again help us to make this clear. An overplus of the necessary energy of Mars (Geburah), the energy that budges inertia and clears away that which is effete and outworn, would be certain to occur during the period prior to the emanation of Tiphareth, the Redeemer. As soon as emanated, the Redeemer would compensate the severities of Geburah, even as Our Lord said: "A new law give I unto you. Ye shall no longer say, an eye for an eye and a tooth for a tooth . . ." Now this uncompensated severity of Geburah gave us the jealous God of the Old Testament and all the religious persecutions that have ever been done in His unbalanced Name. It forms the Qliphah of Geburah, and every cruel and oppressive nature is in sympathy with it. To its Sphere goes all the overplus of the force they emanate that is not absorbed by the opposing force in the universe—all the unslaked revenge, all the unsatisfied lust of cruelty; and these forces, whenever they find a channel of expression opening up, rise through it. Consequently the man who gives way to cruelty soon finds that he is not merely expressing the impulses of his own undeveloped or misshapen nature, but that a great force like a stream in spate is urging him on, driving him from one outrage to another till finally he loses his self-control and discretion, and is swept away to self-destruction by some incautious expression of his impulses.

24. Whenever we make ourselves the channel of any pure force, that is to say any force which is single and undiluted by ulterior motives and secondary considerations, we find that there is a river in spate behind us—the stream of the corresponding Sephirothic or Qliphothic forces that is finding a channel through us. It is this that gives the single-minded zealot his abnormal power.

CHAPTER XXVII

CONCLUSION

1. Having ended my study of that portion of the Holy Qabalah which is concerned with the Ten Sephiroth upon the Tree of Life, I can find no other words to say than: "The little done, the undone vast——."

2. This book will, I hope, be followed by other books. The Twenty-two Paths form a system of mystical psychology, being concerned with the relationship between the soul of man and the universe. As the Ten Sephiroth, being concerned with the Macrocosm, are the key to illumination, so are the Twenty-two Paths, being concerned with the relationship between Macrocosm and Microcosm, the key to divination; and divination, taken in its true sense, is spiritual diagnosis, a very different matter to fortune-telling.

3. The Spheres of the gods upon the Tree is also a matter of profound interest and immediate practical application, for they give the key to the rites that were performed as a means, and a very effectual means, of contacting and equilibrating those different forces that are personalised under the names of the gods.

4. All these things, however, require detailed knowledge, and that can only be got together gradually. It is more than one pen can do unaided, and I should welcome the correspondence of those who are interested in these subjects, not as research into antiquity, but as living forces that come home to men's business and bosoms.

5. All that remains to us of ceremonial in the West is in the hands of the Church, the Masons, and the producers of cabaret. All three are effectual after their kind: the Church

evoking love of God; Masonry evoking love of man; and cabaret evoking love of women.

6. Viewed as a means of invoking the spirit of God, ceremonial is pure superstition; but viewed as a means of evoking the spirit of man, it is pure psychology, and that is how I view it. It is a lost art in the West, but an art that is well worth reviving.

7. In these pages I have given the philosophical basis on which this art rests. Its practical application depends not only upon technical knowledge, but upon the development of certain powers in the mind by careful and prolonged training, of which the first is the power of concentration, and the second the power of visual imagination. It is concerning the power of the visual imagination that we are so lamentably ignorant in the West. Coué just missed the turning when he sought in prolonged attention a substitute for spontaneous emotion.

PART IV

The Mystical Qabalah was first published almost fifty years ago and it remains probably the finest basic exposition of the principles of the Qabalah. In preparing this edition the Editors, members of the Society founded by the author, have taken the opportunity to bring up to date the transliteration of Hebrew, to correct some inaccuracies in the text, to make a few additions and changes to the lists at the beginning of the chapters on the Sephiroth, and to introduce some new material which follows this editorial.

In connection with the transliteration of Hebrew into English, the author's position is clearly stated on page 20 in paragraph 5; and the Editors are similarly placed. However, Dr I.R.M. Bóid of the Department of Jewish Studies, Victoria College, Victoria, Australia, has been kind enough to give much helpful advice and guidance in the matter; and following his suggestions, amendments have been made in the text. Furthermore, he has drawn our attention to inaccuracies which are too widely spread through the book to render correction feasible and therefore they are noted here:

1. 'Tiphareth' is better written 'Tiph'ereth' or 'Tiphereth'.
2. 'Geburah' is better written 'Gevurah'.
3. 'Qliphah/Qliphoth' are better written 'Qelippah/Qelippoth'.
4. 'Assiah' is better written 'Asiyah'.
5. 'Jehovah' is not a possible pronunciation nor a satisfactory rendering of YHVH. It has been retained for traditional reasons only.
6. 'Qabalah' is better written 'Qabbalah'. This involves the title of the book which, of course, we are unwilling to change and so 'Qabalah' remains throughout the book.

The Editors wish to express their appreciation and thanks to Dr Bóid for his interest and help.

As regards the additional material, much work has been done on the Tree of Life and the Sephiroth within the Society of the Inner Light and some extracts from their papers are included here as a supplement in the hope that they will be of help to students.

The 'Holy Guardian Angel' is mentioned in the Chapters on Tiphareth, Netzach and Malkuth and it is said to correspond with the 'Higher Self'. In the Society of the Inner Light the present view of that 'Angel' may be stated as follows: Among the concepts held in the consciousness of the Creator is one of the function and evolution of humanity and as each human unity or Spirit has its part to play in this, every unit has its individual contact with the overall concept; to put this another way, there is an individual application of the overall concept of every human Spirit. These individual differentiations are called the Holy Guardian Angels.

From one point of view they equate with each Spirit's realisation of its particular part, its work of Destiny; from another they equate with the Divine Idea of the same thing; from yet another they equate with the individual contact of each Spirit with God and God with each individual Spirit. People have been aware of them in various ways — but for all they frequently manifest as conscience.

The nomenclature of the division of the human being into parts is varied, a rough and ready threefold division being 'Spirit, 'Soul' and 'Body'. In the Society of the Inner Light the soul and body parts were formerly known as the 'Higher Self' and 'Lower Self', or 'Individuality' and 'Personality'; but now and in the following extracts from the Society's papers they are referred to as 'Evolutionary Personality' and 'Incarnationary Personality', the former comprising the microcosmic aspects of Chesed, Geburah and Tiphareth and the latter the microcosmic aspects of Netzach, Hod, Yesod and Malkuth.

The expression 'The Fall' is used in the following extracts as well as in the text of the book, and our present understanding of that phrase is as follows: Spirit is pure being, an individual centre of potentiality in God. It is the source of all its manifestations, underlying yet transcending them, and is in a sense independent of them. With the activation of Will comes Immanence, the Spirit Immanent; here the

Spirit conceives the concept of itself as a manifesting Being and its drive is to manifest the Will of God which on the level of Spirit Transcendent is one with the Will of the Spirit.

We can imagine the God-centred Spirit considering how, having freewill, it can manifest the Will of God and it is not hard to imagine how easily the focus can shift on to its own Self. 'How can it be done?' becomes 'How can I do it?' and the focus almost innocently shifts from God-centredness to self-centredness. The stories of 'The Fall' in Genesis, of Pandora's box and elsewhere, illustrate this falling away from God-centredness to self-centredness.

THE TREE OF LIFE IN GENERAL

The Archangel of Kether, Metatron, is said to have given the Qabalah to Man. This means that he 'sent through' an 'idea-chart' of evolution which was imprinted on the Essential Self and through meditation brought down to the 'lower' mind (i.e., the mind of the Incarnationary Personality). Language as we understand it is not used by non-humans but great concepts can be received from them and put into human language by human beings. This verbal form is only approximate and its adequacy depends on the development and ability of the receiver and the conditioning of the cultural background, etc.

The anthropomorphic forms of angels and archangels come from the human mind (see page 240, paragraph 7). More appropriate forms might be pillars of vast force or geometrical shapes in accordance with the basic nature of the Sephirah involved.

— — — — — —

The Qabalistic method has the advantage over other schemes of esoteric development in that it unfolds the make-up of Man in more precise accordance with that of the Great Being of which he is the child. That is to say, the 'Spheres of Becoming' are recapitulated in Man in much the same way as the major outlines of creation have been traced. The King is chosen in Tiphareth, defends his Kingdom in Geburah and finally is anointed in Chesed. It should always be kept in mind that the Tree of Life represents the gradual unfoldment of Kether-Ehyeh;

the 'Becoming'. The same system of unfoldment of 'becoming' is found in Man who does it from above downward in his spiritual faculties, from below upward in his psychological faculties, and on earth through his creative expression in activities.

— — — — — —

The archetypal Man can be thought of as standing with the Earth under his feet and the sky above his head, and the line of force as representing the Middle Pillar descending straight through from the crown of his head to the soles of his feet. The Sephiroth on the Middle Pillar form the Centres. You will observe that Kether, the Crown, is above the head, it rests on but is not in the head; and Malkuth, the Kingdom, is beneath the feet; these are both in the aura extending from the physical body. Between these two poles of Kether and Malkuth in the aura, Man the microcosm, the individual, lives his life and works out his evolution. Kether is his spiritual Centre.

BINAH

The polarisation of Chokmah and Binah creates the Web of Life and the realisation of this gives the understanding of the cyclic nature of Life and therefore the acceptance of Life as it is. One who has this realisation has contact with Reality. The result of the realisation is the disappearance of conflict because the one who has realised becomes part of Life as it is, knowing its changes, its rhythms and its cycles. This knowledge and realisation produces a state of serenity and peace in the face of all things. In other words, the Macrocosm and the microcosm are in alignment.

The result of such a realisation is manifested in an ability to gauge conditions from day to day and to accept people as they are at any given moment, seeing the stage they have reached — not seeing only what they might become, though that has to be envisaged as a future possibility.

These matters relate to Binah and give rise to the 'Compassion of the Adept'. It is a great art to be able to see the difference between a soul as it is and what it can become as a result of further training. To some extent *all* Personalities are limited, but they *are* the instruments of the Spirit. In so far as the Incarnationary Personality is willing to do its utmost to achieve within its limits in order that the Spirit may put forth and use power in Malkuth, thus far can the incarnation be counted a success. It is essential to assess with detachment the limits of the Incarnationary Personality and to avoid despondency or undue resignation lest the limits be narrowed more than is necessary.

The one who combines Force and Form is an exactitude of precision and who also allows for the 'human element' in his calculations, and combines these faculties with the ability to see his work in that right relationship which gives ries to compassion is an 'adept'.

The keys to a Sephirah are probably most easily found from the three 'V's — the Vision, the Virtue and the Vice. Applying this to Binah, there is first the Vision of Sorrow. This Sephirah, perhaps more than any other, is shunned because of the Vision. It is often difficult for the ill-conditioned human consciousness to separate the idea of sorrow from calamity, sin, death, cruelty, etc. Perhaps it is more truthful to say that very few people try to make that distinction because their emotions shy away from sorrow; reasonably so, because the sorrow they experience is little compared to the Divine Sorrow of the Vision in Binah, the Principle of Limitation.

This Vision of Sorrow is an essential part of the consideration of Form. It has to do with change of state and focus. For 'fallen' Man it produces sadness at realising the vast difference between what should have been and what now is; and realising what had to be done, and how much, to bring back into line with what should be what is now out of line. It is consequent on the realisation of the redemption made necessary by the 'Fall' — but had there been no 'Fall' the essential Vision of Sorrow would still exist.

Realisation of the Vision of Sorrow is a state in which the Cross of all manifested Life is accepted. It is not the same as the suffering and pain caused by the action of the Dark Mother through Geburah upon the Personality which action is in the emotional realm and related to the Tipharetic Mysteries of the Crucifixion, Mysteries of which the experience should be completed in Geburah.

Can it be wondered that when the true Vision starts to impinge on the human being his earlier reactions may well be inertia or avarice? By avarice is meant the refusal to give up what he has or even what has been achieved, and also to share his achievement with others, to give to others the help he has had himself.

The Virtue is silence and its need is obvious; silence here is the exact measuring of what not to say and when not to speak. In everyday life do we not see how very few people refuse to answer questions when they do not clearly know the answers, or when the one asking the question could and should find the answer in himself — and is deprived of that opportunity by the eagerness of the one questioned to display his knowledge or to air an opinion? Silence is Divine non-action on one plane.

Binah is the *idea* of Form and therefore gives rise to the basic form or 'plan' of the Divine Intention; this is the basic Cause which will eventually insist on an effect consonant with Its Nature. Time is rightly attributed to Binah for it is an aspect of Form.

In Binah is the Principle of Understanding; not the understanding of the mind but the understanding that comes from the deepest levels of feeling which is of the nature of the Feminine. There is also a supernal awareness of a consciousness whose 'Roots are in Amen'; a Wisdom and a Faith beyond the sphere of thought and quite unlike what the concrete mind usually considers as 'faith'. In Binah is the Feminine Power of Jehovah and it is through Binah alone that Wisdom is applied.

Binah is one of the two heads of the Sephiroth of Function — the Side Pillars — and the Hebrews realised these Powers as exercised by God on different levels both in the macrocosm and the microcosm. Binah is the 'Female Function' rather than the Female herself. A god-form can be useful in building a clear representation to the mind. It is best for each to work out for himself the Sephiroth according to his own Inner Light. The Qabalah provides stepping-stones of symbols and symbolic representations on which each plants his foot differently in order to cross the Abyss.

Binah represents that Aspect of God which brings force into outer manifestation — that which gives this force 'shape' for the mind (and sometimes for the eye) to understand it. Binah gives a mental form to the highest idea and, being the Principle of Form, can also give the crudest primitive shape or symbol to the 'lowest' earthly force. One cannot, humanly speaking, have understanding of a force unless that force be shown forth and interpreted by form. Form, of course, is a limitation but force cannot manifest in the Solar Universe without it.

DAATH

Daath may be considered as the point of unity in which all knowledge is contained. Being unity, it necessarily contains the synthesis of Law, Justice and Equilibrium. Daath represents the unity and unification of all on the Tree of Life. It represents the Wisdom of God uniting in itself Power and Love.

Daath is not a Sephirah though it is a very important point upon the Tree. It is not usually given attributes, for it is not generally developed in evolution as yet but only in some who are moving in the forefront of evolution, at present in the scientific field.

Daath is the state of knowledge — of knowingness — as well as the awareness of eternity. In it is garnered the essences of experiences of its projections. In Christian language Daath is the sphere of the 'Upper Room' at the descent of the Pentecostal flames. In pre-Christian times it was the sphere of the Creative Fire in the realm of mind; in Druidism it was connected with Beltane, though Beltane was also the festival of the earthly Creative Fire as well. Daath holds the key to man's knowledge of himself but it takes much inner development to use that key. Daath on the Tree in the individual human aura holds knowledge of the way in which each Evolutionary Personality has been affected by the development of Earth.

Daath is, of course, far removed from what is often miscalled 'mysticism' — that false, vague denominator of transcendental matters. Daath brings the correct understanding of that much-abused word. Mysticism is not to be found in a confused state of purposeless or ill-directed 'spirituality'; Daath is nothing vague. Daath is that mind which is clear, simple and certain and which links and understands both sides of the Abyss; the genuine mystic holds in his mind a clear-cut realisation of the various potencies shown on the Tree of Life and of their unity with God and with himself. Daath represents the Unity which links the Supernal Triangle with its manifestation — the mind of God working through Man and evolution. Here the balance and realisation and absorption of these potencies meet together in the light of the abstract mind; thus it is said 'In Daath are the Conclaves assembled'.

A good symbol for Daath is the cloud-hidden peak of the Sacred Mountain of any race. It was Daath-consciousness that Moses contacted when he received the Tables of the Law from the top of Sinai, the Moon Mountain. The situation of Daath is upon the Abyss, the Abyss which separates the Supernals from the rest of the Tree of Life, and which separates the vast powers of Eternity from practically all that the human mind can conceive or know at all. Chokmah and Binah unite in Daath in a sense of supreme Divinity which is impossible to describe. Above all, Daath is Realisation in its supremest meaning, understanding united with knowledge, and bringing forth within the human mind at its most abstract level a complete awareness of all. In such a complete awareness the human mind is absorbed within the Eternal Mind and is made one with it. Daath represents, therefore, the supreme Wisdom and supreme Power of Realisation.

Within each of the Sephiroth there is a Tree in miniature, and in these ten miniature Trees there is a Daath. Until the student has been in contact with the Daath of each Sephirah he does not know that Sephirah absolutely. There is, for example, a Daath in Malkuth, and when it is contacted there is realisation of the smallest waves and atoms and their meaning and inter-relationship, not only with Malkuth but with the Whole — which realisation would not be possible without this contact. The same applies to the other Sephiroth, and where there is an effort to realise Balance and Justice, help may be obtained through contact with Daath in so far as the student is able to make it, for by this means some degree of realisation of Justice is bound to come if the desire for it be deep and sincere.

Thus, as regards man, Daath is the supreme Realisation. As regards universal things it may be visualised under the symbol of the Mind of God. Daath may be considered as aligned with the workings of the Mind of God. It can therefore be imagined that when the human mind in its abstract level contacts the Supernal Mind there will follow realisation of some kind, an awareness in some very deep manner. The supernal revelations of ancient times which have come to great Adepts, and through them to the Race, have been received through contact with Daath. The 'formula' that expresses the nature of Daath is that of the 'Empty Room' or 'Empty Tomb'; the phrases have analogues on several levels. The symbol refers to the absence of symbol and contact with reality.

In the final contact with the 'Empty Room' this, the 'last symbol', is absorbed into the consciousness and thus the 'Empty Room' no longer exists. The Empty Room, as its name implies, has no furniture, no forms It is a narrow confine at first filled with 'Essences' and 'Light' but these will fade out at the end. The Spirit realises this narrow confine as its symbol of itself and absorbs this symbol. Thus does the individual soul attain to perfect freewill through recognition of his own 'field of limitation' which is the complete acceptance of the past which in turn gives realisation of the future *within* the integrated and illuminated man. Thus are past and future synthesised in the present, and this *is* Daath.

— — — — — —

The Abyss is a symbolic indication of the difference in the mode of functioning of the Spirit through Kether, Chokmah and Binah focussed through Daath, and the mode of functioning through the Sephiroth below the Abyss. Above the Abyss the Spirit functions through states from which emerge the qualities of Love, Wisdom and Strength; below the Abyss the Spirit's functioning is conditioned through sensations, emotions, feelings and the mind, through which man reproduces the spiritual qualities of love, wisdom and strength, tinged and distorted by the deviations and lack of development as well as enriched by the growth of man.

The consciousness of Daath is not achieved through the abnegation of the mind, the emotions or the sensations; rather are these factors extended to their uttermost so that there is a change from what would be called normal functioning of that factor. Transmutation or alchemy takes place and on the evolutionary aspect there is transcendence; on the level of intelligence there is what could be called intuition, light in extension, wisdom. On the emotional level there are the feelings extended to the ecstasy of divine union which is love, and on the sensory level there is perception extended to the ecstasy of immortality which is strength.

Generally speaking, individuals recognise sensations, emotions, feelings and the mind, and remain in their grip until their recognition of 'states' and practice in their creation grow — hence the negative approach to life of those who go from one effect to another. Many who have aspired to the state and experience of the Empty Room of Daath (the symbolism of the womb after another manner in which there is birth not into a physical body but into that state summed up in the words: 'Then shall I know as I am known' — a self-awareness state of causative creativity beyond the mind but conceived through attitudes) have found numbness, emptiness, aridity. These are not attributes of the Daath state but are the accretions surrounding it, the accretions made by the human mind in its impingement — another manifestation of the deviations on another level.

The Empty Room could be said to be empty in terms of the mind in that it does not contain forms, but it is not empty in terms of consciousness; it is concerned with states and attitudes and the experiencing of qualities. In faith and the many harmonics of it is the power to bridge the gap between the tools of consciousness and function used by the Spirit 'below the Abyss' and the causative core of creative beingness of the Spirit, symbolised on the Tree as being 'above the Abyss'. It is not a matter of being in a different place or environment but of being in a different state. The basic Intelligence of the Spirit is one of creativity which is used or abused or neglected by the mind and the emotions and sensations according to the 'state' of the individual concerned. Man has within himself all the qualities he needs; he does not need to develop them; what he has to do is to create and demonstrate the necessary states for their growth and flowering. The seed contains the flower and God made man in His own Image.

CHESED

The Virtue of Chesed — Obedience — means acceptance of the Law not because of obligation or fear but because man knows himself as a part of the Law.

GEBURAH

Geburah is the Sphere wherein an individual enters upon or turns aside from the path to Achievement. It shows the joint action of the Pillars of Energy and Endurance perhaps more clearly than any other Sphere. There are souls which can face a terrible death in some religious, dynamic or other cause — this is a sharp Geburic action, but there is also the 'routine' side of Geburah which is liable to be underestimated. This side is symbolised not by the sharp sword so much as by the scourge which lashes to *continuous* action, and the chain which holds captive through great stretches of time and prevents any escape. Fury and fear are so often associated with the Holy Fifth Sephirah that the *constant* vigilance and control of its *continuous* working are often overlooked. This latter might be described as the 'steady' side of Geburah which needs not only the drive of the will but also the detached observation and understanding.

Geburah often has sharp and quick workings but its slowness is one of its most potent methods. The poetical extract which has become a saying: 'Though the mills of God grind slowly, yet they grind exceeding small; though with patience He stands waiting, with exactness grinds He all' is very sound — and also contains a reference to the Endurance of God (His Patience); Erasmus has the same idea in his 'Sero molunt deorum molae'.

NETZACH

The 'Vision of Beauty Triumphant' is the realisation of achieved perfection, such as God had when He found His work was good and 'rested on the seventh day'. This Vision is the achievement of all in perfection. With Man such realisation can come only after the Sacrifice of Tiphareth and he will have to overthrow all the false ideals of 'Beauty' and 'Peace' before this Triumph. He must have Victory over the false ideals evolved since and because of the Fall. Some usually accepted notions of Venus-Aphrodite are responsible for some of these false ideals. The Vision should really be of the Triumph of Truth and Law.

The 'gods' are emanations of the One seen as aspects of Adonai through the lens of racial feeling and are often in actuality real beings who were in remote times racial guides and leaders and who have been built up into '*forms*' by racial memory. Their *forces* can be real enough if used with skill and potency even today.

Netzach might be described in one aspect as the Sphere of Romance. Romance contains the Beauty of, and Victory after, Strife — the fierceness and force of opposing circumstances which make tragedy

— the glory of fighting overwhelming odds and overcoming them. Netzach is also the Sphere of 'Faerie', of gods and of certain nature-spirits of great power as well as of great beauty.

The title given to Netzach of 'Firmness' is a realisation of the Netzach necessities. Netzach refers to relatedness and this should be firm, stable and not confused so that each relationship (whether referring to people or things) is in its right place. It is the formula of the Many-which-are-One. The disorderliness of Netzach is very usual and well known — that disorderliness which leads to the particular vices of that Sephirah. Yet Netzach has its own type of order — an orderliness which does not become confused and unstable with the many aspects but draws them together, not separates — makes the many into the one. There is meant to be order in the 'Green Ray'; it is wrong delineation of Netzach which brings about confused and overexuberant aspects.

HOD

Hod is the Sphere of Truth, but there is also, as in all the Sephiroth below the Supernal Triad when expressed in the microcosm, the adverse conditions — trickery and falsehood. We have to remember that these untoward or adverse qualities are usually shown in the god-form of the planet associated with each Sephirah, not the pure or divine state of the Sephirah. Hod is the Sphere of Truth and of those who know it and equally of those who distort it. The truth is crystal clear so that one does not see a mere reflection but can look down through it into the depths beneath. It is the Sphere of the Wise Men and Wise Women of history and romance — some of whom worked with Truth and some of whom distorted Truth.

— — — — — —

The Sephirah Hod is the basal Station of the Pillar of Severity, even as Binah is the apical Station. No Sephirah can ever be considered by itself for it stands in terms of relationship, evolutionary and functional, to other Sephiroth according to circumstances. In considering problems arising in the Sphere of Severity the Pillar of Severity as a whole must be taken into account. The function of the Sephirah Binah is, however, of so abstract and universal a nature that it does not require separate consideration when practical applications are under discussion. It represents forces of stability and inertia and is the basis of all organisation. It reflects into Chesed and thence into Hod; whereas Chokmah the dynamic factor reflects into Geburah and thence into Netzach, thus imparting to the central Sephirah of the Pillar of Severity its dynamic aspect.

Hod is a many-sided Sephirah, as is indicated by the symbolic form of a Hermaphrodite attributed to it. It is associated with Hermes who lent his sandals, and Pallas Athene who lent her shield, to Perseus for the slaying of the Gorgon in the name of Justice — by which myth we may discern the nature of its connection with Geburah. The winged sandals lent the swiftness of thought to the feet of the hero and in the polished shield he saw reflected as in a mirror the deadly head of the Gorgon, thus sustaining no harm from her glance.

Hod, or Mercury, represents the human mind; for evolution has advanced up the Tree through its sphere, thus causing it to become organised in terms of consciousness. It is therefore no formless sphere of force, as is Geburah, but a sphere wherein mind operates in terms of that consciousness developed in Malkuth.

YESOD

Yesod has the substance of water and the moon and yet is aligned with great force and strength. Yesod is rightly called the Machinery of the Universe. There is behind all outer appearances an inner mechanism which never fails and which works on its own laws.

The forces of regeneration as well as of generation are at work within the Machinery of the Universe, and the foundations of the Holy City as well as of the Earth may be thought of as in Yesod; the foundations do not alter but the structure alters from age to age — even in the mundane sense — for more and more of the etheric atmosphere is drawn into the arena of Yesod, atmosphere of such different tensions and uses that the 'appearances' seem to vary and man and his nature display cyclic differences as time goes on.

The same type of mechanism also works behind the body of Man. In this present Age scientists are beginning to recognise that there are forces working within Man which cannot be seen or assessed by the physical eye or the physical ear. It is on the knowledge of these laws behind Man, the more intimate knowledge of the human unseen mechanics, that the Aquarian healing will be built — and has already begun to be shown in various ways. Forces which work in the mind of Man affect his body. By thoroughly understanding these laws working in the mind of Man his body can be helped if it is sick in any way. A better form of working in this sense is to put man in touch with his own mechanism and it is the knowledge of that which more and more can influence the new type of healing.

Yesod is also the Storehouse of Images. Images are of many kinds and words themselves are only images at best. Equally there are different kinds of pictures. Take for example the images by the hundred of Our Lord. Some are ill-conceived, low in perception, yet they may to some people bring a strong Christian contact. There are, equally, great pictures by famous artists. There are forms of great music which can express our Lord in quite another way, and all these things belong in their final instance to Yesod before they can contact the Earth. Yesod is indeed the universal Storehouse of Images and there are many symbols which, thought out carefully, have great bearing on these matters.

MALKUTH

He who properly understands Malkuth has set his feet firmly on the path of evolution. It can be seen that its titles show that it is the gate or entrance to the supernal contacts, to transmutation and joy.

It is the Sephirah of every possibility but has not yet come to its perfection; therefore is the image a *young* woman crowned and throned to achieve her full growth as the Daughter of the Mighty Ones. She has still to come to the status of Binah on whose throne she sits. The whole Tree is in Malkuth, and Malkuth has a special connection with Netzach, Hod and Yesod.

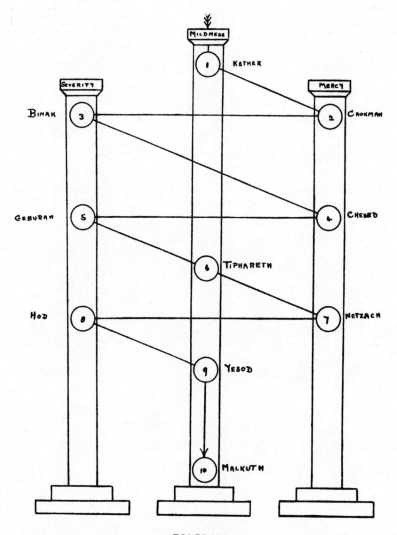

DIAGRAM I
THE THREE PILLARS AND THE DESCENT OF POWER

321

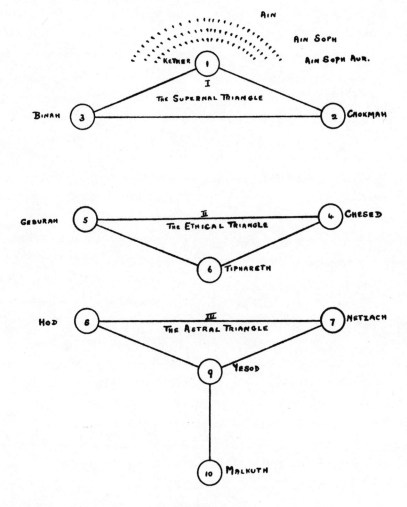

AIN

AIN SOPH

AIN SOPH AUR.

KETHER ① I

THE SUPERNAL TRIANGLE

BINAH ③ ② CHOKMAH

GEBURAH ⑤ II
THE ETHICAL TRIANGLE ④ CHESED

⑥ TIPHARETH

HOD ⑧ III
THE ASTRAL TRIANGLE ⑦ NETZACH

⑨ YESOD

⑩ MALKUTH

DIAGRAM II
THE THREE TRIANGLES

323

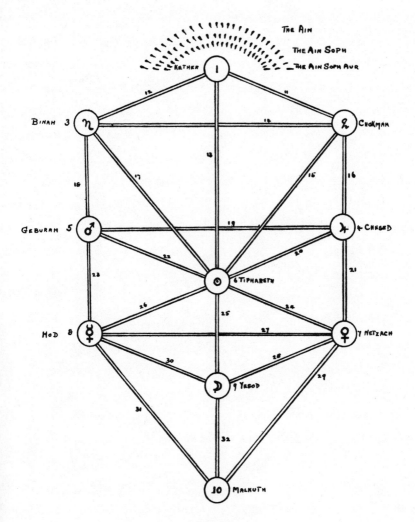

The Ain
The Ain Soph
The Ain Soph Aur

Kether 1

Binah 3

Chokmah

Geburah 5

4 Chesed

6 Tiphareth

Hod 8

7 Netzach

9 Yesod

10 Malkuth

DIAGRAM III
THE TREE OF LIFE AND THE THIRTY-TWO PATHS

DION FORTUNE'S SANE OCCULTISM

In *Sane Occultism,* Dion Fortune deals with the many pitfalls of occultism, not only from the standpoint of the serious student, but also from that of the ordinary person learning of occult matters for the first time. One of the greatest dangers for those who interest themselves in occult science is the lure of the Left-hand Path. Whereas the Initiate of the Right-hand Path is god-centred, the Initiate of the Left-hand Path is self-centred. Here she explains how to recognize and avoid these temptations.

Practical Occultism in Daily Life reveals the many minor magical rites that can be used by anybody to achieve a steady concentration to deal with the everyday problems of life. Dion Fortune teaches these things not as rule-of-thumb methods, but with explanations of the occult principles on which they rest, so that those who try to use them may use them intelligently.

DION FORTUNE'S THE COSMIC DOCTRINE

This classic work explains much in the esoteric sphere which has hitherto been inaccessible to the general reader. Its revelations are designed to induce in the occult student a deeper understanding of Cosmic Law and lead to a significant expansion of consciousness and esoteric knowledge. Various images are given, under which the student is instructed to think of certain things. But the author does warn that these images are not descriptive but symbolic; they 'are designed to train the mind, not to inform it'.

Dion Fortune was an exceptionally gifted psychic and seer who wrote a number of remarkably powerful books. Following a nervous breakdown in her twenties, she embarked on a study of analytical psychology which ultimately led her to the occult Mysteries and to widespread acclaim.

DION FORTUNE'S APPLIED MAGIC

Dion Fortune is now recognised as one of the most important figures in twentieth-century occultism. Her books on various aspects of the occult tradition, as well as her highly acclaimed fiction, have made the complex theoretical foundations of psychic development comprehensible to thousands of readers.

Applied Magic is a selection of Dion Fortune's writings on the practical applications of magical and occult techniques. Written from the point of view of a gifted psychic, they provide invaluable and suggestive pointers to anyone intent on increasing their inner awareness.

Aspects of Occultism looks at nine specific aspects of the Western Mystery Tradition, including, God and the Gods, Sacred Centres, The Astral Plane, The Worship of Isis, Teachings Concerning the Aura, and the Pitfalls of Spiritual Healing.

DION FORTUNE'S ESOTERIC ORDERS AND THEIR WORK

Traditionally, occultists have jealously restricted admission to their secret societies and schools, and have shrouded their practices in mystery. But in *Esoteric Orders and Their Work,* Dion Fortune, one of the greatest occultists of the twentieth century, uncovers the workings of these secret organizations and describes their operations in detail.

From their ancient roots, the Western Esoteric Systems have an unbroken tradition of European initiation that has been handed down from adept to neophyte. In *The Training and Work of the Initiate,* Dion Fortune indicates the broad outlines and underlying principles of these systems in an endeavour to illuminate an obscure and greatly misunderstood aspect of the Path. Thanks to her work, even those who cannot give up their whole life to the pursuit of esoteric science can evolve a philosophy of life and so discuss their individual relationship to the cosmic whole.

PRIESTESS

*In the meantime I had my dream of moon-magic and sea-palaces,
and day by day I lived more in another dimension where I had
that which I knew I should never have on earth, and I was very happy.*

Dion Fortune was the pen-name of Violet Firth, one of the most luminous and striking personalities of the twentieth century, and Womanhood's answer to Aleister Crowley.

This is the first full biography of a woman who hid behind a veil of secrecy and who became a cult figure in the years after her death in 1946. A brilliant writer and pioneer psychologist, her whole life was devoted to living out an eternal Myth in a story that can be told in terms of Virgins and Dragons, Moons and Oceans, and the spirit of the land itself.

A powerful psychic and medium, obsessed with the study of magic, her career was never entirely within this world. And in her own eyes at least she was a Priestess, a channel for the Great Goddess, an exponent of the time-lost Mysteries of Women.

From her birth in Llandudno, through her years in the drowned lands of Somerset, Alan Richardson unfolds the patterns of her life in what is his best book yet: her early career as a Freudian analyst, her nervous breakdown, her time as a Land Girl and her developing psychism; her romance with a man whom she believed to be non-human, her fraught marriage to a doctor whom everyone knew as Merlin; the foundation of her own group devoted to the practice of her peculiar philosophies — and the start of her long, hard, always stormy journey into the Otherworld, toward the heart of the Goddess that she saw as sleeping within the Earth itself.